**SAGE** was founded in 1965 by Sara Miller McCune to support the dissemination of usable knowledge by publishing innovative and high-quality research and teaching content. Today, we publish more than 750 journals, including those of more than 300 learned societies, more than 800 new books per year, and a growing range of library products including archives, data, case studies, reports, conference highlights, and video. SAGE remains majority-owned by our founder, and after Sara's lifetime will become owned by a charitable trust that secures our continued independence.

Los Angeles | London | Washington DC | New Delhi | Singapore | Boston

# GRIEF and DISAPPEARANCE

Thank you for choosing a SAGE product!
If you have any comment, observation or feedback,
I would like to personally hear from you.

Please write to me at **contactceo@sagepub.in**

**Vivek Mehra,** Managing Director and CEO,
SAGE Publications India Pvt Ltd, New Delhi

## Bulk Sales

SAGE India offers special discounts
for purchase of books in bulk.
We also make available special imprints
and excerpts from our books on demand.

*For orders and enquiries, write to us at*

Marketing Department
SAGE Publications India Pvt Ltd
B1/I-1, Mohan Cooperative Industrial Area
Mathura Road, Post Bag 7
New Delhi 110044, India

*E-mail us at* **marketing@sagepub.in**

## Get to know more about SAGE

Be invited to SAGE events, get on our mailing list.
*Write today to* **marketing@sagepub.in**

This book is also available as an e-book.

# GRIEF and DISAPPEARANCE
## Psychosocial Interventions

## Barbara Preitler

*Translated by Julia Skala*

www.sagepublications.com
Los Angeles • London • New Delhi • Singapore • Washington DC • Boston

Copyright © Barbara Preitler, 2015

All rights reserved. No part of this book may be reproduced or utilized in any form or by any means, electronic or mechanical, including photocopying, recording or by any information storage or retrieval system, without permission in writing from the publisher.

First published in 2015 by

**SAGE Publications India Pvt Ltd**
B1/I-1 Mohan Cooperative Industrial Area
Mathura Road, New Delhi 110 044, India
www.sagepub.in

**SAGE Publications Inc**
2455 Teller Road
Thousand Oaks, California 91320, USA

**SAGE Publications Ltd**
1 Oliver's Yard, 55 City Road
London EC1Y 1SP, United Kingdom

**SAGE Publications Asia-Pacific Pte Ltd**
Church Street
#10-04 Samsung Hub
Singapore 049483

Published by Vivek Mehra for SAGE Publications India Pvt Ltd, typeset at 10/12 pts Minion Pro by vPrompt eServices Pvt Ltd and printed at Sai Print-o-pack, New Delhi.

**Library of Congress Cataloging-in-Publication Data**

Preitler, Barbara.
  Grief and disappearance: psychosocial interventions / Barbara Preitler.
    pages cm.
  Includes bibliographical references and index.
  1. Grief. 2. Disappeared persons. 3. Missing persons. 4. Psychic trauma—Treatment.
    I. Title.
  BF575.G7P735         155.9'3—dc23         2015         2015008750

**ISBN:** 978-93-515-0242-5 (HB)

**The SAGE Team:** Supriya Das, Neha Sharma, Megha Dabral, Rajib Chatterjee and Ritu Chopra

# Contents

*List of Abbreviations* — vii
*Preface* — ix
*Acknowledgements* — xi

1 Reaction towards Loss—Grief — 1

2 The Social Consequences of 'Enforced Disappearances' — 47

3 Collective Forms of Coping — 88

4 Psychotherapeutic Work with Traumatised People — 114

5 Individual Reactions to 'Enforced Disappearances' — 128

6 The Family and 'Enforced Disappearances' — 151

7 Interventions for Communities after 'Disappearances' — 167

8 If a 'Disappeared' Person Comes Back — 186

9 Self-care for Professionals — 195

10 Conclusion — 203

*Bibliography* — 207
*Index* — 223
*About the Author and Translator* — 229

# List of Abbreviations

| | |
|---|---|
| AHRC | Asian Human Right Group |
| CEH | Comisión para el Esclarecimiento Histórico |
| CPC | Centre for Psychosocial Care |
| DPM | Dual process model |
| ECCC | Extraordinary Chambers in the Courts of Cambodia |
| FEDEFAM | Federación Latinoamericana de Asociaciones de Familiares de Detenidos-Desaparecidos |
| IASC | Inter-Agency Standing Committee |
| ICMP | International Commission on Missing Persons |
| ICRC | International Committee of the Red Cross |
| IDP | Internally Displaced Person |
| JVP | Janathā Vimukthi Peramuna |
| MIA | Missing in Action |
| NHRC | National Human Rights Commission |
| PAHO | Pan American Health Organization |
| PTSD | Post-Traumatic Stress Disorder |
| SOC | Sense Of Coherence |
| UNP | United National Party of Sri Lanka |
| URM | Unaccompanied Refugee Minors |
| WTC | World Trade Center |

# Preface

In my psychological and therapeutic work with severely traumatised individuals, I have, time and again, met people who had no information whatsoever about the whereabouts of a close relative. Trauma in and of itself is already characterised by immense feelings of helplessness. When relatives 'disappear' without a trace, these feelings of helplessness and impotence become constant in the lives of those left behind.

In trauma-focused psychotherapy, we mainly work with the concept and the diagnosis of post-traumatic stress disorder. 'Post' means 'after'. We assume that the traumatic situation has passed. In the case of people having 'disappeared', the traumatic situation the relatives of these people find themselves in is not over; a sense of closure with regards to the worries for the beloved person can only be achieved with great difficulties. The loss cannot be accepted as final. Again and again despair, hope and fear intrude into their lives.

While researching and working in this field, I was continually astounded by the sheer number of people who were affected by this phenomenon in the course of human history or are affected by it today. Considering this, I was surprised to find that comparatively little has been published on this problematic issue.

This book hopes to do its part in bridging this gap and promoting an academically as well as practically oriented discourse on the topic of 'enforced disappearances'. The quotation marks around the term are put there on purpose to point out that these people have not really disappeared. They did not dissolve into thin air. They are either alive somewhere, or if they have died, then there is a real spot somewhere in this world where their death has taken place. Then their human remains exist in a tangible place. We just do not know where. The questions of when and why remain equally unanswered.

In this book, I attempt to approach the topic of 'enforced disappearances' from various angles.

In Chapter 1, I introduce a number of theoretical models dealing with grief in general and complicated grief in particular. They form the basis for an understanding of the particularly complicated ways of dealing with loss in the context of a 'disappearance'.

The Chapter 2 deals with the historical dimension of 'enforced disappearance'. It spans a wide array of topics, from example, from Greek mythology to a range of different situations in which people are forcibly 'disappeared' and to natural disasters like the 2004 Indian Ocean Tsunami. The central issue covered in this chapter is that of dealing with 'enforced disappearances' in the context of war and political violence.

Throughout the world, people have developed different strategies for dealing with the infeasible situations of the 'disappearance' of one or more relatives. In Chapter 3, a number of communal coping strategies are compiled and introduced.

Chapter 4 then provides a short overview of psychotherapeutic approaches to severe traumatisations. It forms the basis for further discussions in the two chapters following after, the first one (Chapter 5) being concerned with the therapeutic work with individuals, and the second one (Chapter 6) with families dealing with the 'disappearance' of one or more relatives.

In certain situations such as wars or natural disasters, a large number of people 'disappear'. Many families are affected; hence, therapeutic work in the form of one-on-one interventions becomes virtually impossible. With this in mind, Chapter 7 focuses on coping strategies for communities. The manual introduced in this context is the result of my own work in various crisis areas, as well as that of colleagues working in cooperation with me in South Asia. Since having first been drawn up, it has been used after a number of different disastrous events in Central America as well as Africa. The text is purposefully kept simple, in order to be approachable and understandable even in situations of extreme stress. As the traumatic situation is not over even once the initial crisis has been dealt with, descriptions of long-term programmes in communities that have been most grievously affected by 'enforced disappearances' constitute the final part of Chapter 7. In rare cases, 'disappeared' people do return. Chapter 8 briefly outlines this issue.

Whenever people approach or encounter the difficult issue of 'enforced disappearances', they are confronted with the feelings of helplessness and uncertainty that come with it. The unresolved grief and fear the relatives experience affects those who set out to help them as well. Therefore, Chapters 9 and 10 deal with the important matter of mental hygiene.

Many of the topics addressed in this book warrant discussions on a much wider base. Scientific studies would help us to further our understanding of the complicated situation relatives of people who have 'disappeared' find themselves in. With this book, I hope to spark off further academic discussions and new views on practical approaches to the issue of 'enforced disappearances'.

# Acknowledgements

In the many years that I have worked with traumata in a psychotherapeutic as well as an academic context, I have met many people who were willing to talk to me about the 'disappearances' of their relatives. I was privileged to be a companion to them during these trying times. First and foremost, this book is dedicated to them.

Many thanks also go to all my colleagues in Austria, in other European countries, in Asia and in America, who have supported and advised me in manifold ways in my work as well as in the writing of this book.

The first three chapters of this publication are based on a previous book of mine, *Ohne jede Spur...*, which I was able to publish in 2006 at Psychosozial-Verlag Gießen. I would like to express my gratitude to this publishing house for their amicable support in reworking the book and translating it to English.

I owe my heartfelt thanks to Zukunftsfond Österreich for their generous funding as well as their moral support. I also greatly appreciate Bent Soerenson Fond's simultaneous sponsoring of the translation into Russian.

Last but not least, I want to thank the team at SAGE, who, across borders and time zones, encouraged and supported the making of this book. Only through their work has this publication become possible.

# 1

## Reaction towards Loss—Grief

### Loss without a Goodbye

The 'disappearance' of an attachment figure always means a loss under particularly difficult circumstances. In the majority of cases an 'enforced disappearance' implies being confronted with the absence of one or more important attachment figures in an especially sudden, unforeseeable and inexplicable manner for relatives and friends. People who live in regions of political tension might be apprehensive of an 'enforced disappearance'. They may worry about it and even fear it, but the actual act happens without prior notice. It comes without the opportunity to say goodbye; but a conscious, deliberate parting is essential for the time of separation—which is usually a permanent state in the case of a 'disappearance'.

### *The Significance of Saying Goodbye*

In order to be able to accept the dreadful enormity of the death of a beloved, rituals are necessary. For many people it helps to see and touch the body of the deceased one last time. For one person, this can prevent fantasies about the status quo still being intact, about the person still being alive and about to come back. For another, this act creates a situation in which saying goodbye to the person, the familiar features, the well-known face, is possible—especially if death came suddenly (Kübler-Ross 1983). Only then, when the physical death is accepted, does it become possible to also let the person go on a social level, to permit the 'social' death, mourn the deceased and move on towards planning a future without this person. This is an extremely painful process. In Sri Lanka, for example, the rituals surrounding death and mourning are characterised by a clear visibility of death, which is quite reasonable and productive from a psychological point of view: The departed is placed on a bier or in an open casket and displayed for everyone in the family and community to see. It is customary to take pictures of the deceased. Death is perceived as one of the realities of life; the rituals give form to the act of saying goodbye and thereby often facilitate this process.

In all this, the needs and wishes of the bereaved should be taken as the touchstone. If after a violent death, the family and friends of the departed decide not to view the body, wishing to hold on to the image of the deceased as alive and whole, this naturally needs to be accepted as well. The act of saying goodbye can then be conducted via pictures and other mementos. It is essential that people have the possibility to express their grief and their emotions. According to Kübler-Ross (1983: 65), the use of sedatives mainly serves to mask the pain and can lead to delayed and intensified mournful sorrow.

The relatives of people who 'disappeared' do not have any such opportunities for ritualised goodbyes, for funerals. The pain caused by the immeasurable loss cannot be expressed since this would mean to concede death. It would imply that all hope of the beloved 'disappeared' still being alive has been given up. In the context of structural violence, of which 'enforced disappearances' is an example, David Becker, who works as a psychoanalyst in Chile, even talks about a ban on mourning. In order to not perish under the pressure of despair, the grief is suppressed, and any acts of mourning are avoided (Becker 1992: 41).

Nicoletti (1988: 58) describes loss in the cases of 'enforced disappearances' as something confusing, something inconceivable:

> From a factual point of view: does a disappearance ... imply loss? If it does, it has very particular characteristics since to begin with, one does not know what has been lost. The missing person is someone who is not any more where he used to be, no one knows where he is now and his existence is denied. ... to consider the missing people dead without even giving their names: that is to say, to be missing is like having one's existence denied both as a living and as a dead person.

The person who has 'disappeared' seems to be doubly lost: The physical absence—alive or dead—calls into question the very existence of the person.

## 'Enforced Disappearance'—Terror Prevents Mourning

A violation of human rights, 'enforced disappearance' is a powerful form of terror against political/ethnic/religious opponents. This adds to the difficult situation relatives of 'disappeared' find themselves in. They are often in no position to enquire after the 'disappeared' or conduct any kind of research about the person's disappearance or whereabouts. They often have to face threats and other forms of intimidation.

If people get separated from each other during a civil war, their search for each other often takes place under anarchic conditions—there are no, or at least very few, institutions or organisational structures that aid in the search for missing relatives or furnish information about them. Quite to the contrary, in order to ensure one's own survival, any such searches have to be foregone completely in most cases.

Instead of receiving support from their social network, as would be usual in an event of death, relatives of victims of 'enforced disappearances' are often abandoned by their families and friends.

## Lack of Rituals

There was no conscious act of saying goodbye to the person who has 'disappeared' and there is no body that can be buried. There is no documentation to prove that the separation is a permanent and final one. Consequently, there are usually no rituals to help accept the separation. The support of the social network that accompanies the mourning rituals in many cultures is conspicuously absent in cases of 'enforced disappearances'.

## The Separation Is—Possibly—Not Permanent

The hope remains that the 'disappeared' might return. This leads to a state of freezing and raises the question whether or not one can even talk about mourning in these cases. Especially in the first weeks, months, often even years, any kind of grief or mourning is perceived as a betrayal of the 'disappeared'. All energy is put towards holding on to the hope for a reunion.

At the same time though, the loss is already an undeniable fact: The relationship that had existed before the 'disappearance' is lost for good. Even if the 'disappeared' should 'reappear', an irretrievable time span has been spent apart from each other. 'Eight and a half years of feeling my heart being torn apart ... my entire youth without a family. Eight Christmases, all the birthdays from the 11th to the 18th, uncountable evenings in which I longed for a word from her [the mother], a touch'[1] is how Kampusch (2010), who was kidnapped as a young child and counted among the 'disappeared' for years, describes the separation from her mother.

## The Absentee as the Centre of the Family

The physically absent—possibly already deceased—person becomes the centre of the life of the social circle, the family. This often leads to psychopathological reactions.

Becker (1992: 88), for example, describes how the state of exception in these situations often becomes normality, a normality characterised by taboos, bans and prohibitions: Precisely the situation that puts such strain on everyone involved cannot be addressed. Any expression of grief or fear is prohibited. Together, the relatives develop intra-familial patterns of depressive behaviour.

The 'disappeared' is either idealised or gets blamed and degraded. Drastic leaps from one extreme to the other are possible. The glorification of the 'disappeared' constitutes the helpless attempt of those remaining at home to do something—anything—for their beloved by retaining an ideal image of the 'disappeared' and thereby letting the person live on. In their vilification on the other hand, relatives project their anger and aggressions onto the 'disappeared' person. 'If he/she hadn't been politically active, hadn't behaved in such an irresponsible manner, then we would have been spared this terrible plight.'

In this book I try to approach the complexity of this difficult topic via the grieving processes typical in 'normal' mourning situations, i.e., in those cases where the circumstances of the person's death are clear to all involved and where the body can be laid to rest with all the culturally entrenched rituals. By means of reflecting upon and understanding these grieving processes, I want to arrive at a clearer understanding of what the loss of a beloved person through an 'enforced disappearance' can mean for the relatives and friends of the victim, and what it takes for these people to move on and keep on living.

## A Person's Development into a Social Individual

In order to be able to approach the topic of people's reactions to 'enforced disappearances', it is necessary to first understand how and why human beings build relationships in the first place, and what the loss of such relationships entails.

Loss and separation can constitute a part of any phase in the life of a human being. Lifton (1979) writes that we need to see life and death as a natural unity. The experience of birth already inherently contains within it the potential for the experience of life as well as death. 'The birth experience activates the infant's innate potential for both life and death imagery and even more, provide the first model for combining these two. Extrauterine life begins with an extrusion' (Lifton 1979: 58).

Human life starts out with a drastic physical separation from the mother's body. The environment is suddenly and utterly changed; the newborn child is surrounded by a host of new stimuli. Consequently, birth can be understood as the origin of many subsequent fears.

> In the separation and encounter with the new environment, the infant might also experience an opening out—a rush of vitality and movement, the beginnings of bodily autonomy. Extrusion and emergence, death equivalents and vitality, the prefiguring of death and renewal—the dialectic is there from the beginning. (Lifton 1979: 59)

Our conceptualisations of death are based on 'death equivalents': separation, disintegration and stasis. These three experiences are possible from the very beginning of life on. They form the basic models for the emotions experienced at a later point in the context of death. All three 'death equivalents' have their specific vitality-affirming counterparts. Separation stands in opposition to connection/attachment, disintegration stands vis-à-vis integrity and stasis forms the counter-pole to all movement and development.

None of the three parameters can be conceived without its respective oppositional force. For Lifton, separation and connection/attachment are the most fundamental experiences in human life.

In order to gain an understanding of the psychological consequences of a separation—and, hence, of the consequences of the 'disappearance' of a relative—it is important to first examine the different forms of affectional bonds with attachment figures in a human life.

## *The Security of the Mother–Child Attachment*

What Erikson (1968) understands as basic trust is the first infantile perception of life as reliable: The mother or attachment figure reacts to the child's needs and satisfies them. If the infant's needs are too frequently disregarded or if the reaction to them is not an adequate one, a basic feeling of mistrust is established within the child. Children are relatively slow in their development of attachment behaviour. This facilitates the development of a repertoire of inner imagery which the child in turn makes use of in learning to cope with connection/attachment and separation. 'That imagery in turn provides him with a variety of imaginative possibilities, but also renders him uniquely vulnerable not only to separation from specific nurturing figures but to more indirect suggestions of separation as well' (Bowlby 1969: 60).

Bowlby describes three stages in the grieving process of children aged 15–30 months that have to cope with a separation from their mother: protest—despair—detachment.

Protest is usually expressed in the form of anger and tears. This constitutes the child's efforts to call back the lost mother. After a couple of days, despair sets in. The loud protests cease, but the child's desperate longing for the mother, for her return, is clearly apparent. In the phase of detachment, the child resigns itself to the fact that the mother is irretrievably lost. Detachment is again accompanied by anger and aggression.

Underlying all the different historical and cultural models of socialisation, we find one central, common tenet: In order for a child to develop in a healthy way it needs affectional bonds it can trust in. Emotional connections are essential for survival; they constitute a crucial necessity in every human's life. The attachment to the mother is of vital importance, even in frameworks that attempt to understand humans primarily as biologically determined beings. B. Van der Kolk (1987: 31f.) writes on this topic:

> A person is a biological organism that develops from the moment of birth in a social context, which begins with the mother–infant bond.... By attaching themselves to caregivers, children put themselves in constant touch with a powerful protector. The assurance of a safe base to which children can return after exploring their surroundings promotes self-reliance and autonomy.

Only if the child feels safe and secure under the parental care—which, in this context, is meant in the widest sense of the word, including the care of foster parents, etc.—only then can it start to explore and become acquainted with the world. It follows from this that these early traumatisations of an infant or toddler through the loss of an attachment figure also constitute a loss of the confidence and safety contingent on this attachment figure.

The loss of eye contact with the mother is enough to make children feel insecure and induce anxiety about the separation. As long as the infants lack the concept of a future, they cannot bear the separation from their mother. Only once children have developed the concept of object permanence, it becomes possible for them to await the mother's return.

All this depends, however, on the time frame set for the separation and the accompanying explanation the child receives for the mother's absence. Winnicott (1971) states that a child separated from its mother can experience her absence as a death. For a while, the child trusts in her return, but once its limit of tolerance is reached—and this is an individual limit, ranging from days for one child to mere minutes for another—the mother is effectively perceived as dead by the child. This phase is characterised by intense feelings of anger, fear and desperation.

## Bowlby's Theory of Attachment

The theory of attachment used throughout this book was developed by John Bowlby. He starts out from the premise that the affectional bond with the loving mother, or with another first attachment figure, forms the basis for all subsequent affectional bonds.

> During the course of healthy development attachment behaviour leads to the development of affectional bonds or attachments, initially between child and parent and later between adult and adult. The forms of behavior and the bonds to which they lead are present and active throughout the life cycle. (Bowlby 1980: 39)

Bowlby describes the primary social bond between mother and child as a bond that then acts as a prototype for all future social relationships. Bowlby's associates have investigated the age-specific forms of affectional bonds with a primary attachment figure. Infants aged three months typically start learning to differentiate between the different people approaching them. When they have reached the seventh-eighth month, children are usually rather fixated on a single person; by the 18th month, most children have foregone this single fixation in favour of having a number of trusted persons (Schaffer & Emerson 1964).

Ainsworth (1978), who worked in close connection with Bowlby, has conducted a study on the reaction of a one-year-old towards the mother leaving the room and returning after some time. Later, the study was extended to include older children. From these, three typical attachment styles could be derived:

1. *Secure attachment*: The children are able to express their feelings at the time of separation from the mother/attachment figure.

Some children cry, others get angry. The children make active attempts to cope with the situation such as searching for the mother, pondering her absence and processing the situation by transferring aspects of it into their playing. Upon the mother's return, they express their joy about the reunion, seek contact with the mother, and then return to their interrupted playing.

2. *Insecure-ambivalent attachment*: The children show signs of intense distress and fear when the mother leaves. They try to prevent the separation using all their available means. They cannot be consoled and do not calm down at all during the mother's absence. When the mother returns, those children demand her full attention and need her comfort for an extended period of time.
3. *Insecure-avoidant attachment*: The children appear to ignore the mother's departure as well as her return. Ainsworth's study revealed, however, that these children do show physical stress reactions such as increased pulse rate and high cortisol levels. This indicates that young children already try to mask their feelings of fear and helplessness (Bowlby 1980; Rehberger 2004).
4. *Insecure–disorganised attachment*: Later, Main et al. (1986) described a fourth attachment style, namely that of the insecure–disorganised attachment. Children falling into this category show only inchoate reactions to the separation (for example, when parents return, children turn to them for only a very short amount of time) or exhibit behavioural stereotypes such as turning on the spot. They appear apathetic and benumbed.

Bowlby saw the original role of attachment in the biological need to secure one's survival. Humans need meaningful long-term relationships in order to be an active part of their social environment and to reproduce. Attachment relationships are, therefore, seen as something logical and necessary from an evolutionary perspective. While this primary function has ceased in importance throughout the cultural development of humanity, the reflective function, that of being able to empathise with others' mental and emotional state, has remained. The capacity to envision the psychological state of others forms the basis to make sense of one's own. This is in line with Rehberger (2004: 27), who stresses the importance of understanding others as a fundamental condition for developing an understanding oneself. According to him, the complex interplay between a child and any kind of care giver is strongly influenced by the attachment relationship in the mother–child dyad, the triangular constellation with mother and father and the plurality within the family, including the interrelations between the child, its siblings and the parents.

A secure attachment provides safety and confidence. The aim of a successful attachment strategy can thereby be described as attaining such a feeling of safety and confidence. According to Rehberger (2004: 28, 30), there is a direct correlation between the extent to which an attachment figure can alleviate the child's uncertainties expressed through crying and clinging, by picking the child up, holding, soothing and comforting it, and the child's trust into attachment bonds as sources of feelings of security and confidence. Rehberger writes further that, therefore, a secure attachment relationship promotes the development of lasting self-confidence and self-respect as well as the acquisition of instrumental and interpersonal competences.

A secure attachment enables the child to also move away from the attachment figure and explore its surroundings. Veith (2008: 6) describes in this context that an infant or toddler who feels safe and secure can explore the surrounding world. Faced with any kind of threat, the child can return to its 'safe base'. Lacking a secure attachment, such explorations become virtually impossible.

If the desire for attachment and connection is continually frustrated, this can lead to an increase in insecurity and anxiety, or to a suppression of the need for attachment.

The attachment styles described above, secure attachment, insecure-avoidant attachment, insecure-ambivalent attachment and insecure-disorganised attachment, can be found in the behavioural patterns of adults as well (Ainsworth 1978; Rehberger 2004).

If a child experiences a secure attachment, it can develop a positive self-image and gain an empathic understanding for others. Attachment promotes autonomy as well as confidence in one's own abilities. Another important element in an attachment relationship is that of affect regulation. In a secure attachment, fears are allayed, pain is soothed by comforting, and anger is acknowledged and simultaneously assuaged. Affirmative feedback on positive emotions can enhance these.

Attachment also forms the basis for the concept of belonging to a certain family, social group or culture, and thereby fosters the development of a number of different context-dependent identities ranging from occupational and social to those within the family. The need for a secure attachment and the mounting desire of the growing child for autonomy both represent basic human needs and further a child's development. For Rehberger (2004: 32), the interplay between these two desires, that for attachment to and approval of others and that for autonomy and independence, is still of vital importance for the establishment of meaningful relationships between adults, which, in turn, constitute an essential component of a successful, prosperous life.

## Transitional Objects and Transitional Phenomena

While children at first experience the world as a part of themselves, and, thereby, the mother's breast as intrinsically connected to them, a differentiation between the 'I' and the external world soon becomes necessary.

> The object represents the infant's transition from a state of being merged with the mother to a state of being in relation to the mother as something outside and separate. This is often referred to as the point at which the child grows up out of narcissistic type of object-relating ... it leaves out the idea of dependence, which is so essential at the earliest stages before the child has become sure that anything can exist that is not part of the child. (Winnicott 1971: 14f.)

Transitional objects facilitate the necessary process towards an acceptance of such differentiations. They represent something that belongs to the child, while not literally belonging to it in the sense of being a part of the child.

> Transitional objects serves as an intermediary for the infant's discovery of the difference between inside and outside. It is an actual object but also has symbolic meaning. It is the not being the breast or the mother....
> A fully developed transitional object is temporarily more important than the mother for the child. (Winnicott 1951: 233, 235)

At first glance it might seem most uncalled for to let a mere object take up a more important role than one's own mother. Closer consideration reveals, however, what immense relief this can bring to the child as well as the mother and/or any other attachment figure. The child can take this symbolic representation along in its search for a wider external world. Meanwhile, the mother can detach herself to some degree from the intensely symbiotic relationship shared with her child.

The transitional object is characterised by the child being its sole owner and assuming all rights of loving and bestowing affection upon it, as well as venting anger and frustration on it. This transitional object must never be

changed, unless by the infant itself. It is a real object, not a hallucination. If, after a while, its importance diminishes, it can slip out of conscious memory without having to be grieved for (Winnicott 1971).

If, however, a child is faced with a difficult separation process at a later point in life, the transitional object present in early childhood can regain its importance:

> Patters set in infancy may persist into childhood, so that the original soft object continues to be absolutely necessary at bed-time or at time of loneliness or when a depressed mood threatens.... A need for a specific object or a behaviour pattern that started at a very early date may reappear at a later age when deprivation threatens. (Winnicott 1971: 6)

Transitional objects can remain important throughout a person's life or at least retake their place of importance in situations of crisis. Greenson writes about one of his patients who comforted herself during the psychoanalytical sessions by patting the textile wallpaper. This wallpaper takes over the place of a transitional object from early childhood and conveys a feeling of emotional security (cf. Greenson 1978). In another case study, Greenson demonstrates clearly how a person's separation anxiety can be soothed via the use of a strongly symbolic transitional object. Upon being told that the psychoanalytic sessions would have to be suspended for a number of weeks as the therapist would be abroad for that time, the patient at first reacted with distress. Then, however, she found an object that could symbolise Greenson for her:

> ... I looked like the white knight of her chess set. The realization immediately evoked in her a feeling of comfort, even of triumph. The white knight was a protector, it belonged to her; she could carry it wherever she want, it would look after her, and I could go on my merry way ... without having to worry about her. (Greenson 1978: 207)

Here we can clearly see how the patient as well as the therapist experiences a sense of relief. Of course, it does take a certain measure of maturity on the side of the patient to be able to overcome her separation anxiety with the help of the transitional object and reach a point where she can let her therapist leave.

In my psychotherapeutic and psychosocial work with people who have suffered difficult and painful losses, transitional objects have become ever more important. Such objects can be deliberately used to help in coping with the separation from a beloved person.

A real-life example from Austria:

A six-year-old boy is brought to therapy by his mother who at that time is in the late stages of pregnancy. The boy cannot stay at school without her anymore; he needs her to always be either in the classroom with him, or at least right outside in the hallway, in order for him to not lapse into panic. Also, he has started to wet the bed again. A few weeks ago, his father was arrested for a crime by a special force unit in the middle of the night. The policemen, clad in black, hooded and masked, broke into the family home in the middle of the night and woke up and scared the sleeping family.

In the therapy room, there is a basket filled with various dolls and stuffed animals. The young patient gets permission to pick one of these and take it home with him. He chooses an approximately 6 inches tall, black stuffed devil, which has red horns, but a really friendly face.

Two weeks later, the therapist asks the boy whether he still wets the bed. He answers in the negative, explaining proudly that now he is not afraid of going to the bathroom at night, because the little devil accompanies and protects him now. A few days later, the boy can allow his mother to leave him at school, since he now has a figure there with him that symbolises security and safety for him.

Mementos of loved ones who have passed away or have 'disappeared' are often essential in the process of facilitating grieving.

An example from Sri Lanka:

A counsellor tells the story of a 10-year-old girl who has been paralysed from the waist down for a number of months. Additionally, she suffers from severe attacks of dizziness and fainting spells. There is no recognisable organic cause for this severe condition. In a supervision session, the counsellor further relates how about half a year earlier the father of the girl died of a sudden heart attack while riding his bike. We can understand the physical symptoms the girl displays as a symbolisation of the father as a person as well as of her continuous connection to him.

By taking over the symptoms that her father in all likelihood experienced during the last moments of his life, she attaches him to herself and thereby 'prolongs' his life.

We developed another, healthier way for the girl to remain connected to her father while at the same time also accepting his death and the necessity of letting go of him as a physical entity in her life, as represented via her own body. Pictures, bracelets and gifts given to the girl by her father should be given primary focus in a deliberate and purposeful way during the psychological counselling. If the girl succeeds in conceptualising these objects as representing her connections to her father, then she can let go of the physical symptoms plaguing her body.

## Between the Parental Home and the Peer Group

For adolescents, the peer group represents an increasingly central part of life. As young adults, they have to leave the parental home and establish their own independence. The peer group facilitates a transition from fulfilling the role of a child within the fold of the nuclear family to living up to the part of someone who has reached emotional maturity.

For younger children, school friends and play mates already become more and more important, even if their families still represent the primary point of reference. For adolescents, the group of peers becomes even more central. Blos (1979) describes the period of adolescence as the 'second great chance'. For young adults, the peer group can to a certain degree compensate deficits and instabilities existent within the family life. New roles can be observed, tried out and practiced. Within the circle of friends, new feelings of belonging and accepting form the basis for a redefinition of one's own personality. Adolescents from an unimpaired, stable parental home have an easier time integrating into a peer group and establishing their identities there than adolescents from less fortunate family backgrounds.

The time of adolescence signifies a change from the natural dependence of a child to the autonomy of an adult. During this phase of radical restructuring, the world is often perceived and understood in terms of absolutes: Everything is either good or bad, active or passive; there is either love or hate. A middle ground cannot be seen, let alone accepted (Blos 1979).

In most cases, this phase of adolescence represents a transitional stage that facilitates the acquisition of the ability of a mature kind of differentiation. During late adolescence, this processual second detachment from the immediate family should be completed.

In those respects where adolescents mistrust the world of adults, the attachment to the peer group becomes especially strong. This is, for example, reflected in the propensity towards violence often present in groups living under such psychological conditions where the need for a destruction of the adult-made external reality that might threaten the identity of the group is especially prevalent. By putting the group identity above that of the individual, often to the extent of completely relinquishing one's own identity within the group, the collective identity and resultant community can convey a feeling of omnipotence to its members (Kernberger 1984).

Some adolescents perceive this feeling of belonging to their peer group or gang as their sole affiliation. They are completely committed to the group and give up other social and emotional attachment bonds for it, going as far as committing acts of self-destruction. 'Unable to return safely to the parental fold, they tend to develop clinging and dependent relationships, either with someone of the opposite sex or with gang members of the same sex' (Van der Kolk 1987: 158).

While male adolescents tend to hide their fears and loneliness behind juvenile tests of courage and antisocial behaviour, young women are more inclined to attach themselves to difficult male partners, trying to find in these relationships the kind of attention and affection they were denied in their family of origin.

## Experiences of Loss during Childhood

Children whose contact to their primary attachment figure is disrupted or even terminated all together develop a variety of symptoms. They overreact to many situations and have great difficulties enduring states of uncertainty and fear. Their reactions can range from physical hyperactivity to withdrawing into themselves in depressed silence. Grieving children are typically distrustful and cling to their attachment figures, new and old. They rarely join the games of their peers and are rather diffident about establishing new social contacts (Van der Kolk 1987).

Spitz (1967) followed by Mahler et al. (1975) and Bowlby (1980) have all described the consequences that a separation from the mother brings with it for children. If the separation from the mother or the attachment figure lasts too long, this is experienced as overwhelming, even traumatic.

Children perceive themselves as the centre of the world. This world view necessarily entails that they are also the cause for all the goings-on in their lives, which often results in strong feelings of guilt. If a parent 'disappears', the child can build up a scenario in which the father or mother will reappear after the child has done its penance, since their absence is merely a punishment for misbehaviour. Fantasies about further punishment can continue to stress and unsettle the child: 'He may think he is being punished for being bad and the others are going to leave him' (Van Dexter 1986: 161).

## Children's Strategies for Coping with Grief

In children, reactions to the loss of a person they were close to differ depending on their age. Van Dexter (1986) provides an overview of these age-dependent reactions, which is useful in an application to the context of 'enforced disappearances' as well. Van Dexter proposes the following classification:

While children aged between 4 months and 2–2½ years react with continuous symptoms of stress, children aged 2–5 years withdraw into a regressive state. This state manifests itself through extreme clinginess and through their making demands that, by nature, cannot be satisfied.

This description is in line with what I have been told countless times by women working in refugee camps in Sri Lanka. A woman, for example, told me about her niece, whom she had taken in. The woman related that she could barely leave the girl alone, since she needed her aunt close by at all times. The girl's mother had been killed in a bombing raid, the father had 'disappeared'. Other women in the refugee camp, however, also relate this kind of regressive behaviour to significantly older children (up to 12-year-olds).

Van Dexter next describes the group of 5–8-year-old children. At this age, children's cognitive abilities to consciously grasp the concept of loss are much further developed. They might hide their feelings and tears, wanting to not be different from their peers (Van Dexter 1986).

This is the age group at which fantasies that deny the undesired reality and depict the beloved person as alive are especially common. If the person who has been lost has been 'disappeared', then these fantasies can impede the grieving process even further.

Children aged 8–12 often react with shock and denial. At that age, the concept of mortality can already be grasped.

> The child is threatened by the idea of mortality now. He may resist communicating with adults. He may also try to act grown-up in an attempt to conquer the pain and sorrow of his loss and helplessness. Often, in this age group, grief goes unnoticed, especially if the child tends not to act out grief, but withdrawn until, in time, he can acknowledge his sorrow and grieve.
> (Van Dexter 1986: 160)

The behavioural patterns described here have to be taken seriously, particularly in children who have lost one or both parents in a time of political unrest. This is even more true, if the parents were victims of an 'enforced disappearance' during such a time, a situation that is complicated by additional insecurity and uncertainty. The general instability and incertitude of such a situation, combined with the politicalisation of the mourning process, leads the adults to pay little attention to the children reacting in such a quiet, unobtrusive manner. The children's apparently mature behaviour makes it easy for them and their needs to be overlooked.

Finally, Van Dexter describes the group of grieving teenagers. Outwardly, they also tend to display a mature and composed stance.

> When an adolescent cannot grieve directly, he may exhibit it through exaggerated pseudo-adult behaviours: identification with the dying person; depression and withdrawal; sexual acting out, and care eliciting behaviours designed not only to secure care but to release tension; selfpunish and sometimes replace the dying person. (Van Dexter 1986: 160)

This description may form the basis for an explanatory approach as to why it is so particularly easy to recruit child soldiers in civil war countries.

Van Dexter bases her descriptions on her work with grieving children in schools. She has developed her own model for how school teachers can best support grieving children. Central to this model is that the school should serve as an island of stability during this time of uncertainty and instability. Stability here also means that the child should remain within the structured routine of a school day, including mandatory attendance and fulfilment of the required workloads. The familiarity of these routines provides them with a sense of dependability and stability. Beyond that, Van Dexter emphasises though that the teacher should make sure to devote special attention to these children and give them room and time for their grief. 'The child needs reassurance that he is loved, that he is not at fault' (Van Dexter 1986: 160).

## *Sequential Traumatisation (Hans Keilson)*

Keilson's (1979) work on the sequential traumatisation in children can be described as seminal in several respects. He shows that a trauma cannot be understood as one specific isolated event, but needs to be recognised as a process that extends over a number of stages—the sequences. Psychological understanding is, therefore, only possible if all these sequences are taken into account.

In the Netherlands, Keilson conducted a systematic long-term study with Jewish survivors of the Holocaust who had been separated from their parents during the time of Nazi persecution. Drawing on this data, he developed a model based on three major phases of traumatisation.

The pre-traumatic sequence is characterised by a significant deterioration of the living situation the child finds itself in, and by the first experiences of persecution. This phase encompasses all those experiences of fear that are connected to the all-pervading crumbling of the rule of law, the suddenly mandatory wearing of the yellow star (which both culminated in the raids and deportations), the assault on the dignity and the integrity of the family, the destruction of entire economic livelihoods, the confinement to ghettos, the tense, fearful anticipation of atrocities to come, the sudden disappearance of relatives, acquaintances, friends, schoolmates and playmates, in short, the complete disintegration of their familiar environment (Keilson 1979: 56).

The traumatic sequence per se, in which the interviewed children lived separate from their parents in secret hiding places or concentration camps, is actually the second traumatic sequence. Here, the traumatogenic elements are much more clearly discernible. They consist not only of the direct threat to the child's life, the lack of any secure legal status and the feeling of being at the mercy of a hostile environment, but also the continuous strain stressors such as privation, hunger and illness put on them. Furthermore, they also include the psychological experiences of a 'general atmosphere of menace' such as progressive attrition, calling into question and destruction of social behaviours—especially in comparison to the culturally established norms—due to the continuous confrontation with terror, death and the brutal use made of power (Keilson 1979).

Finally, Keilson describes the time after the fall of the Nazi regime as the post-traumatic sequence. In the post-war period, the children either had to return to their families of origin or had to integrate into society in another form. But the world they 'reappeared' into had been changed significantly from the one they had been forced to leave. The state of constant threat to their lives suddenly over, the state's measures for rehabilitation just in the beginning stages, the children or young adults are faced with the difficult task of processing and coming to terms with the wide gulf between them and others, the gaps in their knowledge and the difference between the worlds they had left and the one they had to re-enter. This often leads to an intensification of the confrontation with their traumata, which in turn leads to new damages to their psyche (Keilson 1979).

Keilson included children of six different age groups in his study, based on the assumption that the effects of the separation from their parents and consequent life under constant threat would differ depending on the stage of development the children were in.

In the two groups made up of the youngest children (0–18 months, 18 months–4 years), character-neurotical developments connected to difficulties in making contact and general personal and social insecurities were most prevalent. In comparison, those older than 4 largely suffered from chronic-reactive depressions. A striking number of the children in the prepubertal group (10–13 years) developed anxiety neuroses. In fact, the figures were so significant in this respect that Keilson identified this as an age-specific reaction.

Age-independent reactions were general emotional disturbances, conflicts of loyalty and identity and various forms of grief disorder. Even those people who were generally able to come to terms with the traumatic experiences connected with the separation from their parents had troubles coping with certain situations in their later life. One of these situations, recurring within the group of participants, is, for example, the point in life where the children themselves reached the age their parents had been at the time of the separation. Follow-up studies also showed that the time after the birth of a child is one where the memories and feelings of identification with one's own mother are especially vulnerable (Keilson 1979). However, according to the clinical part of Keilson's study, all of those study participants generally coping well, independent from their respective age at the time of the separation from their families, experienced a similar form of reception into the foster family during the post-traumatic phase (Keilson 1979). This reception (also independent of the foster parents' religion) is described as being characterised by the new attachment figures conveying a strong feeling of safety and security to the children. From this it follows that such a reception is crucial in preventing children of any age who have been traumatised by a family separation from developing serious, chronic illnesses.

Becker and Weyermann (2006) adapted Keilson's model, expanding it from three to six sequences:

1. *The pre-conflict phase*: All the experiences a person has made prior to the actual traumatic event have their influence on how the affected person perceives this situation of extreme violence or particularly tragic loss, and how well this situation can be processed on a psychological level.

2. *Beginning of the persecution*: This sequence is largely similar to Keilson's pre-traumatic sequence.
3. *Direct persecution, acute terror and relative calm chronification*: Here, Becker and Weyermann distinguish between the experiences of direct acts of war or abuse and the long, subsequent periods of waiting while the thread looms. They point out that in times of war or oppression, the by far larger amount of time is spent waiting for the next catastrophe than actually experiencing one. In fact, this time of waiting is where most of the psychological effects of terror take root in the victims psyche, condemned to biding time considering one's own inner hurts and injuries and lingering on the feeling of threat, the fear of what atrocities are yet to come, a fear which gets chronificated more and more and intensifies over time (2006: 191). This is especially significant in the context of 'enforced disappearances': Here the fear and worry about what the beloved has to endure, in general as well as right at that moment, puts a permanently encumbering strain on the relatives.
4. *Phase of transition*: This denotes the time of ceasefire after a civil war or the transitional period right after the end of a dictatorship before a new, stable kind of government has been established. Such a time is typically characterised by an increase of freedom, but not really by an end of acts of repression. A prime example for this could be found after 2011 in North Africa and the Middle East, during the transitional period following the uprisings of the Arab Spring Movement. During that time, a vision of a future suddenly becomes possible again, while at the same time it becomes clear that such a future will never be free of the irreversible experiences of the past (Becker & Weyermann 2006: 191). In this instability and uncertainty, there are many similarities to the situation people seeking asylum find themselves in; they have arrived in a safe country, but it is not yet clear whether or not they will be allowed to stay.
5. *Following persecution; the post-conflict situation*: This sequence, which again corresponds largely to the third sequence described by Keilson, is the most complex in nature. How the general situation as well as the vulnerabilities of the victims develops, depends to a large degree on the conditions provided for them through political decisions and by the way they are received by society.

Central in all phases of sequential traumatisation is the loss of a relationship, an attachment to an important person (as it is the case if a relative 'disappears'). The children live in separation from their parents, their siblings, their extended family, the entire social environment they are familiar with and in almost all cases this separation is a final one. It is often impossible to attain any kind of information about the circumstances of the relative's death. The resulting grieving process is oft pathologically prolonged, as could be seen in Keilson's follow-up study in 1972, a time at which the child victims of the Holocaust had long reached adulthood. Keilson (1979: 235f.) illustrates this through the story of Esther, who, at the age of eleven, had to witness her mother and grandfather being arrested and carried off. Following this, her aunt took her in and hid her. After the war, she was apparently completely convinced that her mother would return to her. Every day she was sure that this would be the day she would come back to her. This conviction was further supported by the return of an uncle and another aunt, who had been detained in a concentration camp. Young Esther was so certain that her mother was still alive at that time that one day she impatiently asked her uncle, who functioned as her guardian, when her mother would finally come back. Irritated, her uncle replied by asking how he could possibly know that, and snapped at her, telling her clear off at once. This response shook her to the core. She never forgot it. From then on, she kept her thoughts and fantasies about her mother to herself. Only years later did she understand that she had inadvertently hit a tender spot in her uncle's heart. Keilson explains further that at the time of the follow-up study, she had spent many a time in the previous years sitting apathetically in a chair, startling at every sound. Only rarely did she leave the house in these phases. During such times her children ran her errands. These periods alternated with times in which she travelled to her aunt in order to talk about 'those times'. She still saw herself as the child waiting for the mother's return. During the day, she has to slip into the role of a mother, raising her children and caring for them. Leading this double life, however, takes its toll. At times, she suffered from severe states of exhaustion.

If children have to experience the loss of an attachment bond under traumatic circumstances, it prevents a natural grieving process and can have long-lasting after-effects. In countries plagued by war or terror, children are frequently confronted with the sudden death and/or the 'disappearance' of their parents. Only rarely do these children receive adequate help in coping with this loss and overcoming their grief.

## Telling Children the Truth

Surviving parents often feel that they can protect their children by keeping the truth about the 'disappeared' family member from them. For the children, though, being barred from information obviously available to the adults generally presents a much larger burden. Because of the reactions displayed by the adults surrounding them, the children of course realise that something terrible must have happened. The placations they get to hear do not correspond to the actions and emotions they can watch in their remaining parent or other attachment figure. The children have to rely on their own imagination, picturing all kinds of inconceivable horrors. They cannot address their fears in a conversation with an adult, since, officially, everything is perfectly in order. At the same time, they might even feel responsible for the 'disappearance'. In this situation of complete denial they are denied access to any kind of explanation that might relieve them of such thoughts.

Even very young children can sense that it might actually be the adults who cannot cope with the situation and have to flee into denial. This can then result in a reversal of roles, where the children try to protect their own parents by playing along and keeping up the web of lies. Of course, this puts an excessive strain on the children.

A mother, who has concealed the father's death (of a serious illness he had gone to hospital for) from her daughter for months, overhears the girl talking to one of her playmates. To the question where her father might be, the girl answers that he is dead. The mother is quite taken aback by this, as she has talked almost daily with her daughter about the bed-ridden father, unfortunately too gravely right now for any visitors to be allowed. Together, the two have imagined what life will be like together, once the father has recovered and returned to them. The little girl protects her mother from the terrible truth. This, of course, puts a serious strain on her relationship with her mother who is concealing essential information from her.

In August 2005, eight months after the tsunami in Sri Lanka, a nurse relates the following case: The only reaction a father can get out of his five-year-old son is one of almost violent aggression. The father had told his son that the mother, pregnant at that time, has travelled to India for the birth, but is well and healthy. In truth, he has not heard from her since the tsunami. With every passing week, the son's questions became more insistent: He demanded to know why his mother had not returned.

At a loss as to what to do, the father has asked the nurse for professional help. In our supervision sessions with the nurse, we come up with a plan for how to best create a situation in which the father can tell his son the truth, supported by the nurse herself and an acquainted pastor. (Psychotherapeutic support did not constitute an available option in the East of Sri Lanka at that time.) Afterwards, both had the chance to talk about their thoughts and feelings individually, the son meeting with the nurse alone, and the father with the pastor. The goal of this intervention is to provide the boy with a situation in which he can express his anger on the father who has lied to him, which in turn is necessary to establish a new basis for re-establishing a trust-based relationship with his father. In order to avoid volleys of accusations and verbal attacks between father and son in this first phase of confronting the truth, these individual sessions with familiar people who are nevertheless not directly involved in the situation are of particular importance. The husband and father has to acknowledge that his wife is indeed not abroad in a safe country, but has in all likelihood perished in the flood; the son has to, in an age-appropriate manner, come to terms with the loss of his mother and the fact that his father has lied to him in such an important matter. Through this careful form of intervention we make a grieving process for both possible. They are not alone in their grief, but are connected by the shared pain, which can be a chance to hopefully re-stabilise the father–son bond.

When working with parents faced with loss, helping them towards a willingness and ability to tell their children the truth constitutes an essential goal.

## Grief and the Grieving Process

Grief is a highly complex process consisting of feelings, cognitive elements as well as actions. Its purpose is coping with and overcoming experiences of separation, abandonment and loss. Freud (1914/16: 244) writes:

> In what, now, does the work which mourning performs consist? I do not think there is anything far-fetched in presenting it in the following way. Reality-testing has shown that the loved object no longer exists, and it proceeds to demand that all libido shall be withdrawn from its attachments to that object. This demand arouses understandable—it is a matter of general observation that people never willingly abandon a libidinal position, not even, indeed, when a substitute is already beckoning to them.

This opposition can be so intense that a turning away from reality takes place and a clinging to the object through the medium of a hallucinatory wishful psychosis. Normally, respect for reality gains the day.

Shapiro talks about the time of mourning as 'frozen time'. In Freud's words:

> We bury our hopes, our wishes, and our desires with the dead, we are inconsolable and refuse to replace our loss. We act in this case as if we belonged to the tribe of the Asra who also die when those whom they love perish. (Freud 1918/2011: 7)

Often, the time of grieving is described by those affected as a nightmare they simply cannot wake up from, no matter what, as a time in which they are completely incapable of facing the truth and managing their ever-day life. In addition, they are also confronted again and again with the lack of understanding on the part of those people in their social environment who have never had to experience such a painful loss.

Another important point to consider is that grieving takes time.

After the death of a spouse, coping with the bereavement will need two to three years, according to Shapiro (1994: 48). In this, however, she does not describe the grieving process following a sudden and unexpected death. In those cases, grieving takes significantly longer.

## Grieving Process

Throughout the grieving process, a number of different, sometimes even contradictory feelings may arise. These differ from person to person, in nature as well as in the stage of the grieving process during which they occur. According to Rehberger (2004: 18f.), the most basic emotional conditions the bereaved go through are pain, longing for who and what has been lost, hopelessness, dejection, anger and a number of fears such as the fear of falling, of breaking down, but also of remaining in this state of feebleness and weakness and even of dying themselves. These conditions often show themselves in the bereaved via a stooped body posture, inner or outer paralysis and reticence. Rehberger describes further that grieving people often withdraw, focusing inwardly on all they have lost, and on related dreams and fantasies. They devote themselves to thoughts about shared experiences, at times to a point where they are literally lost in their thoughts, making them hard to reach for others, especially in cases of strong grief. Often, the bereaved attempt to consciously take action as a means of responding to their feelings of being helpless and overpowered (Rehberger 2004: 18f.).

There are a number of different models that try to subdivide the grieving process into its main stages. In an exemplary fashion, three of these are described here.

## Rando's Six 'R' Process

Rando (1992–1993), for example, describes the grieving process as consisting of six different stages—the six 'R' process:

1. Recognising the loss.
2. Reacting emotionally to the separation, via pain, identification, etc.
3. Recollecting and re-experiencing the lost relationship.
4. Relinquishing the past attachment to the late beloved and the bygone world of which the beloved had been a part.
5. Readjusting to a new world without forgetting the old one.
6. Reinvesting themselves into this new world.

The aim of the grieving process is to arrive at a stage of acceptance of the now permanent absence of the beloved person (or object, in fact), and to integrate this absence into one's own life in a meaningful way. Rehberger (2004: 28f.) stresses that a successful grieving process does not have deletion at its centre, be it deletion of the symbolic representations of what has been experienced in emotional closeness with the lost beloved or that of concrete memories of the love lived together. Grieving is not about inner disengagement. While a presence becomes an absence, an open, accessible present with a possible future becomes a past without a chance of further development, it is the retention of the loving attachment to the deceased that explains the bouts of grief that flare up again quite unexpectedly at times (Rehberger 2004: 28f.).

## J. Bowlby's Four Phases of Mourning

Bowlby (1980) describes the grieving process in four phases, focusing, in contrast to Rando, on the difficulties inherent in accepting the loss.

1. *Phase of numbing*: This phase can last from a few hours up to a week and can be interrupted by outbursts of extremely intense distress, pain and/or anger.
2. *Phase of yearning and searching*: In this phase, which can take anything from a couple of weeks up to a number of years, the bereaved searches for the lost beloved in spite of the certain knowledge that the attachment figure is lost forever.

   On the one hand is belief that death has occurred with the pain and hopeless yearning that that entails. On the other is disbelief that it has occurred, accompanied both by hope that all may yet be well and by an urge to search for and to recover the lost Person. (Bowlby 1980: 87)

   Anger and rage feature commonly in this phase. On the one hand, this anger is focused on those perceived responsible for the loss while on the other hand, the deceased themselves are sometimes the recipients of the bereaved's rage, as they are the ones who withdrew from the relationship bond.

   In the context of the present project, this phase is especially significant. If a person has been 'disappeared', it is sheer impossible to verify that the beloved will never return.
3. *Phase of disorganisation and despair*: The unsuccessful search for the lost person or object is met with despair.

   Only if he can tolerate the pining, the more or less conscious searching, the seemingly endless examination of how and why the loss occurred, and anger at anyone who might have been responsible, not sparing even the dead person, can he come gradually to recognize and accept that the loss is in truth permanent and that his life must be shaped anew. (Bowlby 1980: 93)

   If this can be achieved, then the next phase within a successful mourning process can follow.
4. *Phase of reorganisation*: Patterns of thinking, feeling and acting that have the lost person as a focal point are now separated into two groups. There are those that have become redundant as they depend on the physical presence of the lost figure, such as household chores, shared hobbies, etc. These are set apart from shared goals and values that can prevail. The memories of the shared past are integrated and a new future without the lost person is planned.

These phases are not to be understood as absolute in any way; mourning is a very individual process and depends on a variety of different factors. Bowlby (1980) has identified a number of these and categorised them into five groups of variables.

1. *Identity and role of the person lost*: If there had been a strain on the relationship with the lost person, the grieving process is commonly exacerbated. The same is true if the lost person was younger than the bereaved, as this kind of loss is much more unexpected. The death of a child constitutes a particular high risk for a long and complicated mourning process for the parents (Bowlby 1980; Rehberger 2004).
2. *Age and sex of the person bereaved*: Men generally try harder to control their emotions during mourning than women do. This results in lapses in concentration and general inefficiency in their task fulfilment for them. Rehberger (2004: 40) relates this suppression of emotions to the achievement of a more realistic acknowledgement of the loss, while stressing the incapacity to work in men as an indicator for their suppressed fears and pains.

    In his study with Vietnam veterans, Van der Kolk (1985, 1987) found that the age of the male soldiers constituted a significant factor in their post-traumatic stress disorder (PTSD) risk; In those cases where the men were still adolescents when brought into action, they developed much stronger attachment bonds to the other soldiers in their troop and, consequently, the death of one of their 'buddies' effected them in a much more traumatic way.
3. *The causes and circumstances of loss*: The main topic of this book is the particularly difficult situation surviving dependants find themselves in when they lose a beloved person through an 'enforced disappearance', a situation which significantly exacerbates the process of grieving. Studies about mourning generally show that losses that are sudden, especially if connected to violence, complicate the grieving process considerably.
4. *Social and psychological circumstances affecting the bereaved at the time of loss and after*: The support the social environment can provide for the bereaved is most essential for a successful mourning process. This issue is also of special importance to the relatives of victims of enforced disappearances and will therefore be expanded on at a later point in this book. If a person, rather than clearly dying, 'disappears', this does not only, by its very nature, bring with it a very difficult grieving process, but often also goes hand in hand with a lack, or even a withdrawal, of social support.

5. *The personality of the bereaved, with special reference to his capacities for making love relationships and for responding to stressful situations*: Pre-existing stable relationships have a positive effect on the mourning process. Previous traumatic losses, on the other hand, make people particularly valuable to the effects of a fresh loss. In order to understand the process of mourning, as Rehberger (2004: 72) points out, one needs to be familiar with the bereaved's affect regulations prior to the loss. He also names a number of other factors necessary for a profound comprehension of the grieving process, such as the significance of the loss, the way it was experienced by the bereaved and the consequences the loss has on this person.

## Stroebe and Schut's Dual Process Model

Stroebe and Schut (1999, 2010) have developed the so-called dual process model (DPM) in order to better understand the process of coping with bereavement. The bereaved perceive themselves as oscillating between two poles, one loss-oriented and one restoration-oriented.

The loss-oriented pole is characterised by a strong feeling of sadness, the intrusion of the loss and grief on all activities and thoughts and the denial and avoidance of any kind of acceptance of the loss. The restoration-oriented pole on the other hand is typically characterised by an interest in new things, by distracting oneself from the grief and by trying out new roles and entering into new relationships.

The continuous yearning for the lost person and the despair over the loss stand in opposition to a re-orientation and dedication to new opportunities and possibilities life offers. The desire to completely live in one's memories and be consumed by grief can exist simultaneously with the wish for new experiences. The DPM extends the professional perception of mourning by focusing on this simultaneous presence of opposing emotions and desires, as well as the oscillation between these poles as part of the process of coping with bereavement.

## Coping with Bereavement and Dissociation

For J. Kauffman, dissociation constitutes a normal element within the grieving process, during which the bereaved moves through a number of emotional stages, starting with denial and ending with an acceptance of the loss as reality. In his approach, acceptance and denial can again co-occur simultaneously. 'We partially accept and partially deny a death at the same time.... Dissociated fragments of the self persist and contain the wounds of death that are not accepted into consciousness' (Kauffman 1993–1994: 34).

These fragments of the self are in dynamic interplay during the mourning process. Some of the conscious fragments deny the death while others comprehend and accept it as reality. What forms acceptance and denial take is mainly influenced by three central factors:

1. What internalised images of and opinions on death and loss does the bereaved have?
2. In what kind of relationship to each other were the bereaved and the deceased?
3. What were the circumstances surrounding the death or loss?

If the bereaved has already had prior traumatic experiences with death and loss, then the division is experienced with increased intensity.

> The mourning process is always a matter of simultaneously believing that the deceased is alive and not alive. Our understanding of the mourning process needs to grasp the relationship between these two in the mourner. It is not a matter of being 'in denial' or not, but a matter of identifying specifically where the denial is and how it is functioning relative to what is recognized. (Kauffman 1993–1994: 35)

Symptoms that might appear pathological at first glance can actually constitute normal reactions of mournful sorrow. Kauffman notes that even drastic manifestations such as the hearing of voices can under certain circumstances in fact be part of the normal grieving process and need not be seen as a disorder.

If the circumstances surrounding the death or loss are extremely traumatic, then dissociation has to be put into the right perspective. The pathological state of splitting is no longer seen as such within the context of traumata, but as an independent defence mechanism better described as 'dissociation' (Zepf 2001).

When working with the relatives and close friends of people who have 'disappeared', one does not only have to keep in mind all those elements present within a normal mourning process, but also those coping mechanisms commonly found in people who have had to experience external traumata, as the loss of an important attachment figure through an 'enforced disappearances' certainly constitutes such a traumatic experience. Other forms of traumatisation may well play into the situation as well and have to be considered.

## Avoidance of Grief

The description of the grieving process can be disrupted at any stage or phase, consequently leading to a prolongation of the mourning process or to chronification. Rando (1992–1993) particularly points out the potential of the bereaved's refusal to believe that the loss or at least certain aspects of the loss are in fact real and true. In order to avoid the pain inherent to grieving, the mourners try to avoid facing these emotions and instead hold on to the relationship bond to the deceased. Here, Horowitz describes an especially interesting phenomenon when it comes to avoidance:

> An important difference in the scientific analysis of trauma and bereavement phenomena is that Horowitz analyses intrusion–avoidance processes as symptomatic of traumatic reactions, whereas in the bereavement area, they have been regarded as coping strategies, and even as coping styles. (Stroebe et al. 1998: 86)

## Complicated Mourning

Grief can be made more complicated or even be inhibited completely by a number of biographical factors in the life of the bereaved as well as by the circumstances surrounding the present loss. Rando (1992–93) describes seven factors that bring with them an increased risk of complicated mourning.

Four of these are directly connected to the present loss or death, namely if

1. death occurred suddenly, especially unexpectedly, maybe even under particularly violent or traumatic circumstances;
2. death occurs after a prolonged time of severe illness;
3. it is the death of a child;
4. the bereaved believe that they could have prevented the death.

The three other risk factors have to do with the bereaved themselves and their relationship with the deceased:

5. if the relationship with the deceased has been a problematic one;
6. if the bereaved has had traumatic experiences with death prior to the present loss;
7. if the grieving person or family does not receive the social support they need.

For relatives and loved ones of victims of 'enforced disappearances', the first and last factors are of particular relevance. The 'disappearance' comes unexpected in almost all cases, and more often than not happens under traumatic circumstances. In the majority of cases, the bereaved are refused the usual social support. They have little to no chance of openly wearing their pain and taking up the role of a mourner in society, or any other of the roles that have changed through the loss.

During therapy it can be possible to make up for the lost rituals to some degree, at least on the level of personal goodbyes. This can be done by, for example, preparing the dishes traditionally eaten at wakes or funerals, and sharing this meal in memory of the 'disappeared' person. Conducting the traditional prayer rituals is another such step. A guided imaginary journey, in which the patient puts him/herself into the position of the mourner at the funeral rituals for the 'disappeared', which could never take place, can be another such measure. If the patient is religious or at least believes in an existence after death, that is helpful too.

## Grief and PTSD

If a person dies after a long, fulfilled life, then those surviving this person will mourn him or her, but the death will not traumatise them. The reversed situation exists as well, of course. There are traumatic experiences (like a hostage situation without casualties) that can lead to PTSD but the victims do not grieve. However, in the majority of cases we do find a close interaction between the two phenomena.

There is a clear difference in the definition of grief and PTSD: Post-traumatic disorders are primarily defined via the diagnostic criteria stipulated in the *Diagnostic and Statistical Manual of Mental Disorders* DSM-V and the *International Statistical Classification of Diseases and Related Health Problems* ICD-10; in other words, they are defined as clearly delineated psychological disorders that can occur in response to a fairly well-defined number of incidents. 'It seems likely that this is a consequence of the general tendency to view bereavement as normal human experience. Nevertheless, there is strong pressure to create a category of pathological grief' (Stroebe et al. 1998: 83).

After traumatic experiences like the Shoa/the Holocaust, grief and mourning is of central importance. Many survivors state that the fact that mourning their dead was sheer impossible constituted one of the most difficult aspects of their experience. This is also echoed in volumes upon volumes of the Holocaust literature, where the impossibility to mourn at a grave since the bodies have been burnt or hastily buried elsewhere, the lack of memorial days since no one quite knows when the beloved has died, and also the feeling of overpowering helplessness in the face of the incredible number of deaths are recurring themes. Henry Krystal (1968: 193) writes already:

> The 'survivor', having unresolved problems of mourning and, in fact, being in a state of pathological mourning, is greatly threatened by any new loss. It is self-evident that the loss of a current love-object mobilizes all the latent conflicts and threatens to overwhelm these patients with depression. As a result, they will typically participate in funerals and bereavements 'without any feelings', and tend to deny their losses, (but may develop insomnia, depression, or hypomania and sleeping pill abuse immediately thereafter). At the same time, however, they suffer chronic depression, and the feelings blocked upon bereavement frequently 'spill' in an isolated fashion upon encounter with diffuse trivial stimuli. What we have found ... is that in the survivor syndrome every loss of one's physical function, capacity, or attribute is experienced exactly as the loss of a love object and consequently threatens the same kind of overwhelming depressive or psychotic disaster.

## Mourning 'Disappeared' Relatives

What, though, happens if reality-testing results in nothing but further uncertainties? What state of normality can be achieved in the lives of those whose beloved attachment figure has 'disappeared'?

The term 'mourning' can be defined; grieving processes have frequently been described—but all of them presuppose that the reality of death can be verified and, therefore, constitutes an irrefutable fact. As discussed at the beginning of this chapter, the 'disappearance' and especially the resultant uncertainty concerning the whereabouts, current situation and faith of the 'disappeared' exacerbates the grieving process for people of all ages. Inner-psychological factors and the type of relationship bond between the 'disappeared' and the patient play a major role in coping with the loss or, respectively, in the chronification thereof.

## Grief Needs Expression, Witnessing and Rituals

Grief has to find its expression in words as well as in rituals. These words and rituals need witnesses to ground them firmly in reality. Additionally, concrete opportunities to say goodbye have to be provided: It is very important that relatives say goodbye to the—now lifeless—body, especially if death came unexpected (Kübler-Ross 1969). 'If the body is not viewed it may take years longer for the survivors to complete their grief because it is difficult to realise the loved one is truly dead' writes Mancini (1986: 147), who works in the field of psychological counselling for families faced with unexpected death. She stresses the importance of encouraging family members to go and view the body, to actively say goodbye to the deceased, even if it should be hard and painful.

### Rituals for Saying Goodbye

Every culture has rituals that specifically provide a way of marking the fact that one of its members has died, and has thereby left the social circle. As much as they may vary across the globe, what all these rituals have in common is that the finality of death is made visible in this world, in this earthly existence. The mourning rituals stabilise the social community, weakened by the loss of one of its members. The surviving members are allowed, even expected, to publicly show their grief for the beloved person. Rehberger (2004) writes on the significance of funeral rites and describes how these rituals symbolically represent the long mourning process in a temporally reduced, exemplary fashion. The mourning ritual points the way towards a gradual detachment from the late family member or friend. The community provides a setting in which dramatic emotional outbursts are allowed, expected, cultivated, even exaggerated, but also restricted and channelled into a specific direction. This is done as a community, providing support and strength for those most immediately affected. The relatives and closest friends of the deceased, who have to face their inner turmoil and outwardly tangible misery of permanently detaching themselves from their beloved, get to experience the support of their social network. Additionally, Rehberger (2004: 23) writes, the mourning ritual also serves to admit the immediate family and friends into their new, changed roles that come with novel rights and privileges.

Where traditional mourning rituals have come out of practice or appear out of place in the face of urbanisation, new forms spontaneously arise—especially when a sudden, tragic loss under violent circumstances occurs. Via mass media, even those that are not physically present or did not even know the deceased can share in these forms of mourning rituals. Places at which tragic deaths have occurred get marked by spontaneous expressions of grief or sympathy, such as putting down flowers, religious symbols like crucifixes or national icons such as flags, also toys or letters. 'Spontaneous memorials are shrines composed of an eclectic combination of traditional religious, secular, and highly personalised ritual objects ... [and] provides a method for grieving such personal, social and cultural losses' (Haney et al. 1997: 162).

## Rituals for Victims of 'Enforced Disappearances'

Mourning rituals usually have the cremation or burial of the body of the deceased at their centre. Therefore, it is impossible to keep to them if the person has 'disappeared'. Rituals that can take place independent from a body, like the ones practiced in a certain fishing village in the Pacific or in the mountains of Mizoram in Northeast India, are the exception rather than the rule. In communities such as these two, where, due to certain geographical or economic conditions such as daily work far out at sea or in the treacherous mountains in the jungle, a lack of a body to bury is unfortunately not too uncommon an occurrence, other meaningful mourning rituals have developed.

Bowlby (1980), following the reports of the anthropologist Raymond Firth, for example, describes the remarkable ritual held for the lost fishermen of Tikopia, a small island in the South Western Pacific, 100 miles south of the Solomon Islands:

A young man went out to sea in a small canoe and disappeared. While Firth's report does not include details of the actions and emotions within the village during the days following the disappearance, it becomes clear that after a couple of moths the assumption that the young man has drowned is accepted as certain by the members of the fishing community.

About a year after the young man has disappeared, during which the family has followed the traditional mourning rituals (like certain keeping to certain food taboos and staying away from social gatherings), the father decides that it is time to hold the funeral. 'In circumstances such as these, which are not uncommon, tradition prescribes a simulated burial in which the usual mats and bark-cloth clothes are buried but in an empty grave. This is called "spreading the grave clothes to make the lost one dry"' (Bowlby 1980: 133).

In this island society, where men time and again perish at sea, leaving no body to be buried, a specific ritual that makes it possible to nevertheless lay those who have been lost to the sea to rest has developed: They are 'made dry'. Bowlby comments on this, writing:

> ... even though, as in this case, there is no body to be disposed of, a society requires that a funeral take place. It was indeed reflection on this Tikopian ceremony that led Firth to insist that the principal function of funeral ritual is not disposal of the body but the psychosocial benefit it brings to the bereaved and to the society as a whole. (Bowlby 1980: 134)

During one of my visits to Mizoram in North Eastern India in 2009, some of the workshop participants told me about a ritual held in their region, which is also designed specifically for people who have not returned home. During the first couple of days directly following the disappearance, they make all possible efforts to find the missing member of their community. After a pre-set period of time, the search is called off and the community begins with the preparations for a symbolic funeral for the disappeared.

On 20 August 2012, a report in the local newspaper (Sevensisterspost 2012) described just such an unsuccessful search for two teenagers who, in all likelihood, drowned in a flooding river. For seven continuous days, the community were searching for the missing youths. As there was no evidence about their bodies on the seventh day, the search was stopped and the community started to prepare for the ritual funeral.

Instead of a body, a symbolic figure of similar height, outfitted with personal belongings of the missing community member was prepared for burial. Using this symbolisation, the mourning rituals were conducted in the normal fashion. One part of the ceremony for the two youths took place on the banks of the river where they had last been seen. The relatives expressed their thanks to all who were involved in the search and said that they were now willing to accept the loss of their children.

## Symbolic Mourning Rituals for Relatives That Have 'Disappeared'

People who enter a new cultural setting as refugees and leave relatives who have 'disappeared' under traumatic circumstances in their home country behind have no cultural grounding whatsoever that might, through traditions and rituals, help them to cope with their loss or support them in their pain and grief. Herein lies a central reason why these people tend to react to the slightest suggestion that the 'disappeared' relative might have died with vehement denial.

Again it helps to conduct a ceremony to say goodbye to the absent relative. Even if this beloved's death would be too terrible a concept to even consider, the current situation of a long-term separation is a clearly apparent fact. The 'disappeared', even if alive, has little chance to determine where the relative has gone to, let alone follow into the European exile. This means that the reality of a life without the beloved person in the foreseeable future is a fact that can be accepted without necessarily facing the possibility of the 'disappeared' having passed away.

Onnasch and Gast (2011) describe 'rituals of remembering' as part of the mourning rituals. These are usually connected to a place, most traditionally a cemetery, but other places that symbolise the connection to the absent person can be used as well, like his or her favourite spot in the home town, a location important to both, such as one where a special encounter has taken place, or, most relevant for the situations of refugees, a place that was created especially for this purpose, by, for example planting a tree or erecting a memorial stone.

If the counsellor can help in successfully reviving the positive elements within the relationship to the 'disappeared' and, from that, can derive wishes and hopes the missing relative has had for the client, then this can help in easing the burden and relieving some of the emotional stress the client is under.

Questions such as 'What would you like to say to your mother/father?'; 'Which plans did your mother/father make for your future?' or 'What did the "disappeared" want for you and your life?' can help in opening up possibilities for the client's life that have been frozen in the ban on grieving that prevented all forward movement. If the concept that the beloved who has been 'disappeared' has had the best wishes for the life of the relative at heart can be successfully internalised, then a revitalisation of these options and plans is possible.

This form is especially appropriate in cases where one or both parents have 'disappeared'.

Concrete acts of saying farewell do not need to make use of important places, but can also, for example, happen through letter writing, by talking to the 'disappeared' family member or via a dinner together with the remaining family, where special dishes are prepared that signify the importance of this meal.

## Redefinition of the Social Roles after the Loss

With the funeral ritual, the social roles of the surviving family members get redefined, and the bereaved get introduced to these new roles. The wife becomes a widow, the husband a widower, the children become (half) orphans. In many cultures, the grave or urn tomb remains as a memorial site that serves as a place for remembering the beloved who has passed away and the grief connected to the loss.

Grief and the process of mourning are embedded in the social context of the community the bereaved live in. Every society has its ways of dealing with loss and grief, most of them consist of transitional rites that are organised into the following three phases:

The first phase mainly consists of a primary reaction to the loss. Rites of separation, which for the time being not only relieve the bereaved of a number of social duties but also withdraw some of their rights, provide the time for this initial, emotional reaction. In central Europe for example, it is (or was) common to stay away from social gatherings at the beginning of the year of mourning, be they part of the mourner's civic duty or entertainments like, for example dances. Both were taboo during initial mourning, and therefore prohibited.

During the second phase of mourning, typically the rest of the year, a visible separation from the rest of society is kept up to a certain degree, making mourning part of the bereaved's everyday life. A family that is in mourning because of the death of a close relative, often decides to, or even has to, wear mourning clothes, making their situation visible to the rest of society. In Austria, dressing in black for a year is the traditional way of signalling mourning. In India and other parts of Asia mourning clothes are white. A widow in the South of Asia wears a white Sari and cuts off her hair. The traditional Jewish mourning rites include the tearing of one's clothes and public weeping, while any kind of self-injury, or the trimming or cutting of one's hair is forbidden.

Different cultures have different rituals within these phases of mourning, such as memorial services, organising a soup kitchen for the homeless or poor in the name of the departed, etc.

The third phase then represents the reintegration into society taking into account the change in identity the loss has caused.

Mourning rituals are rituals of transition that regulate how the changes resulting from the loss are to be incorporated into the social life of those immediately affected by the loss as well as the entire social circle they live in. Some of these rituals are limited temporally, like the tradition to wear black during the year of mourning, others are permanent, like the custom for Indian widows to dispense with the wearing of jewellery and colourful clothes for the rest of their lives.

## Loss of One's Spouse/Life Partner

All psychological coping strategies should be considered in their interaction with the change of the respective social role the bereaved has to go through in connection with the loss. Therefore, a short excursion into the significance of social roles and their change through an alteration of the political or social circumstances seems necessary.

People who have lost their life partner suffer under the resultant feeling of loneliness, which in turn constitutes a serious risk factor for depression. Widows and widowers have to redefine their identities as singles. The loss of a spouse is seen as one of the most difficult life events.

After the death ('disappearance') of a wife or husband, the risk of suffering from depression or anxiety-related disorders is much increased (Prigerson 1997a).

Bowlby (1980) points out that in cases of conjugal bereavement, the phase of yearning and searching appears to be of particular intensity. 'Whereas some bereaved people are conscious of their urge to search, others are not. Whereas some willingly fall in with it, others seek to stifle it as irrational and absurd' (Bowlby 1980: 87).

Many widows and widowers report that they feel drawn to objects or places connected to their late spouse, and consciously touch or visit these.

Maercker et al. (1998) conducted a study with 44 participants aged 20–55 years, showing, in line with Prigerson, that younger people react with a significantly more intense kind of grief than older people. This can be understood in connection with the phase of life the bereaved are in at the time of loss. Younger people do not consider the possibility of death and consequently feel completely overpowered by the death of their partner. Additionally, they are often in the situation of the breadwinner, having to support other dependant with their wages, providing the means of subsistence for the entire family. 'The patient's case was shown to fit well with a model hypothesizing that the loss of a security—increasing partner for an individual with insecure, anxious attachments and self-regulatory deficits could result in symptoms of traumatic grief' (Prigerson et al. 1997b: 1003).

Remmers (2009), who conducted a study with widows and widowers in Germany, found a significant correlation between post-loss depression and a financially insecure situation following the spousal bereavement.

## Political Widows

An example of how political pressure can change the understanding of a social role within society is described by Ramphele (1997). She reflects on the role of widows in South Africa. Under normal circumstances, a South African widow is expected to mourn her late husband for at least a year. A widower, on the other hand only goes through six months of official mourning. During the mourning period, women are banned from all public gatherings, while men retain their social privileges and also their vote within the community.

Such outward signs of mourning are common in many cultures, especially for women. Widows and widowers are often expected to cut their hair and, amongst other things, wear clothes of a particular colour—black in Europe, white in Asia. Some forms of mourning traditions include appearances otherwise almost associated with madness. Ramphele (1997), for example, describes situations where relatives were eating with their left hands, wearing their clothes inside out or only one shoe.

During the rebellion against apartheid in South Africa, these traditional roles of widowhood were expanded to include a new type, that of the political widow. This term refers to the women whose husbands have perished in the fight against apartheid, or were sentenced to a long-term imprisonment because of their political involvement. These political widows were pushed towards fulfilling a new role within the community—

instead of living on the margins of society for a while, they were put into its centre, receiving the hero badges meant for their husband and forming centres of attention. This left them little space or time for personal mourning.

## Not Wife, Not Widow

After the Vietnam War, 1,200 US-American soldiers were listed as missing—'missing in action—MIA' is the term used for those who have 'disappeared' in the context of armed combat.

Spolyar (1975) who made a study of the mourning process of the wives of just these MIAs, describes three different forms of trying to cope with this ambivalent form of loss: The terms he uses for them are identification, substitution and hostility.

In a similar fashion, Benson et al. (1975), working in discussion groups with MIA spouses, identified three different groups of women, each characterised by another way of dealing with their difficult situation:

The first group is made up of those women who actively participate in the efforts of the 'National League of Families', committing their lives to the continuous search for their missing husbands. They travelled to Asia, wrote countless letters, spoke up at public rallies, etc. These women have restructured their lives to a large degree, and have gained a new kind of self-confidence. Boss (1999) encourages the remaining family members during family therapy sessions to do everything in their power to gain access to information about the whereabouts of the person who has 'disappeared': 'The act of seeking information eases the stress of ambiguity. Once that process is exhausted and no more information is available, that, too, becomes information, and helps people conclude, "We have done all that we can"' (Boss 1999: 112).

There are many similarities between the coping strategy of this group and that of many parents whose children have 'disappeared' all over Latin America, such as the group called 'The Mothers of the Plaza del Mayo' in Argentina (cf. section 'The Mothers of the Plaza de Mayo—a Role model for many associations of relatives throughout the world'). These women were also not willing to silently accept their fate, but organised, demonstrated, went public, in short, did everything in their power to learn what has happened to their relatives. They rallied, hoping to find their beloved 'disappeared' alive, but at the same time their efforts were part of the process of overcoming their fear of being confronted with the terrible truth of their offspring's death. The joint struggle and resulting social support makes it possible to then also move on with life.

The second group of MIA wives Benson et al. (1975) describe is made up of women for whom the struggle to come to terms with the ambivalence of the long, uncertain and possible futile waiting period is central. These women try to gradually assume the role of a widow, while at the same time they still hold on to the hope that the missing husband might yet return alive. There seems to be a correlation between the form of coping and the time passed since receiving the information of their husband's MIA status. The husbands of this second group had 'disappeared' more than two years ago at the time of the study.

In contrast, the third group of women have only recently been confronted with their husband's disappearance. Here, the hope that the husband will return clearly dominates. All other possibilities are immediately rejected and categorically denied.

## *The Loss of One or Both Parents*

How a child reacts to the permanent separation from one or both parents depends largely on the child's age and state of development. In principle, it can be said that the conditions identified as beneficial for a normal, healthy mourning process in adults also apply to children faced with loss.

> The conditions required are no different in principle to the conditions that are favourable for adult mourning. Those most significant for a child are: First, that he should have enjoyed a reasonably secure relationship with his parents prior to the loss;
> Secondly that ... he be given prompt and accurate information about what has happened, be allowed to ask all sorts of questions and have them answered as honestly as is possible, and be a participant in family grieving including whatever funeral rites are decided on;
> And thirdly, that he has the comforting presence of his surviving parent, or if that is not possible of a known and trusted substitute, and an assurance that that relationship will continue. (Bowlby 1980: 276)

Grieving children often do not express their feelings in words, but rather in their actions and deeds and their general behaviour. These children often switch rapidly between emotional states, their mood shifting from happiness to profound sadness within the blink of an eye. Regression is also a common form of mourning in children. Physical closeness to attachment figures regains importance; coping with separations becomes harder or even impossible due to the constant fear of another loss (Onnasch & Gast 2011).

## Loss of One or Both Parents through Acts of Political Repression

As Becker (1992) points out that the grieving process is seriously impeded in situations where relatives have died through an act of political repression. In these cases, the regular showings of social support and the cultural rituals connected with the death of a beloved are often withheld by the social environment. The second and third of the conditions identified as favourable for mourning by Bowlby (as discussed earlier) cannot be provided in these cases.

Becker describes how in such situations the child perceives the death of the mother or father as one incident, within a chain of terrible, violent events, which has swept them up like a nightmare. The children are not provided with the kind of information about the circumstances of their parent's death they would need, as the initial shock and then the all-pervading fear prevents the family from talking about it. Helpless, the child makes desperate attempts to reconstruct the tragic event from the scraps of information they receive or overhear. Lacking any means to resolve their confusion, they nevertheless perceive the fear the adults around them experience. Consequently, they hold back, suppressing their emotions and accepting the silence as the behaviour apparently deemed appropriate in this situation. This way, the children learn to connect the lost parent with feelings of chaos and destruction (Becker 1992: 105).

As a result, mourning is perceived as prohibited and the grieving process is prolonged indefinitely. Sometimes it takes years until—often in the course of psychotherapeutic sessions—the bereaved can cry about the loss.

## Loss of One or Both Parents through an 'Enforced Disappearance'

Much of what has been described about the loss of a parent through an act of political repression holds true if the parent or parents were 'disappeared' as well. However, a number of studies, which will be discussed extensively at a later point in this book, show that children regularly suffer significantly from severe pathological grief reactions and disorders following the 'enforced disappearance' of a parent (Becker 1992; Zvidic & Butollo 2000).

Children in this situation are often reported to show regressive or antisocial behaviour, suffer from sleeping disorders and depression, wet their beds again, react in aggressive fashion to minor provocations and neglect their schoolwork. Becker (1992: 88) explains this in relationship to the general state of exception the family lives in because of the 'enforced disappearance'. This state of exception then often becomes normality for the family—a normality characterised by taboos, bans and prohibitions. Precisely, the situation that puts such strain on everyone involved cannot be addressed. Any expression of grief or fear is prohibited.

## Loss of a Child—'Orphaned' Parents

The reactions to the loss of a child are often quite similar to those shown by people who have lost a spouse. There is one major difference, though, which Bowlby (1980) makes explicit:

> Whereas loneliness is a principal feature after the death of a spouse, it seems not to be prevalent after the death of a child. Correspondingly, the sense of loneliness after the death of a spouse is usually not assuaged by the presence of a child. (Bowlby 1980: 40)

Nevertheless, the loss of a child is usually identified in clinical studies as an especially critical event in the life of a person, one in which the bereaved cannot be consoled by the presence of a partner. Children are seen as the future and the loss of a child means to also lose one's presence beyond the boundaries of one's own mortal life (Leahy 1992–1993).

The English language (and, incidentally, the German language as well) has its own words for men and women who have lost their spouses: widow and widower. It has specific terms for children bereaved of one or both parents: half-orphan and orphan. If a child dies, however, there are no terms for the surviving family members, neither the bereaved parents nor the siblings left behind. Are the parents now 'once-more-childless' adults? Are they 'orphaned' parents or siblings?

Leahy's (1992–1993) meta-analysis of grief research showed that parents' grief reactions do not vary in correlation with the age of the child. There is a difference in the reaction of the mother and the father, though. Mothers go through a longer and generally more intense form of mourning than the fathers. Mourning parents suffer to a significantly higher degree from depression than any other group of mourners found in the studies, according to Leahy. This last result, however, could not be verified in other studies (Zisook & DeVaul 1983; Murphy 1988). All studies agree in their assessment, though, that the grieving process of parents mourning a child is not temporally delimited and often lasts a lifetime. This assessment is confirmed in the studies by Stroebe et al. who conducted a long-time study with parents who had lost their sons in two consecutive Israeli wars. The study showed that while the parents on the surface seem to have returned to their normal everyday life after a couple of years, the relationship with the sons has not successfully come to a close for them. The parents manage their daily routines successfully and do not suffer from any psychosomatic symptoms, but their behaviour in relation to the sons they have lost makes it seem as if they had merely moved out, not passed away. In most cases, the sons were idealised by the surviving parents. 'The result appears to be a life preoccupied with the dead, at the expense of the living. From the modernist perspective, the tragedy of death is compounded: Not only are the sons lost to them, but in significant ways, their families are as well' (Stroebe et al. 1992: 1210).

## The Violent Death of a Child

If children die in a violent manner, the coping process of the relatives is an especially difficult and complex one, which often results in a lifelong grieving process and dissociation. Again, many examples for this arose from the horrors of the Holocaust. Langer (1997: 57), for example, writes in her essay on the fate of Bessie K., who unsuccessfully attempted to smuggle her baby through a checkpoint of the Protection Squadron. Handing her little son over to a German soldier felt to her as if she herself was dying: 'For me, I was dead. I died, and I didn't want to hear nothing, and I didn't want to know nothing, and I didn't want to talk about it, and I didn't want to admit to myself that this happened to me.'

When later asked about the whereabouts of her baby, she answered: 'What baby? I didn't have a baby. I don't know of any baby.'

Langer (1997: 58) interprets Bessie K.'s words as follows:

> The death of her child is her own death too, not in fantasy but in reality, a permanent intrusion on her post-Holocaust existence. It is also a form of verbal disturbance, since no language exists ... to describe the role of such durational moments in the lives of those who have lived them.

The reality of the traumatic loss of a child, and the feeling of helplessness connected to one's inability to protect the child are experienced as so intensely traumatic as to result in severe dissonance. Laub (2000) describes a similar case: In response to the question of one of the doctors who had helped in delivering the child years earlier, the patient asks in a fashion quite similar to Bessie K., which child the doctor is talking about, completely denying ever having been a mother. During a therapy session then, can the patient remember the traumatic experience of having a German soldier take the child from her? Even then, though, the patient refers to the child as a 'bundle' that has been taken from her. She describes the situation as overwhelming, as too fast to react to it in a meaningful way. The soldier extended his arms demanding to be given the 'bundle'. The moment of handing it over was the last time the patient had ever seen the 'bundle' (Laub 2000: 864).

These two examples for a violent separation of a mother from her child, which both in all likelihood were followed by the child's murder, cannot be processed in a normal mourning process. The mothers cannot cope with the situation in any other way than by dissociation.

## Parents of Children that Have 'Disappeared'

In his novel *Job*, Joseph Roth (2010) writes about the inability of the parents Deborah and Mendel to communicate at all, after receiving the news that their eldest son, a soldier, is listed as MIA:

> And the Red Cross had informed them that Jonas was missing. He's probably dead, Deborah thought inwardly, Mendel thought the same. But they spoke for a long time about the meaning of the word 'missing', and as if it completely ruled out the possibility of death, they agreed again and again that 'missing' could only mean taken prisoner, deserted or wounded in captivity. (Roth 2010: 138)

The most famous representatives of the group of parents grieving for their 'disappeared' children are the mothers of the Plaza del Mayo in Buenos

Aires. These mothers (and fathers) of adolescents who 'disappeared' during the military dictatorship at the end of the 20th century in Argentina still lead their lives in loneliness and grief. Most of them had never been politically active prior to the 'enforced disappearances' of their children. Through their persistent search for their children, these mothers turned into a strong political power that managed to effectively pillory the political methods of the dictatorship of that time (cf. section 'The Mothers of the Plaza de Mayo—a Role model for many associations of relatives throughout the world').

## *Siblings of Children That Have Died or Have 'Disappeared'*

What kind of destructive effect the death of a brother can have on the entire family, can be gleaned from the following extract from Marguerite Duras' novel *The Lover*:

> My younger brother died in three days, of bronchial pneumonia. His heart gave out. It was then that I left my mother.... Everything came to an end that day. I never asked her any more questions about our childhood, about herself. She died, for me, of my younger brother's death. So did my elder brother. I never got over the horror they inspired in me then. They don't mean anything to me anymore. I don't know any more about them since that day. (Duras 1985: 31f.)

In the many case reviews conducted after the tsunami catastrophe in 2004, it became apparent that those children who had survived the disaster comparatively physically unharmed found themselves in a different, highly problematic situation of psychological abandonment and their inner distress. The children's parents were so intensely fixated on those children who had been seriously injured, had 'disappeared' or had died that as a consequence three different kinds of problematic dynamics developed between the surviving family members:

1. Some parents reacted to their unharmed children in a highly aggressive manner that even cumulated in physical abuse at times.
2. Even more commonly, the children were simply overlooked. Their questions, desires and needs went unnoticed by their surviving parent, and, hence, remained unanswered. Even when in physical proximity to their parents, these children found themselves in a situation of complete abandonment.

3. Sometimes the situation led to a reversal of roles between the family members. The children had to care for their grieving parent and/or their siblings, socially as well as emotionally.

At times, combinations of all three of these reactions could be observed.

Disaster relief organisations should, therefore, in their work pay special attention to those children who were not physically harmed during the catastrophe, so that these children are not left alone in their needs and distress. In the first instance, this is a matter of assessing what resources are available for the support of these children:

- Can other relatives, neighbours or teachers who know the children take them in for the time being, until the parents are up to the role of a parent again?
- If not, what professional institutions can care for the children in what form and for which time span?

Parents, especially if their partner had perished in the catastrophe and they are now faced with the new role of caring for their children alone, are in dire need of support in their struggle to shoulder the responsibility of a parental role again and be able to, in turn, help their surviving children through the loss of their sibling and/or parent.

Central to this is the encouragement to tell the surviving children as much of the truth about their lost family members as is available, and to help the parents to do so in an age-appropriate manner. The goal is to create an emotional platform that can support the new and changed family unit.

## Note

1. Translation from the German original.

# 2
# The Social Consequences of 'Enforced Disappearances'

When I refer to the consequences of 'enforced disappearances' for the relatives of the victims in this book, it becomes necessary to first gain a more specific understanding of the term 'enforced disappearance' itself.

If one takes as a starting point, the systematic violations of human rights in the form of 'enforced disappearances' as they were commonly conducted in the South American dictatorships of the 1970s, and which resulted in presumably more than 90,000 victims in Latin America alone (FEDEFAM 2004), one may, looking closely, arrive at a broader picture of the issue: The wars in former Yugoslavia, for instance, left behind many raw wounds. Countless women are still hoping that their husbands and sons have survived; in Bosnia alone about 300 mass graves containing 16,500 bodies were discovered; the ~~faith~~ fate of 10,000 people is still unknown in 2012 (ICMP 2012).

Looking further back, there is Second World War with its tremendous extent of suffering: the Holocaust with its uncountable victims, the armed combat itself, in which innumerable soldiers were left behind 'in the field', and the countless refugee families, torn apart forever.

If one searches the (specialised) literature for terms such as 'disappeared' or 'missing', one mainly arrives at a list of factual or fictional criminal cases and, at times, speculations about extraterrestrial forces. One also comes upon those people who voluntarily take themselves out of the environment they live in and 'disappear'. Thus, the reasons for people 'disappearing' without a trace are diverse.

Natural disasters, such as the flood disaster that devastated a number of Asian countries in December 2004, lead to people disappearing as well. Their bodies cannot be found at all or have to be buried before they can be identified, owing to the danger of an epidemic spreading.

In this book, I will deal only in passing with those cases where the 'disappearance' was voluntarily, caused by natural catastrophes or through an act of crime. The group of people I focus on are those, whose relatives 'disappeared' as a result of political violence, i.e., in the course of a war or a dictatorship.

About two million people worldwide are registered as having involuntarily 'disappeared' (Österreichisches Rotes Kreuz 2012). Queen Noor (2012: 1), acting as International Commission on Missing Persons (ICMP)-Commissioner, describes the problem as follows:

> When people go missing, particularly through state-sanctioned violence, the family members left behind—usually women and children—are terrified to seek answers about the fate of their loved ones. In most of the world today family members have no legal recourse to demand answers. Those brave enough to ask often fear reprisals from the very authorities responsible for the disappearance in the first place, or who are seeking to cover-up the crimes of previous regimes. After all, it is a fundamental tenet of most systems of law that, if there is no body, there is no crime. And so the silence persists.

## Penelope Waits for Odysseus—the Ambiguous Separation as the Ancient Problem

'Disappeared' and 'missing in action' are concepts as old as the conflict-ridden history of mankind itself. Every war leaves people behind who wait in vain for those who have failed to return, without any knowledge of what has happened to their loved ones.

In our search through history for the first relatives of people who have 'disappeared', we come upon a minor character of the Greek mythology: Penelope, wife of Odysseus, who waits for centuries for her missing husband, though we—the readers—know from the onset that he will return gloriously from the war.

Odysseus was called to war against his will. He himself wanted to stay with his young wife and infant son. Therefore, when the recruiters came he feigned madness, hoping to be deemed unfit for battle. But when his son's life was put at risk, he dropped the pretence and had to go to war. Penelope and her son Telemachus remained left behind. They waited for Odysseus. But even after the war had ended he did not return. Their hopes to ever see him again dwindled.

Especially interesting for their time of waiting are two descriptions: Penelope weaves a burial shroud for her father-in-law—at least during the day. During the night she spends her time unstitching the day's work, undoing what she has made. She is active—doubly active—but in doing so does not move forward at all. The day's work is annulled by that of the night. During Odysseus' absence, there is no development, no progress for her or resulting from her acts and deeds. If her work comes to an end, Penelope would be faced with a decision—her people demand her to take another husband. For Penelope, this would mean accepting that Odysseus is dead. So, to prevent this, she works with twice the energy on making time stand still.

Penelope cannot begin to grief, because the situation she finds herself in is wholly unclear. What feels like a loss to her is nevertheless not concrete, not real. Caught between hope and defeat, this confusion renders all chances of a mourning process impossible (Boss 1999).

Hosts of suitors beleaguer Penelope. She is in no position to refuse them, while at the same time she cannot let herself elect one of them, not knowing whether or not Odysseus might not still return one day. Unable to make a clear decision, she leads a life full of secret schemes and delaying tactics. It is a stalemate situation. Penelope can neither live her life of matrimony, nor is she free of its bonds (Homer 1979).

To me, this description of Penelope seems highly significant, and to a large degree 'archetypal' of the situation of women during all eras of human history. Contrary to Odysseus though, the men the women wait for usually do not return, and in most cases little is known about the circumstances surrounding their deaths or the sites of their burials. If the men have 'disappeared' in the context of a political conflict, the wives are not even granted certainty about their husbands' deaths.

## The Consequence of War: Missing in Action, Lost, 'Disappeared'

The constant history of violence is carved into the memorials of the 20th century. Every cemetery in central Europe serves as a reminder of the cruel history of that time. Omnipresent are the war memorials listing the names of those who have 'fallen' in the war and of those who are 'missing'. This kind of historical awareness is often mediated in a rather undifferentiated manner: The names of those who perished in Second World War were generally carved into the memorials erected already after First World War. No difference was made between victims and perpetrators (Domansky 1997).

A difference is generally made, however, between the 'fallen' and the 'missing'. After First World War, about a million people, mostly soldiers, were listed as 'missing' in Germany. Of these cases, 97,000 were never sufficiently resolved. This number is dwarfed by the 14 million people, soldiers and civilians who went missing during Second World War. In 1992, 47 years after the war had ended, approximately one million of these cases were still open (Smith 1992). The figures of US American soldiers who went missing during these wars are more precise: In Washington, 4,500 soldiers were listed as 'MIA' after First World War and 139,709 after Second World War (Nash 1987).

Apart from the victims murdered by the atrocious Nazi Regime, the world was also faced with the 'normal' consequences of war. About 12 million German soldiers were held in captivity as prisoners of war; the flood of refugees wandering Europe in search of a new home consisted of approximately 15 million people. Practically everyone was directly affected by this situation of uncertainty of loss by having a relative unaccounted for or listed as MIA.

Two new terms were established in this context: that of the 'Sucher' (searcher) and that of the 'Gesuchte' (the person searched for). In Germany, about one out of four suddenly became a 'Sucher' or a 'Gesuchte'.

Böhme (1965) has compiled a report on the work of tracing services active in Germany during the 20 years following the end of Second World War. While his descriptions of the treatment captured German soldiers received at the hands of Soviet officials are certainly biased, he nevertheless contributes largely unknown data about the high number of German soldiers MIA during that time. Since the Soviet Union had not signed the '1929 Convention Relative to the Treatment of Prisoners of War', they were not obliged to provide the International Red Cross with information about the prisoners of war they were holding captive.

In Germany's larger cities, tracing services had teamed up, combining their efforts to collect as much information as possible and pass it on to relatives searching for loved ones. According to Böhme (1965: 160), the motivation for this was the necessity to provide some kind of certainty, as 'to be missing' always means—potentially—to be imprisoned, but alive. Lacking proof of either—imprisonment or death—uncertainty prevails.

'The reduction of all the possible situations the missing person might be in down to the two categories "imprisonment" and "death" is an interesting phenomenon'. Those left behind seem to allow for only these two options, which helps to keep the fear of uncertainty at bay. Deaths such as one through starvation in an unknown prison camp, cannot be classified under either category; Their lack of any kind of possible meaning would lend strength to the feelings of dread and horror; hence, they are denied.

At the point when both sides state that they have released all prisoners of war, the question of those who have not returned still remains. Have all the others really perished at war? Or are they maybe still being detained? Certainly, certainty at all cost is the driving force behind many of the investigations conducted by the tracing services (Böhme 1965: 228).

Another phenomenon that Böhme addresses in the context of people listed as MIAs long after the war has ended is that of the deep-seated belief in the so-called 'silent camps'. The idea is that some of the camps in the Soviet Union were so removed from the outside world that no information exchange has taken place with them yet. Böhme writes on this that those still missing, even if in all likelihood dead, were still believed to be alive as long as irrefutable proof was provided (1965: 227).

## 'Enforced Disappearance'—Terror against the Other Side

'Enforced disappearances' were not only a side effect of war—unplanned for, but lived with—but were also purposefully used against political opponents.

### 'Enforced Disappearances' in the History of Russia

The Russian civil war and subsequent establishment of the Soviet Union— especially the Stalin era—was characterised by severe violations of human rights. 'Enforced disappearances' were a common form of terror under this regime.

On 7 November 1917, Lenin and the Bolsheviks took over Russia. On 3 March 1918, the Treaty of Brest-Litovsk was signed, ending the war with Germany. However, at the same time a civil war flared up, the victims of which were primarily the former ruling class and the intellectuals. On 30 December 1922, a decision was made to annex all soviet socialist republics to the union, the USSR, and seize all lands and means of production. After Lenin's death on 21 January 1924, a bitter fight for succession to his office ensued, which, in the end, was won by Stalin. One of his means of strengthening his position was to create an atmosphere of terror for his opponents. Berija, the head of Stalin's intelligence agency, is quoted to have planned on grinding all their political opponents to camp dust.

Arseny Roginsky writes on these acts of terror, stating that at the beginning of the 21st century, all that remained to remind of them were graves, and of those, only a handful were actually found:

> Today these are mainly burial sites: mass graves of people shot during the Great Terror, and large camp cemeteries. But the secret surrounding the shooting was so great, and so few sources have been found on this topic, that today we only know of around 100 burial sites of people shot in 1937–1938—less than a third of the total, according to our calculations. For example, despite much searching, it has not been possible to find even the graves of the victims of the famous 'Kashketin shootings' near the Brick Factory by Vorkuta. As for camp cemeteries, we only know a few dozen of the several thousand that once existed. (Roginsky 2009)

Between 1923 and 1963, a large number of people 'disappeared' into the system of various different camps. The dissident Aleksandr Solzhenitsyn was one of the chief critics of the human rights violations that affected millions in the Stalin era.

He writes about people seized in the middle of the night, on most elusive charges, without any chance of defending their rights. Many of these people 'disappeared' forever.

> For those left behind after the arrest there is the long tail end of a wrecked and devastated life. And the attempts to go and deliver food parcels. But from all the windows the answer comes in barking voices: 'Nobody here by that name!' 'Never heard of him!' Yes, and in the worst days in Leningrad it took five days of standing in crowded lines just to get to that window. And it may be only after half a year or a year that the arrested person responds at all. Or else the answer is tossed out: 'Deprived of the right to correspond.' And that means once and for all, 'No right to correspondence'—and that almost for certain means: 'Has been shot.' (Solzhenitsyn 2002: 5)

A group that was doubly affected by this situation was that of the forced labourers who had been taken to Germany during Second World War and who, upon returning to the Soviet Union, were stigmatised as collaborators and, hence, again became victims of repressive measures. Under the heading 'Victims of Two Dictatorships', the archivists working for 'Memorial' have collected and publicised information about more than 400,000 of these forced labourers via the database they have assembled (Scherbakova 2002). However, the fate of many of those who have 'disappeared' is still uncertain.

## By Night and Fog

In December 1941 the so-called 'Nacht-und-Nebel-Erlass' (Night and Fog Decree) was issued, making it possible to terrorise the inhabitants of occupied regions with 'enforced disappearances'. The regime was quite aware of the effects this decree had, not only on those immediately affected by an 'enforced disappearance', but on the population as a whole. The aim was to purposefully frighten and intimidate people.

Wilhelm Keitel, who served as the supreme commander of the armed forces from 1938 to 1945 and was executed in 1946, was the one who brought the decree into effect on 7 December. In his writ of command, he explicitly states that 'it is not only justified therefore, but the duty of the troops to use every method without restriction, even against women and children provided it ensures success. Any act of mercy is a crime against the German people' (Wistrich 2002: 137).

In this decree, the only possible punishment for the so-called 'offences against the state' was the death penalty, which was to be carried out right there and then. If an immediate execution proved to be impossible, the convicted was to be brought to Germany without any notice being given to the person's relatives. Following Mittler (2000: 3) it can be said that the aim lay in punishing each and every act of resistance, not through prosecution, but through an atmosphere of terror that successfully eradicates any inclination towards organising resistance the people might harbour.

If a prisoner or someone already executed was mentioned in an official correspondence, the abbreviation NN-prisoner was used. NN stood for 'Nacht und Nebel', German for night and fog, as well as the Latin 'non nominator', rendering the person nameless. It is presumed that in occupied France alone 7,000 people 'disappeared' because of the Night-and-Fog Decree. The Holocaust survivor Leo Eitinger, who has conducted a number of studies with survivors of NS prisons and concentration camps, writes that about a third of all Norwegian victims of the Holocaust had been NN-prisoners, who were supposed to disappear by 'night and fog' (Weisaeth & Eitinger 1991).

## 'Enforced Disappearances' as Part of the Holocaust

The whereabouts of soldiers taken as prisoners during the war can be traced to some extent via registers and lists, their 'disappearance', while often, of course, a personal tragedy, being part of a comprehensible process. This stands in stark contrast to the meaningless, murderous machinery of the extermination camps of the NS regime, which cannot be comprehended by human logic, consisting of nothing but never-ending suffering. Thousands and thousands have died in concentration camps and ghettos. Individual people, their families, their extended families, their neighbours, their friends, all of them were killed. Sometimes, those disappeared were never found because there was no one left to search for them. Daniel Libeskind, in his essay on trauma and the void, touches upon this issue in his description of a walk through 'Weißensee' cemetery. He writes about walking through this place of silence, feeling the void, seeing it in the large marble tombstones that only bear a small number of inscriptions. Libeskind links them to the unwavering trust those who had the stones erected had in the future. Generation upon generation had been expected to be buried underneath these half-empty tombstones. Libeskind, alone in the cemetery, was struck by the sudden realisation that none of the family members would ever return to see the tombstone, to see the emptiness, the void, as they all had already perished (Libeskind 1999: 3).

Many a life story gets lost in uncertainty at the point of deportation. The surviving relatives do know that such kinds of 'disappearances' are, in essence, the same as a murder. Their suffering is increased by the lack of information about how their beloved has died, when and where, and by the impossibility of holding a ritual to say goodbye.

> I am concerned about one particular aspect of the concentration-camp problem: namely, the missing grave. Burial as a ritual has great significance throughout human history. I hear many times from patients, 'If I only could go to the grave of my son, my mother, my father!' (Krystal 1968: 194)

During the final days of Second World War, thousands of prisoners, especially those of Jewish religion, were driven westwards, away from the advancing Russian army. During these death marches, many of the captives were shot and dumped into a mass grave somewhere along the way. A large number of these graves have not been found yet. In many places the search still continues.

Those Jewish children who survived the Holocaust, hidden away all through the war, had to come to terms with the fact that their mothers and fathers would not return to them, in many cases, that none of their family members had survived (for example, Keilson 1979; Fink 1996).

I can only give a brief outline of the relevant aspects of the Holocaust here, despite the fact that the research done in this area forms a central basis of the topic at hand. It needs addressing, even if in brief, as the historical dimension of 'enforced disappearances' and their use as a political means of exerting pressure cannot do justice without discussing these cruel, systematically conducted separations. 'Enforced disappearances' as such have not been the focus of any book or study on the Holocaust. The term is conspicuously absent from all tables of contents and indexes. Almost all biographies and psychotherapeutic case histories of Holocaust survivors, however, tell about the 'disappearance' of relatives and the hope for their return as one of the most unbearable aspect of life after the end of the war. Often, survivor's guilt weighs on them additionally (cf. Klüger 1994; Zelman 1998).

A number of cold figures shall serve to sketch out the historical dimension of the attempt to eradicate entire ethnicities—first amongst them the Jewish people, of course—under the Nazi-made pretext of a 'final solution': About three million Jews were killed in the many NS-execution camps; about the same number was massacred in their hometowns or on execution sites. Another six million—in all likelihood more—died as a consequence of the Nazi machinery of death (Longerich 1989; Heyl & Schreier 1994).

The six million victims of direct murder signalise the Holocaust's unique status in the collective group of crimes against humanity. Statistics alone cannot adequately express this, but nevertheless they need to be cited in order to convey the scope of the genocide that took place: 165,000 Jews from Germany, 65,000 from Austria, 32,000 from France and Belgium, more than 100,000 from the Netherlands, 60,000 from Greece, an equal number from Yugoslavia, more than 140,000 from the Czech Republic and Slovakia, half a million from Hungary, 2.2 million from the Soviet Union and 2.7 million from Poland. An additional 200,000 were killed in the massacres and pogroms in Rumania and Transnistria, others, coming from Albania, Norway, Denmark, Luxemburg and Bulgaria, were equally deported and lost their lives directly or indirectly because of the German racial ideal of the Aryan race (Benz 1995).

These figures also render visible the practice of 'enforced disappearance'—they represent the verified minimum numbers. Many victims of the Holocaust are not documented, there are no exhaustive death registries, nor do we know of all graves.

Mass extermination in concentration camps formed part of the most fundamental structures of the Third Reich. Going there meant entering a part of society completely removed from the rest. Their very existence shows the extent of destructive hegemonic power one group can have over another (Mommsen 1992). Nothing could have prepared anyone for life in this second part of society that existed between the barbed wires of a concentration camp.

After the national Socialist Party had come to power, the 'disappearance' of Jewish relatives and friends was an ever-present concept. In the following, the biographic account of Zelman (1998) shall represent, in a way, the millions of people who have 'disappeared' in those years. In moving words, he tells about the sudden separation from his mother and brother (again, one that lacked all opportunity for a goodbye) and his search for surviving family members after 1945.

## Life in the Ghetto

In the ghetto, it could always happen that somebody was simply suddenly vanished, because they had been deported while the children were at school and the mother went shopping. Many parents tried to save their children's lives by hiding them away in the homes of non-Jewish employees or friends, or in Catholic boarding schools. 'Many mothers fought for their children's lives and prepared them for life without them', Kestenberg and Brenner (1996: 37) writes, but no matter what measures were taken, 'All these children felt abandoned by their mothers.'

If the parents were able to prepare a hideout properly, then at least saying goodbye was possible—if not comprehensible in its entirety, especially for younger children.

In many cases, though, that was not possible. Leon Zelman, for example, writes about returning home from school, together with his brother, and finding his mother gone:

> We began to call loudly, 'Mamusha, Mamusha, Mama, Mama!' Our cries echoed down the lane. No one turned around or paid any attention to us. No one asked us why we were crying. No one spoke to us at all. People passed us as if we were shadows. One often saw crying children calling for someone. Missing or dead relatives were part of everyday life and no one could do anything about it. ... We never saw our mother again. (Zelman 1998: 46)

The 'disappearance' of relatives was just one of the horrors of ever-day life in the ghetto, and so many children were affected that none comforted them, even in the first period of shock and pain. Zelman makes the finality of such 'disappearances' explicit, stating that the 'disappearances' were the rule, reunions the exception (Zelman 1998: 66).

## Separation in the Concentration Camp

The platform for arriving trains in Auschwitz is the place where many people, after days or even weeks of travelling in cramped cattle wagons, laid eyes on his or her loved one for the very last time. Families were separated, usually into those considered to be able to work and those that were not, but sometimes the decision was completely arbitrary.

Again and again survivors talk about how they drew the strength to survive from the fact that they were not alone. Together with a family member or a friend, they were able to find meaning in life and a reason to keep on living. Boys often formed gangs that served as families for them. There were clear rules within the gangs, and their members looked out for each other as much as possible in these hostile surroundings. '[W]ithin their "organization" of friends and family they could preserve trust, respect, and human dignity amid the indescribable degradation that constantly threatened their lives' (Brenner 1996: 111).

Leon Zelman and his brother remained in the Ghetto after their mother had 'disappeared', before they were deported to Auschwitz. Looking back on the situation, alone with his brother, all relatives lost, he writes:

> I had spent four and a half years in Lodz ghetto. I had lost my mother and all my relatives. Only my brother was still alive. How could we bear all these losses? The dead had become our life companions. This procession of spirits, I now realize, accompanied us on all our paths. At the time, however, we looked neither to the right nor to the left so that we wouldn't go crazy. ... And we didn't look into ourselves. Otherwise we would have noticed that our youth was being stolen, our feelings maimed, and that the process of annihilation had taken hold—not only around us—but within us. ... Was it possible to still have goals in this condition? I did not have a mother anymore. I didn't have a family. But I had a brother. I had to protect him. (Zelman 1998: 55)

His main purpose in life—at the age of 14—was to act as mother and father for his 12-year-old brother. Even his brother, though, who stayed behind in the barracks of the labour camp because he was sick, 'disappeared' without a goodbye. 'Shayek was not here anymore. That could only mean that Shayek was not here anymore. Nothing else. I refused to think that he was dead' (Zelman 1998: 72).

The only thing left behind was a piece of bread. Despite being used to eating the bread of the dead, he could not make himself eat that left behind by his brother. 'I was hungry! One ate the bread of every dead person!

That was it. Shayek was not dead, so I had no right to eat his bread. By not eating his bread, although my stomach roared for it, I did not accept his death' (Zelman 1998: 72).

After losing the last member of his family, Leon Zelman grew closer and closer to a friend of similar age, whom he had gotten to know before already. This friend became his new rock, making it possible to keep on living. The hope remained that other relatives might still be alive in another camp.

## Searching for Surviving Relatives after the War

After the war, and with it the Holocaust, had ended, the realisation of what had happened set in, and with it came the question about what had happened to ones relatives. After having spent the first weeks of freedom recovering physically, this question rose in Leon Zelman as well:

> Slowly we became conscious of what was behind us. We had to cope with the realization that we were alone. ... I could not even ask the terrible question about the survival of my relatives, of my mother, of Shayek. ... As soon as we had revived somewhat, we crowded around a large bulletin board, in the hope of finding some news. (Zelman 1998: 87, 88)

Like all survivors, Leon Zelman was searching for his relatives. Every day, he checked the bulletin board with the publicly posted lists of names.

> Possibly this or that cousin or this or that aunt had somehow made it through. We had all lost sight of one another so quickly. By tomorrow the redeeming message could already be hanging on the bulletin board. Talking about these things was like therapy; in spelling out our hopes, we got closer to what we were really seeking—warmth and security. (Zelman 1998: 91)

The search turned into a daily ritual. Answers were sought with an abundance of energy and creativity. The hope prevailed that surviving relatives will be found. It was also a search for truth, though. The survivors wanted to know what had happened. If a reunion had become impossible, then they wanted to know about the events and circumstances leading up to the death. They wanted to know where their relatives died, where they have been buried. More often than not, even these questions are asked in vain. 'Yet many found nothing. Still, those of us who found nothing continued to check the board daily. And gradually, for many of us, the fear became certainty: we were indeed alone' (Zelman 1998: 88).

"'I don't even know where her dust is settled,' he reflected bitterly, "and that hurts me very much. How can one deprive a human being of a space for her eternal rest?'", quote Kestenbergs and Brenner (1996: 34) a surviving adolescent, searching for his mother. The pain of not being able to give his mother a grave is formulated in the present tense, as a question that cannot be answered.

The complete 'disappearance' of relatives, lacking even a grave or burial site, is a continuous burden on the survivors, lasting years, even decades. The search can continue throughout a lifetime.

In a psychiatric evaluation, David Rosen describes the symptoms of a woman living in New York. This woman spent her days searching the streets of Manhattan for her mother, despairing about not finding her. As an adolescent, this woman had been deported to Auschwitz, where, at the platform for arriving trains, she saw her mother for the very last time. She has heard nothing of her since. Despite having led a well-adjusted life in her new home in the USA—she had had a job and two kids—this woman's psychological state started to deteriorate significantly once she was in her 70s. Her last-onset psycho-traumatic stress-disorder showed itself strongest in the misconceptualisation of reality in her continuous search for her mother. The wish to at least know about the place and time of death of a 'disappeared' was often denied. The survivors are left with nothing. 'Their expectation of finding lost parents has waned through the years, as have their nightmares' (Kestenberg & Brenner 1996: 34).

When it had become clear that the war would be lost, many NS-troops tried to erase the traces of the atrocities committed. They opened up the mass graves with excavators and burnt what could be found of human bodies on grills made of railway tracks. What still remained was put through the bone grinder. Finally everything was poured back into the pit (Benz 1995: 115). This attempt to cover up what had happened and destroy the proof for the troop's own crimes against humanity, again affected those who were their victims in the first place—the surviving relatives who are deprived of all information about their loved ones.

## Trying to Retain the Memory: Magic Objects, Transitional Objects

This complete lack meant that other ways of remembering had to be found for those who had lost relatives in the Holocaust. Mementos, small relics and personal items were collected and kept close. These objects could be inanimate or animate ones, like, pets representing the deceased. Kestenberg and Brenner relate these items to the transitional objects described by Winnicott (1953).

After the war, new families, which were often started after a fairly short period of time, served as replacements for all those who had been lost. Children were frequently named after family members who had been killed.

These children, born after the war, had to take up the functions of 'living links' (Volkan 1981). Their presence provided their parents with a feeling of closeness to the 'disappeared' siblings, parents, aunts or uncles. The loss became less permanent and, therefore, easier to bear. Hopes, ideas and fantasies concerning the deceased could be projected onto these living children. Hans Keilson relates the life story of a man named Esra, who survived the concentration camp as a 12-year-old, but lost his entire family. Keilson related how, in order to keep the memory of his parents alive, Esra now kisses his children goodnight twice every evening. The second kiss represents the kiss the grandparents would have given the children (Keilson 1979: 239).

The very fact that children were born, that there was a new generation, signified a triumph over the massacres that had had the total eradication of all Jews, Romani and Sinti as their aim.

## Avoiding Further Losses

After these severely traumatising experiences of loss, attempts are made to avoid further losses. A famous example of this phenomenon is documented by Kestenberg (1996). She describes the reaction of a group of children living in an orphanage in Otwock, Poland, whose caretaker, Franziska Oliwa, was supposed to be brought to hospital because of an infection in her leg. In the experience of these children, people who have been taken away do not return. Faced with the threat of being separated from their attachment figure, they sent the ambulance away. They even managed to convince a surgeon to perform the operation right there in the orphanage.

> When we hide, either we disappear from sight or, in a sense, our identity disappears. For many child survivors, disappearance means death, and aging is a road to it. When child survivors speak of their lost childhood, they tell us that the world owes them a new life. They feel

betrayed once again when they are faced with becoming older without recompense and without having fulfilled themselves. They are lost again. (Kestenberg 1996: 152)

## The Desire for Justice

The German term *Wiedergutmachung* 'reparation', or, literally, 'again-well-making', is interesting in its wording. It implies that a wrong that has been done can be, in a sense, undone. Lozowick (1997) compares the German term *Wiedergutmachung* with the Hebrew *Shilumim*:

> The German term Wiedergutmachung, literally: 'making better again', whatever it may mean, clearly indicates a positive phenomenon. Damage has been caused, and the payment will somehow correct it. The Hebrew term Shilumim stems from a biblical word denoting a form of punishment. The German term seems to indicate that the suffering can somehow be alleviated; the purpose of the payment is to benefit the victim. The Hebrew term doesn't address the damage at all, rather the responsibility of the perpetrator; the purpose of the transaction—in the biblical original—is to save the soul of the culprit more than to benefit the victim. (Lozowick 1997: 205)

To me, the experiences and insights gained after 1945 that found their way into the reports on and descriptions of therapeutic sessions of that time are essential in the process of gaining an understanding for the psychodynamics involved for relatives of people who have 'disappeared', in processing their personal experiences (individually or as a group). Therefore, reflexions and publications on the Holocaust/Shoah constitute an essential basis for this book.

Approaching this topic as a non-Jewish Austrian, I feel a certain shyness. Regarding this situation, I would like to refer to Heidelberger-Leonard (1996), who writes about Ruth Klüger, a Holocaust survivor, and her understanding of history. Comparisons help us in our understanding. According to Heidelberger-Leonard, Klüger stresses her awareness of the concept that history repeats itself. She talks about bridges that can be built between individual, unique events. Following Heidelberger-Leonard, the verbal image of the bridge can be said to fit very well. The meaning of a particular event experienced by an individual is validated, while at the same time historical comparability is recognised (1996: 67f.).

## 'Enforced Disappearances' through War and Terror

People who live in a conflict area and are suddenly confronted with the 'disappearance' of one or more relatives often find that the normal channels for official inquiries are closed to them. Even the most basic measures cannot be taken because of the on-going conflict or the continuous threat of an attack. Just going out with a search party would put everyone's lives at risk.

War zones are not a thing of the past. In the following, I will outline a number of such conflict situations from the last couple of years, the situations survivors found themselves in and the consequences the crisis had on them.

### New York after 9/11

This chapter is based on my own experiences in working with relatives of victims of the 9/11 attacks in the days right after this tragic event, and on the reflections of Pauline Boss and her team (Boss et al. 2003).

The images that characterise this catastrophe remind of those who dominate the media after an earthquake: people using their bare hands, trying to pull their relatives from beneath collapsed buildings, workers and volunteers digging day and night—holding on to the hope that survivors can be found even days after the catastrophe. Almost always 'miracles' take place—people are found alive after days underground. The news goes straight to the heart.

The dream of finding the missing partner, child or parent alive comes true for only a few. Nevertheless, all of those who know of a loved-one buried underneath the debris hope that he or she will be the one for whom this miracle will come to pass. While surrounded by the knowledge that thousands have died, the hope remains that my child, my brother, my wife ... will somehow be saved. Like those who have survived through an earthquake, the relatives of the victims are the last to give up hope. But this was not a natural catastrophe, but a terrorist attack, consciously planned and executed. The death of all the people in the World Trade Center (WTC), the Pentagon and on board the airplanes were accepted as casualty.

I experienced these September days in New York 2001 directly, during which hopes became slimmer, turning slowly into the horrible certainness of death or into a chronic state of uncertainty. Since I had been in New York for a conference at that time, I volunteered to lend psychotherapeutic support to the relatives of the victims of the attack on the WTC. For three days, from 13 to 15 September, I worked as a counsellor for the employees—and, of course, their relatives—of a company that had had their offices in one of the top floors of the collapsed skyscraper. The management of this firm had reacted quickly, and, in the light of the magnitude of this catastrophe, in a very coordinated manner: They rented a hall in a first class hotel to be used as a meeting place for the survivors and the family members of the 'missing' employees.

I am using the word 'missing' here, because this was how the victims of the attack on the WTC were commonly referred to at that time. Just as after an earthquake, everyone was acutely aware of the fact that there were a large number of fatalities, but the use of 'missing' reflects the hope for survivors—which was alive much longer in the hearts of those whom we supported throughout these difficult first days than in our own.

On 13 September, a young woman who had lost her husband told me frequently about how strong and fit her partner was, how he surely was strong enough to survive this situation and hold on. When I saw her two days later, she had given up the hope that her husband might still be alive. At that time, she then clung to the idea that he must surely have passed away quickly and had not had to suffer before he passed away.

The safe frame, as it has been described by Herman (1992), was provided in an exemplary manner for the employees of a number of large firms. The rented hall was a beautiful, safe place people could retreat to and spend time together in. For many of the mostly middle-class families, there was an element of paradox to this—the banquet hall of a famous hotel, known from TV or newspaper pictures as a place for high society parties, became the space for their personal mourning and grief.

Journalists were not permitted in, providing a chance for the relatives of the 'missing' to find a moment of peace. Those who wanted to publicise their stories had ample opportunity elsewhere. Inside the hall, families and friends were also provided with details and information by the firms. On the first day, this was still done in accordance with a schedule, where everyone got the same information at the same time. However, many relatives, especially the victims' parents, felt burdened by information such as what continual payments the companies would be able to provide. They perceived this kind of basal information about lucre an imposition on their grief about the loss of their child. On the other hand, this kind of information was vital for many of the wives and children of the 'missing' employees, as they needed to have a modicum of financial safety for the upcoming weeks. Quick on the uptake, the organisers rearranged their plans and set up a number of tables where those who wanted to get information could do so, talking directly to legal representatives, bookkeepers, etc.

What remained as part of the daily schedule was an address given by the head of the firm (sometimes videoed in) and ecumenical masses held by a rabbi and a number of priests of different Christian affiliations.

On 12 September—the day right after the catastrophe—it was mostly the employees of the company, most of who had survived because, by mere coincidence, they had not been at the office at the time of the attack, who organised the impromptu support centre. Most of them were relieved by Red Cross volunteers on the next day. Their own trauma began to become apparent: They began to realise how close they had been to dying themselves. At the same time they began to grief for the large number of colleges and friends they had lost.

### The Offer of Psychological Counselling and Support

Psychologists and therapists who had volunteered their support wore orange pins in order to be recognised. Apart from that, the organisation of the psychological counselling was rather chaotic. While on 13 September, my French colleague and I were welcomed enthusiastically as much needed psychological support (especially because of our knowledge of languages other than English), on the 15th there seemed to be more counsellors than relatives of 'missing' people.

It also was unclear what type of counselling would be taking place. No one took the offer of a group-debriefing. This comes as no surprise, considering the circumstances. This measure would have made sense, had the traumatic event been over, but these people were right in the middle of it, faced with the unimaginable reality of death, their horror ever-present. Pauline Boss was invited by the trade union to work with the employees of the WTC's building administration and its cleaning personnel over the period of a number of weeks. Having worked in the research field of ambiguous loss for a number of years, she also criticises the attempts to apply prefabricated therapeutic models to the 9/11 attacks: 'Ambiguous loss is chronic trauma' (Boss et al. 2003: 458).

Interestingly, it was mostly the distant relatives (uncles, cousins) who accepted the offer to talk to psychologists during the first days following the catastrophe. Survivors who had managed to escape in time, or had not come to work yet that day were also amongst those who made use of the psychological support during that time.

On my first day of counselling, only one set of relatives, a couple that had lost their son, came to me for a session. The mother had been in therapy for some time and therefore knew what she expected from our talk. This family's specific tragedy lay in the fact that their son had been severely depressed and had repeatedly voiced suicidal ideations. For years, the parents had been worrying for their son's life. That he had then died as the victim of a terroristic attack at the age of 26 was confusing and irritating for both parents. Nevertheless, they were the only ones who had accepted the reality of their child's death already two days after the incident.

## RITUALS HELP

The first people with missing-person-flyers came already on the evening of the day of the terrorist attack. All these flyers had the same design: a picture of the—for now—missing person in the middle, framed above and below by the name, the company they worked for, what floor their office had been on, and contact details of the relatives. The hotel we worked in had an office where family members could create and print such flyers for free. A whole wall in the banquet hall was dedicated to these flyers, becoming a memorial site in its own right. When it became necessary to change to a different hall on the 15th, all these flyers were taken down and put up again in the new room. People made certain that there would be enough space for all of them. These pictures were visited like graves, providing a place to grief at and to remember. Many stood in front of the flyers for a long time, weeping loudly or crying in silence.

Since, contrary to all expectations, my flight left as planned on Sunday the 16th of September, I flew home that day. My feelings were ambivalent; I felt like I was abandoning the people in New York, while at the same time I knew that there were plenty of psychologists and therapists to continue the work.

According to reports that arrived from New York during the following weeks, allegations against the counsellors were made after I had left, accusing them of reacting in a wrong way or not helping at all. I do think that in individual cases this critique was certainly justified. After all, many of the psychologists who volunteered had never been confronted with traumatised people. Those who had learned about methods to approach the situation might have applied them in an overly structured way that was simply too much for the traumatised people. On the whole, however,

I think that this critique was really an outlet for people's despair. The pain could only be softened by a margin—and, hence, a vent for the helpless desperation was found. It would have been illusionary to expect anything beyond basic support through the first days of grief from the psychologists. I am convinced that, generally, the range of psychological services offered helped the people of New York in making it through these first days and in their attempts of coping with their loss. Nothing can take away the pain and grief, though. The difficult circumstances surrounding this violent death, and the destabilisation of everyday life all through New York City were additionally burdening factors. The grieving process was further complicated by the lack of bodies. In most cases, nothing was found that could be buried. The official death toll was made public a year later, in September 2002: 2,819 people were killed in the terrorist attacks of 9/11, 289 bodies were found and identified. From the debris, 19,858 body parts were retrieved, and still, 1,717 families have no real evidence for what has happened to the person they lost (Boss et al. 2003).

The collective ritual of posting and visiting the missing-person-flyers has certainly played an important role.

## Families Torn apart by Political Arbitrariness

Staub (1989) calls the time between 1975 and 1979, when Cambodia was ruled by the Khmer Rouge, a time of auto genocide. About 2 million people died through executions or of starvation. While the term 'enforced disappearance' is not mentioned in the literature about Cambodia under the Khmer Rouge, biographical accounts show that relatives and friends again and again 'disappeared' suddenly without a goodbye.

After having triumphed in the civil war, the Khmer Rouge wanted to turn Cambodia into the perfect communist agricultural society. The urban population had to leave Phnom Pen as well as all other major cities immediately. This resulted in three million people on the road at the same time, which by necessity led to problems with hygiene as well as a shortfall in supplies.

People from the same ethnic group as the group in power (Khmer) were killed for incomprehensible reasons (Staub 1989: 11).

Those whose relatives had disappeared had little or no way of inquiring after them, let alone searching for them. In most cases, they had to assume that the person had been executed, but sometimes he or she had only been moved to another camp. Ung (2000) describes her childhood under these conditions. One day, her father is taken away by a group of soldiers. The first days are spent waiting.

> We sit on the steps waiting for him together in silence. No words are exchanged as ours eyes search the fields waiting for him to come home. We all know that Pa will not return, but no one dares to say it out loud for it will shatter our illusion of hope. (Ung 2000: 105)

The family spends the days between hope and despair. As atrocities are committed frequently and publicly, even the youngest children know what being taken away by soldiers usually means. Ung describes movingly, how the knowledge of the present terror and the lack of knowledge about her father's situation combine to horrifying thoughts, dreams and fantasies:

> My mind races and fills my head with images of death and executions. I have heard many stories about how the soldiers kill prisoners and then dump their bodies into large graves. How they torture their captives, behead them, or crack their skulls with axes so as not to waste their precious ammunition. I cannot stop thinking of Pa and whether or not he died with dignity. I hope they did not torture him. (Ung 2000: 105)

The family is almost certain that the father has been killed. Nevertheless they cling to the hope that he might be alive against all odds. Loung Ung remembers herself praying as a seven-year-old, saying:

> Dear gods, Pa is a very devout Buddhist. Please help my Pa return home. He is not mean and does not like to hurt other people. Help him return and I will do anything you say. I will devote my entire life to you. I will believe you always. If you cannot bring Pa home to us, please make sure they don't hurt him, or please make sure Pa dies a quick death. (Ung 2000: 107)

Later, her mother and her younger sister 'disappear' as well. Nothing is ever heard of them again.

Sadly, the story of this family is a typical example of life in Cambodia under the rule of the Khmer Rouge leader Pol Pot. Kinzie et al. (1998) write about the drastic changes made during that time, which have affected Cambodia for years after, and still show themselves today. Religious concepts were called into question by the terrible losses and by the chronic grief induced by the widespread deaths. The personal identity built on the concept of a family was largely destroyed. With a large number of men being murdered, women had to act as single parents without having a cultural basis for that concept. The surviving family members clung to each other in fear.

Surviving family members need to remain particularly close to each other for emotional and physical survival. Anything affecting that closeness may be seen as a threat that can reawaken frighteningly vivid memories of prior losses. This threat may be perceived even in positive transitions, such as marriage, or the move to another city for a better job opportunity. (Kinzie et al. 1998: 213)

Kinzie and his team conducted a longitudinal study (examinations in 1984, 1987 and 1990) with 40 adolescents who had come as refugees to the USA. The initial examination showed that 50 per cent of the adolescents were suffering from PTSD and 50 per cent fulfilled the diagnostic criteria for depression. Three years later, these figures had barely improved. Those of the study participants who lived with foster families were less likely to have PTSD than those living in residential institutions. Of the adolescents, 72 per cent felt extremely burdened by their worry for Cambodia and the relatives they had left behind.

In 1997, the Cambodian government asked the UN for support in the legal process dealing with the genocide. In 2001, the National Assembly of Cambodia passed the law that established the Extraordinary Chambers in the Courts of Cambodia (ECCC) as the Cambodian court for the Khmer Rouge Case trials.

That the trials took place in Cambodia using Khmer was a deliberate decision. That way, the public was able to follow the trials. The cooperation with the UN ensured an international standard for the trials. Witnesses that testified in court were promised psychological counselling.

The court cannot grant compensations to individuals. It can, however, sentence individuals to giving symbolic compensations and support to the community.

However, the judges may award collective and moral reparations such as an order to publish the judgment in appropriate media outlets at the convicted person's expense or an order to fund any non-profit activity or service that is intended for the benefit of victims. (ECCC 2012)

Freeman (2012) describes a study conducted with 775 survivors of the Khmer Rouge regime, all of who have lost at least one family member through the acts of the regime. Conducted in 2008/09, the study showed that 30 years after this time of terror 14 per cent of the study participants were suffering from prolonged grief disorder. As especially difficult for the survivors proved the fact that those killed by the Khmer Rouge rarely received a proper burial.

## Powerless Wives

In Sri Lanka, 'enforced disappearances' were used by a number of different war parties as a means of exerting pressure during the war. In the period from 1988 to 1990 alone, up to 60,000 people had 'disappeared' there (Black 1999). The majority of them were young men aged 15 to 35. This period was marked by serious confrontations between the Singhalese-chauvinistic 'People's Liberation Front' (Janathā Vimukthi Peramuṇa, JVP) and the reigning government under prime minister Premadasa (UNP). The brutal attempts of the JVP to overthrow the government by destabilising the country was met with even more drastic acts of brutality by the government forces. On roadsides and rivers, large numbers of bodies, mutilated beyond recognition, were found in these times. Ondaatje (2011: 184) writes in his novel *Anil's Ghost*, in which he addresses these years of terror in Sri Lanka:

> We have seen so many heads stuck on poles here, these last few years.... You'd see them in the early mornings, somebody's night work, before the families heard about them and came to remove them and took them home. Wrapping them in shirts or cradling them. Someone's sin. These were blows to the heart. There was only one thing worse. That was when a family member simply disappeared and there was no sighting or evidence of his existence or his death.

Today one has to assume that none of the people who have 'disappeared' up to 1999 are still alive. Thousands of bodies, mutilated beyond any chance of identification, were buried in anonymous graves. The state-of-emergency legislation permitted government forces to bury bodies without any autopsy having been conducted. In November 2012, a mass grave holding the remains of 154 people was discovered in the highlands of Matale. Archaeologists date the grave to the time between 1986 and 1990 (Haviland 2013). The people buried in it have clearly been murderer. In a statement concerning this discovery, the Asian Human Right Group (2013) writes:

> However, the key question is as to whose remains these are. Identifying the exact names of those whose remains are inside this mass grave is of importance, not only for future initiatives relating to justice but it is also important from the point of view of the families who lost loved ones during this period. For many families what happened to their loved ones who 'disappeared' is a vital psychological and emotional issue.

As of today, thousands of people still live in uncertainty as to what has happened to their son, their husband, their father.

The civil war in Sri Lanka lasted from 1983 to 2009. People kept 'disappearing' throughout the entire time span. There were victims in each and every social demographical group; virtually all parties involved in the conflict were responsible for such 'disappearances'. Any remaining hopes on ever seeing one of these 'disappeared' alive again are in vain, by all objective criteria. From a psychological point of view, however, they are quite understandable.

In her study, Thiruchandran (1999: 92) points out how women are doubly powerless in a conservative, patriarchal society. Women's identity is defined through the social and economic position of her husband. A widow loses both forms of identity, his and hers.

In many cases, the women were stigmatised. Tamil women are held responsible for the karma, the fate of their husbands. Therefore, they and their children have to face a form of prejudice so irrational in nature that there is no arguing against it.

Mothers whose husbands have 'disappeared' or died feel guilty not only for being incapable of maintaining the family's economical status, but also for not being able to protect their children from these prejudices.

In a large number of cases, the children turned on their mothers in these situations, showing anger and aggression and blaming their mothers for their fathers' 'disappearance' and the deterioration of their living conditions.

> The children had often reacted with a lot of hostility and bitterness towards the mothers and the mothers had a lot of emotional outbursts—they cried, sobbed when they related the many episodes of the revolt of the children. Disobedience of the children they felt was the worst behaviour but the verbal attack of the children caused them even more pain....
>
> 'If appa (father) were alive, he would give rice (food). You are starving us. You have no job, no money. We have no education. What kind of a mother are you. To go to school we have no shoes. When we come home we have no food.'
>
> 'Why did you give birth to us. Give us rice or squeeze our necks and kill us.' ... A few of them even beat the mother. (Thiruchandran 1999: 89)

The poverty the fatherless families live in after the death or the 'disappearance' of the father is seen as the most central problem these families have to face.

There is a significant difference though. Widows and half-orphaned children can collect a small pension from the government to support themselves. The relatives of 'disappeared' are excluded from such financial support. Their social status remains unresolved as well.

I would like to illustrate the resulting difficulties of this situation by relating the story of a young woman I met during my stay in Sri Lanka in March 1996:

> M., a 26-year-old Muslim woman, is about to remarry. Eight years ago, her first husband was dragged off during a night time police raid only months after they had been married. Together with him, a number of other young men 'disappeared' as well. M., who was 18 at that time, has therefore been neither a wife nor a widow ever since. She has never heard from her husband again. Now, she would like to turn over a new leaf. She is planning to marry a young doctor whom she has met at work and fallen in love with. But she is plagued by the question: What if her husband is still alive? (Here we find a parallel to Europe after the war: There was no proof of life to be had for the thousands of men who had become prisoners of war.) As a Muslim women, she attracts attention in Sri Lanka: She constantly shows her widowhood by wearing a black chador—an unusual garment in Sri Lanka. She wants to continue to wear a veil after marrying again. This outward sign of mourning is her way of striking a compromise between her loyalty to her deceased husband and her love to her new spouse.

M.'s first husband was taken because of his origins and his religion, and has 'disappeared' never to be seen again. Her situation is similar to those of the wives of the Sri Lankan soldiers who have been listed as 'MIA' since the war. Piyanjali de Zoysa of the University of Colombo interviewed 2,000 of these women. He also conducted an in-depth study with 22 of them, the results of which he summarises as follows:

> Young wives of soldiers who are gone missing-in-action may feel guilty about getting attracted to other men and would be in a dilemma as to whether to assume a new relationship, as that would mean that she has considered her husband to be dead. In the conservative Sri Lankan society, this would generally have adverse implications for the woman, as her in-laws and the community to which she belongs tend to frown upon such behaviours ... all 22 of the wives of soldiers ... indicated that one of their main problems was having to wait in hope 'forever' that the husband would return one day.
>
> These women also had fears about their future, especially in regard to concerns about their personal security in relation to the possibility of future

marriage, inability to ward off unwanted sexual advances from other men and a feeling of degradation because there husband had disappeared. The wives were also concerned about the future welfare of their children and of not being able to make long term plans. (De Zoysa 2001: 205)

A significant step in the process of overcoming this nationwide trauma was the establishment of three commissions charged with the task of solving such cases of 'disappearances'. Within the first year, the commission worked on 8,543 cases of 'disappearances' (Fernando 1998: 6).

If a death was formally recognised by the commission, this was taken as an official confirmation. The relatives were issued a death certificate and could apply for financial compensations. This significantly improved the social and economical situation of thousands of widows and half-orphans.

The commission was taken aback by the large number of enquiries. Since most 'disappearances' had taken place five to seven years in the past; the parents', wives' and children's need for information was great. Since the commission had been instated by a new government that had not been responsible for the 'disappearances', it was considered reliable enough to be entrusted with investigating into the life or death of a close relative.

Another step to help the traumatised population would have been the punishment of those responsible for the 'disappearances'. This, however, seems an almost impossible demand. 'The commissions have made their recommendations, but no legislation has been considered for implementing them', analyses Black (1999: 8) drily. He concludes that the government and many of the public officials are so deeply entangled in the decision process that led to the violations of human rights that have been committed, that this matter could only be resolved with external assistance.

> Even when officers have been transferred, the structural damage to the system has thwarted the search for the truth.... The result of the government's use of the entire legal enforcement machinery in its campaign of mass disappearances is a system that cannot recover without outside assistance. (Black 1999: 8)

While in the Southern parts of the country most 'disappearances' took place in the period between 1988 and 1990, the people living in the Northern and Eastern parts of the island country were almost permanently under threat of getting 'disappeared', since the main conflict between the Sinhalese majority and the Tamil minority took place there.

## The Search for the 'Disappeared'—beyond the Realm of Science

In their search for the 'disappeared' loved-one, relatives also turn to religions, mysticisms and other supernatural phenomena. Daya Somasundaram and C. S. Jamunantha from the University of Jaffna, North Sri Lanka, write about one such family and their search for the son and brother who has disappeared. All investigations made with the help of national and international organisations turned out to be futile. Therefore, the family tried to come by information about the young man through oracles. Driven by the hopes they were given over and over by the oracles they visited, the family kept travelling from one to the next. The ambivalent state between hope and despair becomes visible in the deteriorating health of some of the family members:

> A 30-year-old gentleman ... was arrested in mid August, 1996 at Chemmany while he was cycling to his office in the morning. His parents and three sisters searched for him and learnt he had been arrested by the military forces. They had complained to the Army 512 Brigade, Government Agent, ICRC and Human Right Commission. But nothing was fruitful.
> They went to hear the horoscope from the Sasthirakarran. He told them that he had the 'bad period'. Three months later they went to hear the Vaku (oracle) at the Sivahamy Amman Kovil, at Mirusuvil. After performing a ritual, she said that he is living in the South. Six months later, they went to Kokuvil, where the Oracle worshipped Kannan ... and said that he was living, pray to Lord Kannan. (To date they have continued to pray to Lord Kannan). Later, they went to another oracle at Alaveddy where also they were told that he was living.
> Meanwhile, the mother got sick, lost her appetite, found it difficult to speak and died one year later. Father also became depressed and started to neglect his self-care. Sister also has poor concentration in her normal work. But they said with tears that they are praying that one day their beloved one might come back. (Somasundaram & Jamunanantha 2002: 244)

All earthly means of searching for the 'disappeared' brother and son had proven in vain, but the supernatural oracles and predictions also fail to provide information about the whereabouts of the 'disappeared'. The risk that advantage might be taken of the people who have become desperate in their search for the beloved gets higher the farther away they move from verifiable means of searching.

Scientific methods such as exhumation and forensic procedures that would offer a chance for identification of deceased are rarely performed

74  Grief and Disappearance

in Sri Lanka. Facing the country's history and providing clarity for the relatives of the 'disappeared' does not seem to be part of the political agenda. Instead, those regions in which the late 1980s were characterised by frequent 'disappearances' and findings of mutilated bodies thrive on new ghost stories. Sasanka Perera quotes one such story that was published in the newspaper *Irida Lankadipa* on 8 November 1992:

> One day when a group of fishermen were fishing in this vicinity they heard some terrible sounds from atop the rock. Then suddenly a well-built man wearing a black jacket and a hat appeared. Making a loud noise he jumped into the sea. After a while the fishermen saw the man climb on to the rock again. Then another man appeared and both of them jumped into the sea. The fishermen returned home and consumed a fish curry made out of the fish they had caught. That night all three started purging. Their excrement was black. Other fishermen have seen groups of strangers sailing towards them in the darkness who disappear before contact can be made. (quoted in Perera 1999: 95)

The place described in the story had been the sight of the execution of four young people who had gone into hiding. After being shot, their bodies had been tossed into the sea.

S. Perera sees this type of ghost story as a way of remembering the 'disappeared' as well as an expression of survivor's guilt.

> More importantly I would also suggest that it is also an expression of their own personal guilt. In other words, despite being alive, they could not prevent the deaths of many in their community.... As we know, in the context of the terror in the south, floating bodies in rivers or the sea were one of its most enduring legacies. Thus the fishermen clearly ate tainted fish, fish that had fed upon humans, possible members of their own community. (Perera 1999: 96)

## The Children of 'Disappeared' Soldiers

After the Balkan war in the 1990s, about 40,000 people were listed as 'missing' or 'disappeared' (Schmidt-Häuer 2002).

The psychologist Sibela Zvizdic (Zvizdic & Butollo 2000) documented the effects the loss of the father, who had either died or had 'disappeared', had had on the children.

From 14 different schools in Sarajevo, 816 children aged 10–15 participated in the study. They had been somewhere between 6 and 12 years old during the war. The mothers of these children were alive. For the study they were split into four groups.

The first group was made up of 201 children whose fathers had 'disappeared' during the war with no information about their whereabouts having ever reached the family. Most of them survived the war living in refugee camps in Bosnia. The second group of children had been separated from their fathers during the war. They had fled the country together with their mothers, while their fathers had remained in Bosnia.

The 208 children that made up the third group had lived with their mothers in Bosnia throughout the war. Their fathers were killed in the war, and the families were told about this fairly quickly. The last group of children was a control group. The 203 children in this fourth group had spent the duration of the war together with both parents in Bosnia and were not affected by any losses.

Zvizdic examined the children, using two questionnaires she herself had drawn up, namely the 'questionnaire for war-related traumatic events—ITRR' (consisting of 34 closed items, one open question) and the 'questionnaire for postwar-related stressful/traumatic experiences—INRR' (10 closed items), as well as the Birleson depression scale for children—DSRS. Describing the results, Zvizdic and Butollo's results show that children whose fathers had been killed during the war had less traumatic experiences than those children whose fathers had 'disappeared' (Zvizdic & Butollo 2000).

In an analogous fashion, the children whose fathers had 'disappeared' also showed stronger depressive reactions than those whose fathers had been killed. The values for depression in both groups were significantly higher up on the scale than those in the third (temporary separation) and fourth (control group) group.

The results of the study were unusually clear: 'We found out that the group of the early adolescents whose fathers had disappeared (and are still missing) was the group exposed most to war-related traumatic events' (Zvizdic & Butollo 2000: 210).

Zvizdic and Butollo concede that this, in part, also resulted from that group having been exposed to the largest amount of additional stressors during the war (threat to their own life, witnessing acts of violence and torture, loss of other attachment figures, loss of home, loss of other social structures). But

It is clear that early adolescents whose fathers are still considered missing persons have been forced to cope with specific postwar-related stressful traumatic experiences as well, which may also be connected with the traumatic disappearance of their fathers. (Zvizdic & Butollo 2000: 211)

Other studies about the children of people who have 'disappeared' have shown similar results (for example, Becker 1992). What makes this study so special is how clearly it shows that the children of men who have 'disappeared' are at a higher risk to suffer from PTSD and depression than those whose fathers had been killed.

## Arbitrariness during Civil Wars

Except for a very brief period of respite, from 1994 to 2009 the people of Chechnya had constantly lived in a war zone. Human rights were violated on a regular basis; the time was characterised by oppression, murder and 'disappearances'.

Hassel (2003) writes about the lies that lay at the basis of the Second Chechen War. Everybody told the truth that suited them best, the rebels themselves, of course, but even more so the Russian officials, their armies and secret service agents. A major problem, according to Hassel, lay in the lack of independent sources. Instruments of democracy, such as a fairly extensive legal system and local and national newspapers did exist, but for the most part they were dependent on the state and told the version of reality they were expected to (Hassel 2003: 10). Such an atmosphere of disinformation and half-truths becomes the breeding ground for circumstances in which even severe violations of human rights cannot really be controlled effectively. Especially the 'enforced disappearances' became regular occurrences in the terror that was the everyday reality of war.

The authors of the Amnesty International Annual Report 2002 enumerate:

> Violations committed by Russian forces during 2001 included arbitrary detention in secret detention centres and pits in the ground, torture and ill-treatment, 'disappearances', and extrajudicial executions. Chechen forces attacked civilians working in the local administration in Chechnya ... and ill-treated and unlawfully killed captured Russian soldiers.

'Disappearances' were executed in an arbitrary fashion. During police raids, villagers were taken prisoners at random. Most of them were granted no contact to the world outside the detainment facility. Often, the prisoners were tortured. The motives for the arrests were not always ones of war or even politically motivated.

> Bribes were so commonly extorted from relatives to secure detainees' release that the act of detention itself often appeared to be motivated by financial gain. Hundreds of people 'disappeared' after being taken into custody; the mutilated bodies of some were later found, along with the bodies of other unidentified individuals, in more than a dozen dumping grounds and mass graves throughout Chechnya. (Amnesty International 2002)

The number of people who 'disappeared' in Chechnya can only be guessed. Hassel's (2003) estimation of 2,800 'disappearances' in the Second Chechen War means that out of 10,000 Chechen citizens, 46 became victims of 'enforced disappearances'. Even under the terror of Stalin's rule, a time where 'disappearances' were actively used to exert pressure on Chechens (and on other minorities as well as on political opponents), the figures were not that high. About 44 out of 10,000 Chechens 'disappeared' during that time.

Reynolds (2000) has investigated the question how such severe violations of human rights were possible. To that end, she interviewed Russian soldiers from eight different regions who had all fought in the Chechen War. The results of her interviews are distressing:

> What they recounted largely matches the picture painted in the human rights reports: The men freely acknowledge that acts considered war crimes under international law not only take place but are also commonplace. In fact, most admitted committing such acts themselves—everything from looting to summary executions to torture. (Reynolds 2000)

The ideology behind this is called 'bespredel' (meaning: without rules). It stands for a situation in which one can act outside the law, and does not get punished for it. Solders report that they took no prisoners. They knew that they were supposed to arrest their suspects and hand them over to the military prosecutor, but they hardly ever did. The general procedure was to kill the persons in question, and sometimes their entire family, on the spot. The bodies were dumped into rivers and well shafts. Whether or not the relatives of those who had been executed in this arbitrary fashion ever learned about their deaths, is rather questionable.

Working with Chechen refugees in Austria, we are confronted with their personal stories. A number of my clients told me about ransom demands being made for their 'disappeared' relatives, or about being 'disappeared' themselves and money being demanded from their families.

Sometimes it was possible to, by getting payment to the right soldier, find a 'disappeared' person again. If the relatives could not put up the money, the person remained lost.

Mr I., one of my Chechen clients, told me that his uncle had already paid ransom for him twice. Then Mr I. had to flee, because his uncle could not have afforded to do so the third time, meaning that I. would have remained 'disappeared' forever.

The kind of warfare where political opponents are simply 'disappeared' is common in civil war. A large, well-equipped army is pitted against a small but tough group of rebels. Like during the 'night-and-fog-campaign' of the NS regime against the French resistance movement, 'enforced disappearances' are used to threaten and terrorise the entire population.

The areas of conflict described in this chapter can be seen as representatives for all war zones in this world. Within the scope of this book, they can only be sketched out in brief, bypassing much of the complexity of the situation in each region. What this chapter does attempt to do, though, is show to what immense extent the entire population is affected by 'disappearances' in situations of crisis, armed conflicts and civil wars.

## 'Enforced Disappearances' as Systematic Violations of Human Rights

Where people 'disappear' for reasons of state terror, relatives usually receive no social or psychological support. Quite the opposite—they get bullied and intimidated. They are even prohibited from searching for the 'disappeared', which means that with any future attempts of getting information, the relatives put their own lives at risk.

The Independent Commission on International Humanitarian Issues (1986) clearly differentiates between the human rights violation 'enforced disappearance' and voluntary disappearances or crime victims:

> To avoid any risk of ambiguity, it should be made clear from the outset that those to whom the title refers are not among the many people who every year decide to exchange one life, and perhaps one identity for another. Nor are they victims of criminal acts whose bodies are never recovered.

## The Social Consequences of 'Enforced Disappearances' 79

Amnesty International defines the term more concretely:

> The 'disappeared' are people who have been taken into custody by agents of the state, yet whose whereabouts and fate are concealed, and whose custody is denied. 'Disappearances' cause agony for the victims and their relatives. (Amnesty International 1993b)

The term 'disappearnce' is written in quotation marks throughout the literature, in order to stress the fact that these people have not really disappeared but are held prisoners in secret places or were killed in a specific location.

'Enforced disappearances' always affect the population as a whole; everyone is threatened and tyrannised by the terror those in power exert. Löwenthal (1988: 16),[1] writing about the situation in Germany under NS rule, describes this phenomenon:

> In a situation of terror, the individual is never alone and always alone. He grows stiff, becomes numb, not only in his relationship to others, but also to himself. The fear prohibits spontaneous emotional and cognitive reactions. The act of thinking itself becomes stupidity. It becomes life threatening. It would be stupid to not be stupid and, as a consequence, communal stupidity seeps into the terrorized population. The people fall into a state of stupor, like a moral coma.

Diana Kordon and her associates (Kordon et al. 1988: 174) analyse the situation of the people living under the Argentinean dictatorship which made wide use of 'enforced disappearances', terrorising the entire population by 'disappearing' political opponents.

> Nobody could escape from this, we were all touched by this situation. No social class or individual person was able to remain unscathed in a country where 30,000 people had been wiped out from everyday life and the course of their destinies interrupted due to the unlawful kidnapping.... Behind each missing person there are many different disappearances; disappearance of the freedom of thought, of action, of speech, of creation, of pleasure. And all this was denied to each and every one of those living at that time. The social body has been deeply wounded, symbolically and literally.

Those who 'disappear' have no way of appealing to the legal system or to human values. Within society, they do not exist anymore—as dead or as living. Those who are responsible for their 'disappearances', deny any involvement. In most cases they are in positions of power high enough that they do not fear inspections or audits. Another common scenario is that of a political situation so chaotic and full of turmoil that an accurate reconstruction of the events at a later point in time is impossible.

'Enforced disappearances' evade all laws and legal system and are, therefore, a powerful tool in solidifying one's power.

> For those who order disappearances or those who ... are its silent accomplices, the technique is extremely 'efficient' and 'convenient': there is no evidence, and no proof, which guarantees immunity from international condemnation and from any internal protest. (Independent Commission 1986: 14)

'Enforced disappearances' are often thoroughly planned attacks, executed by a well-organised group of policemen or soldiers. Governments that make use of this so-called 'safety measure', break their own laws. This particular violation of the law is one, however, where it is particularly difficult, sometimes even impossible, to identify those responsible for it. There is no *actus reus* (tangible evidence for a crime) to report on, there are no witnesses that could be called upon to support an indictment (Amnesty International 1993b). People have simply disappeared. There is no trial, and, hence, no lawyer. The relatives remain in the dark about what has happened. In almost all countries where 'enforced disappearances' are common, they usually have to fear the worst.

> A forced disappearance violates a series of fundamental human rights, including: the right to liberty and security of the person, the right to recognition everywhere as a person before the law, the right to legal defense, and the right not to be subjected to torture. In addition, forced disappearance constitutes a grave threat to the right to life. (FEDEFAM 2004)

In their hopes and fears, the remaining family members are torn between wishing that the beloved brother, father or son died a quick and merciful death, or hoping he is still alive, even if that means he is being tortured and held in prison.

The Federación Latinoamericana de Asociaciones de Familiares de Detenidos-Desaparecidos (FEDEFAM), the Latin American Federation of Associations for Relatives of Detained-Disappeared, estimates that about 90,000 people have 'disappeared' in Latin America since the 1960s. During the time of dictatorship, alone, about 30,000 people 'disappeared' in Argentina alone. Of these, only 1,500 have returned, which means that out of 20 'disappeared', 19 (in other words, 95 per cent, i.e., 28,500 people) were never seen again. Most of the survivors had been held in secret prisons or torture camps for years. At the beginning of the 21st century, Amnesty International (2010) reported on 'enforced disappearances' in 84 countries: They cite more than 2 million documented cases of 'enforced disappearances' having taken place over the last decades.

'Enforced disappearances' result in a terrorisation of the entire population—the all pervading uncertainty and inability to act against this violation of the human rights affects a society as a whole. They act as threatening warnings to everyone: Beware! If you are not willing to comply, you could be the next victim. No legal system can protect you from a 'disappearance'. And once you have been taken, you are completely removed from all forms of audits and investigation since you cannot be found. Wherever you are, you are helpless, without power, completely at the mercy of your captors.

In their search for a 'disappeared', relatives are often informed by officials, that this person has never been seen or heard of, has not been arrested, or been in any contact with the military at all. Diffuse uncertainty is all that remains of the 'disappeared'. Sometimes, this non-information is delivered with degrading comments. In Guatemala, for example, women searching for their 'disappeared' husbands had to listen to snide remarks about their spouses having probably run off with women much prettier than them (Towell 1994).

Enquiring after a 'disappeared' can also become very dangerous—as the following example from Sri Lanka shows: When, on 7 September 1996, the mother and brother of 18-year-old Krishanti Kumarasamy asked military officials for information about the girl, both of them, and the two people accompanying them, were killed. By coincidence, this case reached the public. It garnered a lot of attention—which came too late for the four victims, whose bodies were found 45 days later in an earth hole (Society for Threatened Peoples 2004; Thangavelu 2001). In response to the pressure exerted by international human rights organisations, an official enquiry was conducted, and the soldiers responsible were put on trial. In the course of the trial, it became clear that the murder of Krishanti and her family was really only the tip of the iceberg. One of the accused, D. Somaratne, defended himself, stating that he had never killed anyone, only buried the bodies as he had been commanded to: 'We only buried bodies. We can show you where 300 to 400 bodies have been buried' (quoted in BBC 2004).

Michael Ondaatje, who addresses 'enforced disappearances' in his novel *Anil's Ghost,* writes on this topic:

> In a fearful nation, public sorrow was stamped down by the climate of uncertainty. If a father protested a son's death, it was feared another

family member would be killed. If people you knew disappeared, there was a chance they might stay alive if you did not cause trouble. This was the scarring psychosis in the country. Death, loss, was 'unfinished', so you could not walk through it.... All that was left of law was a belief in an eventual revenge towards those who had power. (Ondaatje 2011: 56)

In almost all parts of the world there are people searching for 'disappeared' relatives—either because of political systems that had been in power in the past, as is the case, for example, in Sri Lanka, and in almost all countries of Latin America, or because of current political conflicts.

In Latin America, relatives have organised into groups, and have been fighting together for their 'disappeared' spouses, sons, daughters or grandchildren since the 1970s. Aribal Blanco Araya, whose husband 'disappeared' in Honduras in 1981 (quoted in Amnesty International 1993a), says:

> There are thousands of cases like ours in the whole of Latin-America ... there is the grief of mothers, the hope of wives and the sorrow of children ... and we will not give up because we believe in the right to life, to full respect of human rights, justice and peace.

This kind of self-organisation into groups in their common fight for justice and for information about the whereabouts of their relatives is especially common in Latin America. The members of these groups organising around the issue of the human rights violation, i.e., the 'enforced disappearance' rally, demand the release of their sons, daughters, spouses, etc., or, if nothing else, then at least they want to know the truth about the circumstances surrounding their deaths (Taylor 1997).

On 20 December 2006, the UN passed the International Convention For The Protection Of All Persons From Enforced Disappearance. It came into force on 23 December 2010, was signed by 92 countries and has since been ratified by 39 of these (United Nations Treaty Collection 2006).

Article 1 of the convention states:

> No one shall be subjected to enforced disappearance. No exceptional circumstances whatsoever, whether a state of war or a threat of war, internal political instability or any other public emergency, may be invoked as a justification for enforced disappearance. (United Nations Human Rights n.d.)

It is made clear here, that no exceptional circumstance whatsoever can be accepted as a justification for an 'enforced disappearance'. 'Enforced disappearances' are a crime under all political and social circumstances.

## 'Disappearance' of Refugees

Loss of Contact

People flee their homes for a number of reasons—because of wars, dictatorships, the threat of torture, etc. Fleeing one's home often means a permanent separation from everyone there, and the loss of all means of communicating with the relatives and loved ones left behind. Despite the advances in communication technology made in the 21st century, refugees often have no ways of contacting their families at all.

Refugee families left their homes fearing repressive measures, and went as the so-called 'internally displaced persons' (IDP) to other, safer parts of the county, or left their homeland altogether and fled to Central Europe, the USA, Australia, etc. Often, they started out without concrete plans or a clear destination. Especially for relatives living in Africa or Asia, it is impossible to find their relatives in these foreign countries. In the Additional Protocol to Geneva Convention (1949, 1977) in the chapter 'Missing' it says:

> As soon as circumstances permit, and at the latest from the end of active hostilities, each Party to the conflict shall search for the persons who have been reported missing by an adverse Party. Such adverse Party shall transmit all relevant information concerning such persons in order to facilitate such searches.... (International Committee of the Red Cross 1977)

The Red Cross does important work in the field of reuniting relatives living in different countries. Often, however, this is a challenging, sometimes an impossible task, especially if the relatives are asked to help search for those living in a region that does not have resident registration.

Because of the lack of communication, especially with people who are in the process of fleeing a country, 'disappearances' often go unnoticed. Escape routes are often dangerous, and the refugees lack the knowledge or experiences necessary for, for example, crossing the open sea in a boat or a mountain pass in winter. They do not have the necessary equipment, clothes or simply the physical fitness, and they know little or nothing about the cross regions. In most cases, the refugees are totally dependent on migrant smugglers. Often, they have no choice but to risk life-threatening situations on their way to their new homes (boats barely seaworthy, narrow and poorly ventilated hide-outs, etc.).

Under these conditions, many people die, and their relatives are never informed about it. Only if the bodies of these refugees are found, or if survivors report disposing of them, do their deaths gain public notice, become official and can be reported back to their families. Completely exhausted refugees who are picked up in cramped boats at the coast of Italy, Greece or Spain tell officials about deaths through exhaustion or thirst. They usually threw the bodies overboard in order to give the remaining refugees a chance to survive. For the relatives of refugees, their traces get lost in uncertainty. Somewhere between the home they left and the longed-for place of safety, a person 'disappeared', never to be seen again.

Over the last years, Mexican families of refugees who have 'disappeared' on their way north have started organising the so-called 'Caravans'. The relatives travel along the route the refugees might presumably have taken, and hand out photos of the 'disappeared', hoping that someone might have information about the whereabouts of their loved-ones (Lenz & Müller 2011).

## Structural Violence and 'Disappeared' Children

It is not only political violence and wars that lead to 'disappearances'. Poverty can also bring about structural violence. Attempts of combating this human rights violation often fail due to a lack of financial and social resources within the affected group.

In India, the public interest in one of the darkest sides of its society, the 'disappearance' of women and children without any trace is currently on the rise. With it, the number of programmes that support the families and children involved in order for the 'disappearance' to not be forever, or at least in order to clarify the fate of the sons or daughters, rises as well.

We do not know how many children are separated from their families in India every year, losing all contact with their parents. The number can only be guessed. The National Human Rights Commission (NHRC) estimates a total of about 44,000. About a quarter of these children are never found again. Other NGOs name even higher numbers.

The reasons for children in India to go missing are varied. The *NHRC Report on Missing Children* (Sharma 2007) lists five main reasons:

- Children are kidnapped or carried off by family members
- Children become victims of human trafficking
- Children run away from home on their own account, or because of circumstances that leave them no other option
- Children lose their way, get hurt and lose their bearings

They usually run away to the glamorous big cities where they fall prey to exploiters and are employed in tea stalls, brothels, beggary, etc. Most of the children come from poorer families who do not have access to police services or whose reports are not taken seriously. (Childline 2013)

In really bad cases, the children become victims of human trafficking or lose their lives as victims of an organ trafficking scheme. Childline (2013) distinguishes between three groups of street children.

The first group comprises those children who live on the streets together with their families; the second group are children who live apart from their families, usually in large cities, and only have irregular contact with their parents; the third group, finally, comprises those children who have lost all contact with their families. In part, this third group is made up of orphans, but also of refugees, victims of human trafficking and those who have run away from home. For this third group, organisations with agencies they can go to and that can support them in their search for their relatives are of immense importance.

The largest platform in India that collects the data of missing children is Missing Child Search. Since 2000, the data of more than 220,000 children has been entered and archived. In 2010, the platform focusing on documentation has developed a homepage to which more than 300 other organisations have contributed information. Via this new online platform, children can now be traced much faster and in a more efficient and professional way. The platform works vice versa as well—children can make use of the homepage in their search for their families. The number of new entries per day show how pressing the demand for such a homepage had been: some of the member organisations list up to 40 new cases per day. Currently, the homepage is reaching its technical limits. Often, the homepage is extremely slow to respond because its servers are often overloaded.

The search for missing children is, of course, only possible in those cases where children were separated from their families due to unfortunate circumstances, not if the parents themselves have sold them or sent them away.

## The 2004 Tsunami—'Disappearances' in the Course of a Natural Catastrophe

The tsunami on 26 December 2004 ended the lives of hundreds of thousands in Sri Lanka as well as other countries in Asia and Africa. Many bodies could be recovered and identified. As so often after natural disasters, a large number of bodies were burnt or buried prior to identification though. Thousands of people simply disappeared, their bodies having been carried out into the sea.

On 29 December, the Red Cross launched a homepage to aid in the search for missing relatives. Its trafficking possibilities reached capacity after only three hours—this new search tool was massively used and proved to be of invaluable assistance in the search for those who had disappeared.

In the following, I relate some of my personal experiences in this situation. On the basis of these experiences I also identify some of the needs that arise after large-scale catastrophes with regards to the psychosocial care of those affected in general and of the relatives of disappeared people in particular.

### Approaching a Familiar Country after the Catastrophe

I had an uneasy feeling while travelling to Sri Lanka in February 2005. I had left that country only six weeks ago, but the tsunami had changed it so much. One conversation from the beginning of December 2004 was vividly in my mind. At that time, we had been discussing the workshop about trauma counselling in Colombo that had just finished. Somebody in the group told us about having experiences of one of the many bombings in the capital, after which he had been searching for a missing friend, whom he eventually found in a morgue. He finished relating this traumatic experience by saying: 'Everybody in this country has seen too much of these things'. This conversation had taken place only two weeks prior to the largest catastrophe Sri Lanka and its neighbouring regions had ever seen, and that, in Sri Lanka alone, cost more than 30,000 people their lives.

While the area surrounding the capital Colombo showed little signs of the catastrophe having taken place, this rapidly changed as we left the capital and travelled up north. It was sheer incredible how much of the havoc the tsunami had wreaked was still visible five weeks after 26 December. In many places the destruction reached far inland: Houses were in ruins, palm trees lay uprooted, boats could be found hundreds of meters away from the coast like overlarge broken toys. Between the wreckage, strewn about lay personal possessions: a forgotten photo album showing pictures of festively dressed people, a piece of a silk sari, a watch that has stopped. Only occasionally did we see people between the ruins of villages devastated by the tsunami. The fear was too intense, the traumatic memories too overwhelming.

What turned out to be problematic was the extremely large number of psychological and psychosocial support programmes that flooded the country, entering it together with other relief organisations. Often, the term 'trauma healing' was used. Many connected this word with a false promise: Everything will be healed, will be the way it had been before the catastrophe. What caused the most pain though, was the loss of relatives, and none of these people has ever returned alive because of a 'trauma healing' programme. Connected to these programmes was the illusion of a rapid improvement of the emotional pain. These training programmes often had only the alleviation of a single symptom—that of avoidance—as their goal: People learned to reduce their fear of the sea and dare to walk on the beach and go out into the ocean again. This is, of course, of quite central importance for the many fishermen, but it represents only a minute part of the suffering caused by the tsunami. The grieving for those who have been killed or have disappeared without a trace, the homes that have been destroyed and the loss of one's own physical well-being presented much lengthier processes.

Some of the international programmes also did not sufficiently take into account the political and social dimensions of the situation in Sri Lanka at that time. While a ceasefire was in place, peace was still a long way off. Therefore, it was necessary to respond to this situation in a careful, sensitive way. Another problem that needed paying attention to is the fact that many people had been affected and traumatised in a similar manner before. One family, for example, relates how they have just lost their house for the fourth time; three times during the war, now through a natural disaster.

Our task lay in quickly providing a fairly large amount of people with the basic knowledge necessary for them to be able to offer psychosocial support on a long-term basis. Therefore, it was necessary to enable people, who had had little to no psychological grounding, to offer advice and counselling to traumatised victims facing the death and disappearance of their relatives (Preitler 2006b, 2008).

## Note

1. Translation from the German original.

# 3
# Collective Forms of Coping

The outlook for the relatives of victims of an 'enforced disappearance' is a grim one, the prognoses difficult to bear. Life stands still; mourning is impossible. Oftentimes, the social environment further complicates any attempt to move on. Nevertheless, a large number of different individual and collective forms of coping with the 'disappearance' of a relative exists. These represent different ways of transforming—at least part of—the suffering and grief into something new.

In the course of his work with concentration camp survivors in Israel, Antonovsky (1987) began to take special notice of those factors that let people survive even the most severe traumatic situations in a relatively healthy way. Out of the women Antonovsky interviewed, all of who had lived in concentration camps as adolescents, and then had to live as refugees until they finally made it to Israel, 29 per cent classified as psychologically healthy. This prompted Antonovsky to begin studying the factors that enable people to remain healthy or even develop positively, not only in spite of, but sometimes even because of, the immense stress they are under. His theory relates this ability back to a 'Sense of Coherence' (SOC) regarding the traumatic events. According to him, this SOC is based on three components:

1. *Comprehensibility*: Comprehensibility refers to a person's ability to perceive the events in his or her life as inherently logical. For people who have a well-developed SOC see their environment as sensible, orderly and reasonably predictable and clear, not chaotic and random. 'It is important to note that nothing is implied about the desirability of stimuli. Death, war, and failure can occur, but such a person can make sense of them' (Antonovsky 1987: 17).
2. *Manageability*: Antonovsky understands manageability as the subjective, positive evaluation of one's own resources in terms of them being serviceable in coping with the demands on one's life. These resources can be directly available, or indirectly, via a trusted person or group.
    Reddemann (2004) named this component 'Meisterschaft', meaning 'mastership', as the people in possession of this component have the ability to 'master' difficult situations.

3. *Meaningfulness*: In the context of Antonovsky's theory, meaningfulness refers to still having people or things in one's life that are especially dear to the person, and of primary importance. This matters in terms of the attitude a person holds towards the demands and problems they face in life. The same problem can be perceived as completely overwhelming and life-threatening, or it can be put into perspective by being placed into the wider context of one's life, becoming smaller and thereby bearable, even solvable. Other elements in one's life are important enough that it is worth overcoming problems for them. This does not suggest that a positively motivated person does not suffer under the pain of losing a beloved person to death or a 'disappearance', but only that this person will start looking for explanations and solutions.

In the following chapter, I will discuss different forms of coping with 'enforced disappearances' on the basis of Antonovsky's SOC.

The first issue to be addressed in this context is that of political responsibility and of coming to terms with the past as a nation, after a war or a dictatorship ends. Those who find themselves in power after such times of unrest often want to forget as quickly as possible. Corrupt elements within the structure and the guilt parties that remained in office together work towards keeping the past events in the shadows, and thereby prevent the relatives from developing an SOC. Their search for truth, for reason and meaning is hindered. The victims' desire to actively deal with what has happened to them and their 'disappeared' relatives is discouraged, prevented or seen as 'sick'.

How do countries that have recently undergone a change in their political system deal with the acts of violence committed in the past? What kind of answers do those who have been tortured or the relatives of 'disappeared' get from the new ruling powers? Jelin (1994: 51) assesses soberingly: '... there is the factual impossibility of bringing to trial all those responsible for violations and compensating all the victims.'

She describes the attempts made in Argentina to cope with the past after the fall of the dictatorship in 1983. '... and the wounds will be slow to heal and will re-emerge time and again in different ways, ranging from artistic symbolisations to personal vengeance. Memory can then partially take the place of justice' (Jelin 1994: 51f.).

Elisabeth Jelin calls for an individual as well as collective process of facing and coming to terms with the social catastrophe that this country has had to go through, a process that includes illuminating all the 'voids and "holes"' (Jelin 1994: 53). She makes clear that otherwise the next generation will in all likelihood grow up in an atmosphere of unprocessed trauma characterised by silence and collective paralysis.

Throughout the world, there is an astonishing number of action groups formed by relatives of victims of 'enforced disappearances', where these people actively work on the clarification of facts concerning these 'disappearances'. They are also actively involved in the fight for human rights and, specifically for the prevention of their violation in form of an 'enforced disappearance'.

In this chapter a number of groups of relatives from different countries are described with their ways of coping with the 'enforced disappearances' that affected their lives so drastically. Their efforts towards dealing with this human rights violation stand for those of all relatives of 'disappeared' worldwide.

## The Mothers of the Plaza de Mayo—a Role Model for Many Associations of Relatives throughout the World

The most prominent group of parents of 'disappeared' is probably the 'Mothers of the Plaza de Mayo' in Buenos Aires. They have organised themselves into an action group, demanding that the cases of their 'disappeared' sons and daughters be solved.

The 'disappearance' of relatives throws many people into helplessness and chaos. Nevertheless, they, at the same time, actively take steps in trying to gain information about the whereabouts of the 'disappeared'. First and foremost, they want to find out where their 'disappeared' relative is at that time, and to arrange a speedy return for that person. All three dimensions of Antonovsky's (1979) SOC come into play here:

1. By trying to clarify the circumstances of the 'disappearance' and, thereby, finding out what has happened, the situation becomes comprehensible.
2. As they become actively involved in the search, courageously confronting all threats and attempts of degradation, the Mothers free themselves from the feeling of paralysis. In the midst of the chaos, they develop means of actively handling the situation, which, thereby, becomes manageable.

3. Through their combined efforts to not only find their own relatives, but everyone else's as well, and the successes the Mothers have on a socio-political level, their actions become meaningful, even if they should never get any information about the whereabouts of their own 'disappeared' relative.

The Mothers of the Plaza de Mayo began their search for their 'disappeared' sons and daughters in a maelstrom of fear, hope and frustration. Thornton (2000: 281) writes about the first phase in the search.

> These women, who did not know why their children were taken, nor by whom, immediately went to the authorities to report the abductions. But whether at the local police station, a government office or a military garrison, they were all told the same story—that there was no record of anyone with that name; they would then be sent elsewhere.

For the most part, it was the women who embarked on the odyssey from one government agency to the next. The men, by tradition the breadwinners, often had to return to work, and were thereby kept from this time-consuming kind of search. As they made their inquiries at the same government agencies, the searching women saw each other repeatedly and thereby began to recognise each other and establish contacts between themselves.

At that time, all of them believed that they would only have to wait for a couple of weeks or months for their children to return. Nobody was prepared to consider, then, that their sons and daughters might have 'disappeared' forever.

In April 1977, 14 Mothers organised their first small-scale demonstration at the Plaza de Mayo. They presented a petition for their children and demanded a meeting with the president. Three weeks later, the group had already grown to 60 women supporting the petition. Three Mothers were admitted to the Minister of Interior for a meeting. He played down the issue, suggesting that the 'disappeared' sons and daughters must have secretly migrated to another country or have simply run off. Not willing to be fobbed off that easily, the women announced that they would from now on meet every Thursday on the Plaza de Mayo until they had gotten satisfactory information about the whereabouts of their children.

True to their word, the women have since assembled on the Plaza de Mayo in Buenos Aires every Thursday afternoon and have thereby become 'Las Madres de la Plaza de Mayo'. The peacefully demonstrating women had to face serious threats by police forces as well as the military. Some of them even 'disappeared'.

Despite the intimidations, the women continued in their activism. They gained the support of other human rights organisations, some of them in Argentina, some of them international ones. This support and the contacts they made that way were important to the Mothers. At the same time, however, they insisted on keeping the matter of their 'disappeared' an independent one. They did not want to be swallowed up by one of the larger human rights organisations, but wanted to campaign specifically against 'enforced disappearances'.

Another issue that arose in this context was that of the young women who had 'disappeared' and had been pregnant at the time. Their babies, born in jail cells or secret prison camps, were often secretly put up for adoption, to be raised by members of the military or other trusted workers loyal to the regime. In response to this practice, a new group was formed—that of the grandmothers of these babies, who wanted to find out about the whereabouts of their grandchildren, demanding to be given custody of them.

As the support network for the Mothers grew to include the USA as well as countries in Europe, the Mothers could not be intimidated effectively, nor be ignored any longer. The government changed tacks, and the official newspapers began to call them 'Las Locas'—the crazy women. We can see that here, once again, attempts were made to make victims of human rights violations appear psychologically abnormal.

By 1982, thousands of people had joined the Mothers for their weekly demonstrations. Finally, the military government of the time presented a final report on the situation. 'It said all persons missing but not in exile or in hiding could be presumed dead' (Thornton 2000: 285).

In 1983, the military permitted democratic elections to take place. With this, one of the darkest periods in Argentina's history came to an end. Many mothers and grandmothers are still waiting for information on their children and for the persecution of the parties responsible for the 'disappearances', however. Today, they are still meeting every Thursday, demanding information on the circumstances of their children's 'disappearances'.

> The Madres are still dedicated to denying to government an excuse to forget and move on without acknowledging its complicity and failure to bring the guilty to justice, but have also evolved to include exposing to abuses of other repressive regimes, working for human rights generally, and responding to injustices elsewhere. (Koepsel 2011: 3)

In 1986, the group split into two branches. One, centred around Ms Hebe de Bonafini, was henceforth called the 'Mothers of the Plaza de Mayo Association', and the other became the 'Mothers of the Plaza de Mayo Founding Line'. The former was not willing to accept the compensations for the 'disappeared' children offered by the government. They took particular issue with having to sign death certificates in order to receive these compensations. Hernandez (2012) cites Ms Hebe de Bonafini on this, who said: 'You cannot put a price on life. Also, to accept this compensation you have to sign a death certificate saying when your child died. I cannot sign this as it is the people who took them who know, not me.'

The 'Association' also focuses its work on bringing to justice those responsible for the 'enforced disappearances'. The 'Founding Line', on the other hand has another aim, as stated by their spokeswoman Ms Almeida, whose son Alejandro 'disappeared' in 1977: 'I respect Ms de Bonafini's opinion, but I need closure. I would like to touch Alejandro's bones before I die' (Hernandez 2012).

## The Formation of Support Groups for Relatives of the 'Disappeared'

In Argentina (and many other countries), psychologists and doctors have actively supported victims of violations against human rights, and continue to do so today. Most well-known amongst them are probably Diana R. Kordon, Lucila I. Edelman, D. M. Lagos, E. Nicoletti and R. C. Bozzolo from the EATIP. They joined the Mothers for their group meetings to offer psychological support. During those meetings, the relatives had the opportunity to talk about the fears, sufferings and feelings of guilt they experienced after the 'disappearances' of their daughters and sons. Many found relief in these exchanges.

Evelina, whose son had 'disappeared', was one of the Mothers who participated in these sessions. She was plagued by immense feelings of guilt, because when her son had been taken, she had simply watched, paralysed by fear and helplessness. Again and again, she fantasised about how she might have been able to prevent her son's 'disappearance' by intervening and actively opposing it. Another Mother, Florencia, answered her. When Florencia's son had been seized, she had fought for him with all available means—and now she feels guilty for possibly having made his situation worse through her efforts.

By exchanging their stories and experiences, both women took steps towards being able to accept their individual reactions (Kordon et al. 1988).

These sessions also gave the Mothers the opportunity to address the tendencies of the other members of their (extended) families to keep completely silent about the 'disappearance'. By doing so, they were able to work through this additional traumatisation. The fairly wide-spread opinion that those who 'disappeared' had brought this upon themselves and that anyone associating with them might be endangering their own families had led people to distancing themselves from the relatives of 'disappeared'. These relatives, consequently, felt isolated. They were speechless and helpless. Within the safe confines of the group, they could break the silence in an environment of support and understanding.

Kordon and her team (1988) identified four psychologically significant chances that these group meetings offered to the relatives of 'disappeared'.

1. Reducing survivor's guilt: As the example given above showed, sharing experiences and feelings can open up new perspectives on one's own behaviour and emotional reactions. At the same time, it simply helps to know that others have gone through the similar experiences and emotions. 'The discussion ... has helped us through the exchange of subjective experiences, how ideas held for years by someone who blamed herself for what had happened clash with the guilt feeling of another person who has quite simply, opposite ideas' (Kordon et al. 1988: 46).
2. Alleviating personal suffering and accepting one's own feelings of helplessness and despair: This corresponds with the memories Zelman (1998) relates. The survivors searching—often without success—for other surviving relatives bonded together to support each other during their time in the refugee camp of Bad Goisern.

> During this process, a community slowly began to take shape amongst the survivors. ... Although we knew it was very likely that we didn't have anyone anymore, we did have each other. Together we could discuss hopes of finding relatives again. ... Talking about these things was like therapy; in spelling out our hopes, we got closer to what we were really seeking—warmth and security. ... The friendships made in Bad Goisern lasted a lifetime. ... We don't talk about the ghetto or the camps; we talk about the time afterward, when young people helped each other back to life, substituted for father and mother, brother and sister. There wasn't any psychological therapy. We had to help ourselves to grow up in just a few months. (Zelman 1998: 88, 91, 92, 93)

3. New, unknown or unrecognised elements gain importance, which can lead to a re-evaluation of the individual traumatic experience.
   The group members not only learn that others have felt the same way and have reacted in the same way as they have, but also that there are different forms of coping with the 'disappearances', which should all be tolerated.
4. Through these group discussions and the three elements described so far, the participants strengthen their own self-confidence. '... conservation and strengthening of self-esteem by means of a maintenance and new placement of the relationships between the Ego and its Ideal with the help of the reality principle and intellectual comprehension' (Kordon et al. 1988: 46).

## The Transformation of Grief and Traumatisation into Political Action

At first after the 'disappearance' of their daughters or sons, the mothers needed courage above all else, courage to ask for information about their children at the government offices and bureaus they had never been in contact with so far. The relatives were confused and intimidated. The sudden 'disappearance' of a child constituted a severe personal loss. That nothing specific was known about the current situation of the 'disappeared' was a reason enough to presume that the government had been involved in the 'disappearance'.

Consequently, the relatives were denied the support traditionally provided by other family members and friends. Quite to the contrary: The families of victims of 'enforced disappearances' were often actively avoided by their acquaintances, their friends, even their closest relatives, because all of them feared to throw suspicion on themselves by keeping in contact with the family of someone who had 'disappeared'.

By allying with each other the Mothers created a new psychological frame of reference for themselves. The group they had formed provided opportunities to talk about their situation. Since they had had similar experiences, they understood each other.

Acknowledging the death of their children, which constitutes a basic prerequisite for the grieving process, is something most Mothers were not willing to do. They wanted their children back alive. One of the slogans used at the demonstrations was 'They were taken alive—we want them back alive'. Even when, over the years, it became clearer and clearer that practically none of those who had 'disappeared' had survived, the Mothers demanded to hear about the fate of their children from the government officials responsible. And they wanted the guilty parties to be convicted.

This denial on the part of the Mothers was more a political statement than a psychological reaction: They wanted to prevent anybody forgetting these acts of iniquity and they wanted justice (Kordon et al. 1988).

From 1979 onwards, and especially in their final reports on the violations of human rights committed during the years of dictatorship, the government tried to put pressure on the relatives of the 'disappeared'. They should accept the deaths of their sons and daughters. The government was of the opinion that then the Mother's public searching for their children would come to an end—and with it the search for the parties responsible.

Thornton identifies three factors as especially helpful to the Mothers in their process of coping with life after the 'disappearance' of their children. First, there was the mutual support between the mothers. The 'Madres de la Plaza de Mayo' became the women's new extended family. Second, through working together on their political goals they found a way out of their helplessness with regards to the traumatic events affecting their families. Last, but not least, their political work was a way of going beyond their own personal suffering and influencing society as a whole. Some of them saw their socio-political activism as a continuation of the political work their children had started, which had originally led to their 'disappearance'. S. Thornton sums up this transformation of frozen grief into political activism:

> Although the Mothers may have resolved their grief (or continue to resolve their grief) in an unconventional way because of very unusual circumstances, by publicly denying death and insisting that the government explain and take responsibility for its actions, they have both grown personally and effected positive social change very publicly in a society which generally believes that women, especially middle-aged and elderly women, should remain within the private space of the home.... Through love for their disappeared children they have transformed their grief, born of a horrifying situation, into a positive vision of collective action for a more peaceful world. (Thornton 2000: 289)

## International Networks

Following the example of the Mothers in Argentina, relatives in a large number of other countries have organised into groups as well.

The NGO FEDEFAM, for example, functions as a networking organisation that connects the groups of relatives throughout Latin America. The FEDEFAM has laid down three main aims for itself:

> To rescue alive the victims of forced Disappearance from clandestine detention centers and to restore the children of parents subjected to forced disappearance to their families of origin.
> To demand the investigation of all cases of forced disappearance and the judgment and sanction of those responsible for the crime.
> To promote national and international legal norms which, classifying forced disappearance as a Crime Against Humanity, constitute methods of obtaining justice and of preventing forced disappearance. (FEDEFAM 2004)

The NGO uses a number of different methods in working towards these aims. Its members collect reports, conduct letter-writing campaigns, send letters of appeal to national and international authorities, support publications on the subject, etc. FEDEFAM bases its demands on international agreements such as the UN Declaration on the Protection of All Persons from Enforced or Involuntary Disappearance and the Convention Against Forced Disappearances.

The ICMP was originally founded in Bosnia in 1996, in response to the large number of 'disappeared' after the Bosnian Wars. Today they work on a worldwide basis, focusing on the search for and identification of 'disappeared' persons (ICMP 2012).

The organisation Refugees United was founded in 2006 in Denmark. They understand themselves as a platform that makes use of modern media elements such as the internet as such, and also existing social network sites such as facebook and twitter, in order to provide family members with a way of searching for their relatives that reaches almost all parts of the world (https://refunite.org/ [accessed 2.2.2015]).

Other international organisations such as Human Rights Watch, Amnesty International and Asia Watch also serve as platforms for the search for 'disappeared' and additionally support the relatives in their fight for changes in the social, political and legal structures with the aim of preventing further 'disappearances'.

## Truth Commissions

Truth commissions play an important role in the process of coping with past events.

Probably most famous amongst them was the South African 'Truth and Reconciliation Commission', which worked towards a reconciliation of the different ethnic groups by throwing light on the injustices done and by confirming the factuality of the events that had taken place. However, many other truth commissions existed and still exist, such as those in El Salvador, Peru, Guatemala, Chile, East Timor, Sri Lanka and Ruanda.

First of all, it is important for the victims that the injustices done to them are publicly recognised. This is of special importance to the relatives of victims of 'enforced disappearances'.

If the perpetrators are convicted, then this can strengthen the feeling of security and safety for the relatives and can satisfy their need for justice. 'It can lead victims to feel connected to, rather than isolated from, the rest of the world' writes Staub (1998: 233).

Truth commissions fulfil other functions too, however. Perpetrators have the tendency to perceive themselves as innocent. They excuse their actions as having been necessary at the time and they deny their responsibility, claiming to only having done their duty.

> Direct perpetrators, people involved in supporting roles, and the rest of the group, the bystanders, all tend to see the actions of their group as justified. They see it either as self-defense or as a way of dealing with a group that stood in the way of important, legitimate goals, possibly embodied in a 'higher' ideological vision like communism, nazism, or nationalism. (Staub 1998: 233)

Through the work of the commissions, this self-image is called into question, and at least in the minds of the public, a new image is created: The perpetrators are made accountable for their deeds. Amazingly enough, the victims are often quite ready to go easy on the perpetrators, as long as they admit to being guilty. '... the relatives of the victims showed great generosity ... most of them stressed that in the end, what really mattered to them was that the truth be revealed, that the memory of their loved ones not be denigrated or forgotten' (Zalaquett 1992: 1437).

First of all, they need to base their decisions on the reality as it was perceived by the victims—the reality that needs to be recognised—and all jurisdiction needs to be based upon it. Second, those responsible for the violations of human rights have to be held accountable for their actions in the manner established in the legal system of the country. Then the commission's responsibility lies in clarifying and presenting the fact on which judgement is based.

This seemingly self-evident method is not always put into practice easily. The first model of a truth commission was the set of Nuremberg Trials held in Europe after Second World War. Even in those politically fairly straightforward circumstances, where the responsible parties were all members of a terrible regime that had clearly committed most gruesome atrocities, it was difficult to actually identify and convict the perpetrators.

Since the 1970s, the truth commissions formed in many countries after the fall of a dictatorship often found themselves confronted with a much more difficult situation. More often than not, the people who had been responsible for the human rights violations had found a way into positions of power in the new regime, or held influential posts in the military. Truth commissions formed after a civil war perceived the acute need to preserve the fragile peace and not endanger it by bringing up unsettling truths. The situation becomes even more difficult, however, if the country the truth commission is meant to support by examining cases of human rights violations is still at war. In Sri Lanka, for example, a truth commission charged in 1996 with solving the many cases of 'enforced disappearances', presented the president with a list of 200 army members who had all been responsible for such crimes. For days, deliberate confusion about possible suspensions was created. The result of many discussions was indignation about the denigration of these heroes of war, and about even considering weakening the army in such a way during a critical period in the war. None of the soldiers on the list have ever been suspended from active duty in the war zone (Amnesty International 1997).

The question, in how far state crimes can at all be dealt with while the country is at war, remains unanswered. Nevertheless, there are those cases where perpetrators were successfully held responsible on the basis of the facts provided by truth commissions, and the victims of the human rights violations received justice.

Sangster (1999) points out that the truth in and of itself is already of value, and can have a regulatory and healing effect on the individuals involved as well as on society as a whole.

It is also possible to come up with alternative forms of recompense and penance. The formal apology for the violations of human rights committed that president Aylwin of Chile offered to the victims and relatives of victims of 'enforced disappearances' was taken as more than just an empty gesture. It was seen as recognition and rehabilitation of the dead and the 'disappeared'.

The truth commission in Chile not only dealt with the cases of the 'disappearances' but also drew up a list of recommendations regarding the victim's future. Amongst these were demands for psychosocial care for the victims as well as offering them better access to education.

Hamber (1995), who made a study of the compensations victims of political repression in South Africa received after the end of the apartheid system, draws attention to the difference in the wishes and needs the survivors and the relatives of those who had died or 'disappeared' had: 'Some survivors and families of victims want financial compensation, others a proper funeral for their "missing" loved ones, some simply want the truth and still for others the greatest compensation would be to see the perpetrators brought to justice' (Hamber 1995: 6).

Every society has something like a common understanding of right and wrong, of jurisdiction, of crime and punishment. If the perpetrators were judged and convicted in accordance to these common standards—also in those cases where their actions had been sanctioned by the state—this would go a long way towards helping the victims and their relatives to cope with their trauma. The reason why many refused monetary compensations, according to Hamber, lies in the survivors' and relatives' need to not be paid off for their silence.

In many countries of Latin America, the victims did accept the money offered to them, but immediately passed it on to human rights organisations (Brune 2010).

## The Need for Death Certificates for the 'Disappeared'

In 1995, the then newly formed government of Sri Lanka appointed three commissions to investigate the cases of 'enforced disappearances' in the country. The commissions received reports of about 60,000 'disappearances', most of which took place between 1988 and 1990. In the Southern parts of the country, 5,000 of these cases could be closed successfully, meaning that sufficient evidence could be uncovered for the 'disappeared' person's death to be declared officially, and the relatives be issued a death certificate for the deceased. This, in turn, entitled them to certain financial restorations. It represented a significant step along the path of coping with the past, as well as improving the difficult situation thousands of widows and (half) orphans were in.

Apart from the financial security provided to this large number of women and children, this measure also meant a relief in terms of the psychological strain 'enforced disappearances' put on the remaining family members. In most cases, all of the relatives uncertain of the fate of the 'disappeared' person are continually focused on the possibility of the return of the loved one. A lot of their energy is put into inquiring about and searching for the missing person. The relatives are given to fantasies about places where the 'disappeared' might be at the time and make sure that upon return, the 'disappeared' should find everything just as he or she had left it. This results in the family life freezing in a state of the past with little room for development, for a move forward.

A young woman, mother of two toddlers, whose husband had 'disappeared', earned just enough to ensure her family's very survival by doing part-time secretarial jobs. The NGO that had initially funded her education that allowed her to be a secretary offered her a well-paid fulltime job in the organisation. The woman, however, declined the job, much to the surprise—and also indignation—of the NGO workers. There seemed to be no rational reasons for her doing so. From a psychodynamic point of view, her actions become clearer. She cannot take over her husband's responsibilities as the family breadwinner. Through an enormous effort on her part, she keeps this position open for him. Not doing so would constitute an outright betrayal for her.

If the family accepts the 'disappearance' as something final, the family members usually experience feelings of guilt. They feel responsible, at least in part. In order to truly accept the death of a beloved person it is important to see the dead body. Only if the death is accepted on a physical level does it become possible to let the person go on a social one, to mourn the person and move on towards planning a future without the beloved.

The commissions charged with investigating the 'enforced disappearances' cannot facilitate this confrontation with the mortal remains of the deceased relative, but they can take over the role of establishing the person's 'social' death. As an institution appointed by the state, they have the authority to do so, relieving the family of this task. This represents a significant easing of the burden on the psychological level. At the same time, the relatives' roles within society are clarified. Spouses of 'disappeared' become widows or widowers, children become orphans.

Unfortunately, the truth commissions in Sri Lanka were only temporary institutions that were largely disestablished for political reasons long before the many cases of 'enforced disappearances' had been solved.

The Tsunami on 26 December 2004 led to further 'disappearances' in many Asian countries, Sri Lanka being one amongst them. However, these, of course, were 'disappearances' under vastly different circumstance. In the case of a natural catastrophe, there are no perpetrators who are responsible for the 'disappearances', which makes it much easier for the state to close the cases and issue death certificates for the 'disappeared' persons.

## Exhumation—the Need for Certainty

Since 1996, the ICMP has been working on a pioneer project that has at its goal the effective identification of exhumed persons. Archaeologists, anthropologists and pathologists are working together in developing a programme which, based on extensive DNA-tests, should clarify the identity of the person whose mortal remains had been discovered. The aim lies in retrieving the victims from the realm of anonymity. For the surviving dependants this means finally getting certainty about the fate of the 'disappeared'. At the same time, they also get the opportunity to go through the religious rites surrounding death in their respective cultures.

In his reports on exhumations in Bosnia, Schmidt-Häuer (2002) finds himself reminded of a hero from the Greek Mythologies. He refers to the forensic anthropologist in charge of the exhumations as an Orpheus of the age of DNA-testing, someone who descends into the realm of the dead to find answers about the whereabouts of the beloved who has passed away.

Exhumations are often conducted after the end of a war or after the fall of a dictatorship. Natural disasters with a large number of casualties also make exhumations necessary, particularly if the bodies have been buried hastily, without following any rituals, sometimes even prior to identification. One example for such a situation was the tsunami of 2004.

A large number of the victims were buried in mass graves without anyone knowing who they were. The fear of diseases made such burials a priority. Ideas that dead bodies pose a threat to living human beings, however, are largely based on myths and can be disregarded. Ball (2005), in a report, shortly after the Tsunami writes:

> It is widely believed that swift burial is the only way to prevent the spread of diseases such as cholera. But that is a myth.... Cholera does not appear

spontaneously in the body of a person who did not have it to begin with. And although harmful bacteria or viruses in a corpse can in theory be spread by rats, flies, fleas and other animals, that doesn't tend to happen in practice. The temperature of a body falls rapidly after death, so even the most resistant bacteria and viruses die quickly. Past experience shows that unburied dead bodies pose a negligible risk to those who do not come into physical contact with them. Handling of bodies by relief workers does, of course, require protective clothing.

He bases his information on a statement from the Pan American Health Organization (PAHO 2005). Exhumations are usually conducted in three steps:

The preparatory work consists of historical research pertaining to the circumstances of the 'disappearance', the death and the location of the mass grave. The first two are largely done in the form of interviews, in which the relatives are also asked to describe any distinguishing physical feature of the person they are searching for.

The second phase is that of the actual excavation of human remains and personal objects they might have carried, such as clothing, jewellery, personal documents, etc. The use of archaeological methods is meant to ensure that all useful artefacts are preserved. All body parts and objects are recovered and documented.

In the third phase of the exhumation process, all finds are analysed in a lab. The number of bodies found in the grave, their age, gender, height, sets of teeth and any other distinguishing features are documented and compared with the data known about the 'missing' people reported about. Blood samples taken from relatives make the use of DNA tests possible (Kernjak 2002).

Those relatives who live in countries that perform such exhumations generally like to be close to the exhumation sites.

> There was always the fear, double-edged, that it was their son in the pit, or that it was not their son—which meant there would be further searching. If it became clear that the body was a stranger, then, after weeks of waiting, the family would rise and leave. They would travel to other excavations....
> The possibility of their lost son was everywhere. (Ondaatje 2011: 5)

So far, the literature on the psychological support of relatives during the time of the exhumation is very sparse. There is much demand for it, however. It can be stated as essential, though, that while there needs to be room for the support of the individuals who are immediately affected by the deaths and possible identification, the group in its entirety, as a community, needs to be coached and counselled as well.

In Guatemala, about 28,000 people are said to have 'disappeared' (Agosin 1993). Between 1979 and 1984 thousands of people had been killed and afterwards buried in mass graves. In 1988, the first of these graves was reopened, the bodies in there identified and finally given decent burials. This process of recovering and identifying bodies that turns 'disappeared' into deceased and makes it possible for the relatives to bury their loved ones in accordance with the respective cultural and religious practices is one of the most central tasks that organisations of relatives have set for themselves.

The Historical Clarification Commission (Comisión para el Esclarecimiento Histórico, CEH) recommended an active policy of exhumation, because they perceive this to be an important step towards reconciliation.

> It is an act of justice because it constitutes part of the right to know the truth and it contributes to the knowledge of the whereabouts of the disappeared. It is an act of reparation because it dignifies the victims and because the right to bury the dead and to carry out ceremonies for them according to each culture is inherent in all human beings. (CEH 1997 quoted in Kernjak 2002: 31)

Referring to the hopes she has for the future of her home country Guatemala, psychologist Garcia (2001) describes the necessity of remembering the deaths, of giving them a concrete form and of mourning them in order to be able to live on. In her opinion, the exhumations are of critical importance, not only for the relatives of the deceased but for society as a whole. She sees in them a path towards the truth, a way to recover the lost history of people and a means of acknowledging the sufferings large parts of the population had been forced to go through. Garcia pays particular attention to the feeling of certainty that comes with being able to openly say 'They have been murdered' that comes with excavation and identification. The conflict between the secret knowledge of the killings and the inability to address them is finally resolved (Garcia 2001: 40).

Psychosocial support is of particular importance, since during the years of terror, the spiritual frames of references have purposefully been destabilised, often to the point of complete destruction. Priests (whether they were catholic, protestant or of the Maya-religion) were often denounced or even killed, and generally lost their place as the spiritual centre of the community.

Collective Forms of Coping    105

The concept behind the psychosocial support through the time of the exhumations as it was practiced by Garcia (2001) and her team, which they had entitled 'Salud Mental', can be summed up in six points.

1. The formation of support groups, which often continued to exist after the exhumation had been concluded.
2. The opportunity to relate one's personal experiences to people who are willing to listen to them.
3. Familiar rituals are remembered and re-established by integrating them into the group work.
4. Experts from different fields (ethnology, sociology, pedagogy, medicine, psychology and psychiatry) work together, creating a wide spectrum of information and explanation throughout the duration of the exhumation process.
5. The social conditions within the community are ascertained beforehand. Not only the possible positive effects on the community—such as regaining dignity, acknowledgement of a shared history, etc.—but also the possible negative effects—like the reactivation of fears, desperation and traumatisation—are analysed and addressed.
6. Measures have to be taken already in advance to deal with the unfortunately fairly common cases of 'disappeared' who cannot be found. The relatives of these 'disappeared' are in special need of support and guidance by the team of experts as well as the community, in order to deal with their reawakened feelings of fear and abandonment.

If the bodies of those who have been murdered are exhumed, then they can be buried in a dignified fashion, which, in turn, constitutes a significant contribution to the communal processing of past events. Garcia (2001), in writing about her home country Guatemala, emphasises the importance of dealing with the shared history of violence. While she stresses that nothing can eradicate the 40 years of war nor the consequences of the acts of political violence committed during that time, she also states clearly that, in her opinion, the acknowledgment of what had really happened, the acknowledgment of truths and facts by not a select few but the population as a whole would be the first step in the right direction. If the government faced these facts honestly and made just reparations, then national reconciliation would no longer be a thing of verbose and empty speeches, but might become reality (Garcia 2001: 38).

What positive effects exhumations alone can already have shows a case described by Castello (2010). A young woman, living in the Andes range of Peru, whose mother had 'disappeared' keeps dreaming about the mother. It pains the young woman that in her dreams the mother tells her again and again that she is cold and wet, drenched by the rain. After the mother's body is exhumed and buried in dignity, the dreams stop, much to the relief of the young woman. In the psychological experience of the woman, her mother does finally not feel cold anymore.

## Symbolic and Virtual Memorial Places

### The Pictures of the 'Disappeared'

In this section, I want to briefly advert to the spontaneously emerged ritual of compiling flyers with pictures of the then 'missing' people after the catastrophe of 9/11 in New York. Within hours, the first relatives holding such flyers appeared. These flyers were all very similar in design: In the centre, there was a picture of the—for now—missing person; above and below basic information such as names and contact details of the relatives could be found. In a number of different places in the city, whole walls became memorials, which were visited like graves. Originally intended as aids in the search, they soon became much more symbolic in their function, the walls plastered with them becoming places to remember and grieve at.

Since only a very small number of bodies were actually recovered, the posters became substitutes for the absent mortal remains.

Derek Summerfield writes about a different but closely related function of the picture of a lost person. In Nicaragua, he met Juana, whose two-year-old daughter Liset had been killed by a band of guerrilla fighters two years ago. Juana had since been searching for a photograph of her daughter that had, quite by coincidence, been taken by tourists travelling through her village shortly before the massacre.

> Standing in her almost bare shack she said: 'Now I have nothing of hers ... how can I show that she lived?' Then she said that shortly before the attack some foreign travellers passing through by chance had taken a photograph of her family. Somewhere abroad, she said, there was proof that Liset had existed. It was important for her to be able to demonstrate that Liset was not her private delusion or hallucination, not a ghost, but had definitely lived—until she was murdered. (Summerfield 1998: 26)

Despite her knowing with certainty of her little girl's death, the mother attributed a special importance to this photograph. It would return a small piece of reality to her.

If a person has 'disappeared', the feelings of unreality can be even stronger. The names and pictures of the 'disappeared' can help in remembering them and recognising and acknowledging what has happened as real, even if the events are denied by official sources.

## The Embroidered Names of the 'Disappeared'

The mothers and grandmothers of the 'disappeared' in Argentina have come up with a common symbol. On Thursdays, during their demonstrations, they wear white headscarves, which they have largely made themselves—in part out of their children's old clothes or cloth diapers— and have embroidered them with their children's names. These scarves have become a distinguishing feature of the mothers, a unifying symbol, while at the same time they, in a sense, 'are' parts of the 'disappeared'.

Interestingly, the women who had 'disappeared' in Iran had developed a similar kind of symbol. M. Baradaran writes about her confinement as a political prisoner from 1981 to 1990. She describes the time of 1988-1989 as one particularly marked by fear and terror, as during this time she and her fellow inmates had to live in constant fear of being taken away to be executed. In response to this, Baradaran writes, she and the other women wrote or stitched their names onto their pockets in bright and bold letters. Since their clothes, shabby as they may have been, represented all their earthly possessions and were the only mementos of their imprisonment, of their very lives, it was of the uttermost importance to them that these pieces of clothing were returned to their families (Baradaran 1998: 289). They became external and internal symbols of the lives of the 'disappeared'.

The uniqueness of the local embroidery style is the centre of a project organised in Peru in memory of the 'disappeared'. That every embroidered piece is unique makes the scraps of clothing found in the course of the exhumations unique as well, just as the clothes the 'disappeared' had left at home. One woman relates how, when the mass grave was opened, she recognised the handmade pullover she had sewn and embroidered for her husband, and so found her husband's body.

The relatives of the 'disappeared' in Peru focus on precisely these handmade embroideries in their project entitled 'Scarf of Hope'. Fabricated in hours of needlework, the Scarf of Hope is a cloth of more than a kilometre in length, made of many tiny pieces that visualise the names of the 'disappeared' and the dates of the 'disappearances'.

> The Scarf of Hope has an aesthetic language with a strong visual impact that draws public attention in a non-threatening way. As a quilt, fragments of fabric with the inscribed names and photos of the disappeared are pieced together to tell their stories. With colors and stitches their relatives also give shape to their phantom existence, as in the woman who chose yarn of a milky color ... because her son's favorite dessert was arroz con leche (rice pudding). Or the woman whose panel is knitted ... a stitch named 'forget me not', because she senses her child's cry to be remembered. (Castaneda 2013)

The Mothers in Argentina want to represent their children in their embroidery, the Peruvian relatives use needle and thread to remind of the uniqueness of their 'disappeared' loved ones and the Iranian prisoners wish to at least have their fate known, also in the world outside the prison walls behind which they have 'disappeared', reaching their families as well as the political spheres.

This way, women in three different parts of this world have made a stand against their own 'disappearances' and that of their relatives.

## *Heteronomous and Autonomous Forms of Commemoration*

Robins (2012) describes how far removed from the actual needs of the relatives some forms of remembering can be. In Nepal, the so-called 'Martyr Gates' were erected, commemorating those who were killed or had 'disappeared' in the course of the conflict between the Maoists and the government. These gates, engraved with the names of these victims, were a far cry from being in accordance with the needs of the relatives of the 'disappeared':

> When asked about these, families of the Missing said they did not know if the names of their missing relatives are there, since they are illiterate. This also demonstrates that this memoralisation activity is entirely divorced from the families of those being celebrated, representing the instrumentalisation of the memory of the missing for political purposes. (Robins 2012: 11)

The relatives refuse the concept of their beloved being called martyrs, since this clearly implies them being dead. Many of the relations are not willing to give up hope yet.

In answer to the question, what kind of commemoration would seem appropriate to them, the families often named, amongst other things, compensations in the form of lands or social support. The bestowing of lands would be an appropriate form of justice: Memorials can be torn down, but a property that is given in the name of the 'disappeared' represents something real and solid that the family can benefit from on a long-term basis. Supporting the siblings of the 'disappeared' in their education also seemed a suitable form of compensation—at least the surviving family members would then have a chance for a better life.

The women whose relatives had 'disappeared' in the massacres of the an-Anfal Campaign in the Kurdish areas of Iraq in 1988 fought for years for a form of commemoration suitable in their eyes. They rejected the official memorial, since they did not see themselves represented in an adequate form there. The memorial had a shepherdess at its centre—to the women, this was the most backwards of images, one they could not identify with at all, and which felt devaluing to them.

The aim of the project 'Anfal Memory Forum' was the creation of a memorial that would express the women's grief for their lost relatives. They wanted a representation they could identify with and see themselves and their fate in.

The original idea of a gallery with pictures of the 'disappeared' eventually developed into an exhibition showing pictures that focus on the surviving women, holding mementos of their beloved 'disappeared' in their hands. In the middle of the exhibition hall, there is a statue of a woman standing upright, holding a dead child in her arm, but having a living one by her side. This depiction symbolises the traditional role of mother and the great suffering caused by the deaths of such a large number of children that the mothers were not even permitted to bury, but it also symbolises their strength and their will to live on. For many years during the dictatorship, the women living in refugee camps called themselves 'sitting women', meaning that they felt their lives to be stagnating. They saw themselves as frozen, as paralysed by the uncertainty of their relatives' situations. The statue, standing tall and erect, is in clear opposition to that image, breaking it up and underlining the women's power and their readiness to look forward and face the future (Mlodoch 2011).

## Social Projects in the Name of the 'Disappeared'

E. Varier, who, after years of uncertainty, was successful in clearing up the circumstances of his son Rajan's arrest and 'disappearance', receives a financial compensation for his son's murder. Varier uses the money to fund a hospital ward, which he calls 'Rajan Memorial'. Through this charity work, he was able to see a meaningful element in his son's life even years after

Rajan's death. There is no grave for Rajan, his body having been burned in an unknown place. The 'Rajan Memorial' ward provides a place for Rajan's family and friends to visit and remember him at (Varier 2004).

In a similar fashion, many families in Southeast Asia have set up endowment funds for social projects in the name of the 'disappeared'—wanting something good to be done that is remembered in connection with the names of the lost loved ones. In Nepal, 68 per cent of the relatives polled for a study supporting a form of commemoration that supports the local community. Suggestions were made to erect the so-called 'chautara', roofed resting places, and to build water pumps, both decorated with the pictures of the 'disappeared' and carrying their names.

When asked why such efforts were important, two elements emerged. One was to record the names of the Missing, which appears to be a simple assertion of the importance of recognition that they are missing. Another motivation, unsurprisingly, was to ensure that the Missing and their families were not forgotten. (Robins 2012: 16)

## Memorial Parks and Memorial Museums

A number of projects exist that aim at setting up real, palpable places of remembrance that make up for the missing graves of the 'disappeared'. These can be specially erected memorials, or certain places, buildings or even parks.

The Memoria Abierta organisation in Argentina, for example, took up the task of collecting and archiving the photographs, documents and also recordings of the stories of the 'disappeared', and contributed actively to the founding of a museum—keeping the memory of almost 30,000 'disappeared' alive.

Successful forms of commemorations can contribute to justice. 'Memoralisation can act to boost psychological and emotional resilience and well-being: this is psychological intervention "as" transitional justice' (Robins 2012: 20).

## Memorials in the New Media

For years there was a virtual cemetery online, specifically for people who had 'disappeared'. Lacking a grave at a certain geographical point, they were at least given one on the worldwide web, on www.disappearance.com.

It was impossible to find out why the site could no longer be accessed. In an exemplary fashion, it still goes to show what new forms of commemoration, breaching national and geographical boarders, are made use of in memory of the 'disappeared'.

## The Demand for Justice

National and international jurisdiction should sentence and punish 'enforced disappearance' in accordance with the laws in effect. The surviving relatives need confirmation that what had been done to their fathers, mothers, husbands, wives, sons and daughters had been unlawful and unjust.

This demand—which should be a self-evident one in any democracy—is oftentimes very difficult to assert, despite its immense importance to the relatives of the 'disappeared' as well as to society as a whole.

> When those in power refuse to own up to atrocious acts committed by agents in their name, they seem still to be insisting that the 'disappeared' either never existed or were not the victims but the guilty ones.... It was important in connecting these lost lives to the causes of violent conflict and the motivation of its major players, in measuring the true cost of the violence and mending the holes in the fabric that had resulted. The dead are lost but they may be redeemed to the extent that their names and fates recover a place on the public stage and their stories become part of contemporary history, on whose scales they have weighed something. (Summerfield 1998: 26)

The installation of supranational institutions, such as the International Court of Justice in The Hague, or national ways of dealing with the matter, such as the appointment of the village court 'Gacaca' in Ruanda, are approaches towards justice being done.

In Sri Lanka, Dr Manorani Saravanumuttu became the figurehead of a movement organised by wives/mothers who all demanded the cases of their 'disappeared' husbands/children to be solved. Dr Saravanumuttu's only son, the then in Sri Lanka fairly popular actor Richard de Souza, 'disappeared' in the course of the political unrest in 1989. He was 'arrested' in the family house in Colombo before his mother's eyes. A couple of days later, his body was found on the beach. Dr Saravanumuttu refused to simply accept her son's death. Despite the many attempts to intimidate her, she publicly named the men who had come to her home and had taken her son. Through this, she became a symbol to rally around for many women in Sri Lanka who had lost their sons, daughters, brothers or husbands, most of whom never even got to see the body of the family member they had lost.

In our conversations, Dr Saravanumuttu repeated to me what she had told in public before: However much she might be suffering because of the loss of her son under such terrible circumstances, she was still one of the fortunate ones. At least she had been spared the uncertainty of a 'disappearance' (personal conversations in Vienna 1994 and Colombo 1996).

## Acceptance of Irreconcilability

Where terrible losses had to be endured under such atrocious circumstances, the emotions of the relatives need to be respected. The demands for reconciliation—placed by those who were not immediately affected—can easily glide off into the cynical denying of the reality of suffering and pain. 'I recognize myself only in my irreconcilabilities, they are what I hold on to.... I cannot forget. Forgiving is absolutely sickening',[1] writes Klüger (1994: 279), who survived Auschwitz as a teenager. Her father and brother were murdered by the NS regime. Their bodies had never been found.

Like Jean Amery, Klüger insists that these irreconcilabilities are part of her identity after the Holocaust. They make it possible to live on (*Weiter leben*, meaning 'to live on' is the original, German title of her book).

In the therapeutic and psychosocial work with relatives of victims of 'enforced disappearances', it is of the uttermost importance that the feelings and emotions present are respected. The wish that clients can reconcile themselves with the situation and maybe even find it in themselves to forgive is an understandable one. This would, after all, be an important step towards the clients being able to detach themselves from the traumatic events. In most cases, though, the struggle for reconciliation or—as described by Ruth Klüger—the open irreconcilability remains.

## Sense of Coherence and Resilience

Forms of coping and learning to keep on living differ from culture to culture and from person to person. The forms described in this chapter represent the experiences different people had in their struggle to live with (or live despite) the 'disappearance' of their relatives. These forms, developed creatively in individual or group processes, were provided by social or governmental agencies, or are organised by international institutions.

The strategies of coping with the 'disappearance' of relatives enumerated here represent only a selection of those in existence, limited to those I have knowledge of. They all are reactions to severely traumatising situations. Some of the attempts of coping described are, in a sense, completed, but the majority of them are ongoing processes, developing and evolving all the time.

That people are at all able to react in such productive, creative ways to situations such as an 'enforced disappearance' of a close relative can be understood in connection with the SOC explained in the beginning of the chapter. In their individual ways of actively searching for the 'disappeared', in the exchange with others in similar situations and through the fight for justice and the many, creative forms of commemoration, can the 'disappearance' of the beloved person be viewed in a broader, biographically and socio-politically meaningful context? This goes a long way towards coming to terms with the traumatic experience.

# Note

1. Translation from the German original.

# 4
# Psychotherapeutic Work with Traumatised People

## Social, Cultural and Political Parameters for Trauma-Related Psychotherapy

Trauma-related psychotherapy means always also work on a political level. Since the therapist takes the side of the traumatised person and recognises the inflicted pain, he or she also makes a political statement: Yes, the traumatisation has taken place, or is still going on.

If the traumatising event is a natural catastrophe, acknowledging the victims and providing assistance for them is easier by far. If the traumata were or are induced by other human beings, then there are perpetrators—perpetrators who will deny, cover up and belittle what has happened. If the perpetrator or groups of perpetrators are powerful, then every attempt of intervening in order to help the victims (and be that only in the form of psychotherapeutic support) can become dangerous for the helpers.

Where people become victims of 'enforced disappearances', there must be, by necessity, somebody who is responsible for the 'disappearances'. This somebody has no interest in such cases being solved, nor in any kind of support for the relatives of the 'disappeared'.

The relatives of the victims are often themselves victims, having survived a war, abuse, torture and displacement. Many of them had to leave their homes and now live as refugees or as the so-called 'internally displaced persons' far away from all familiar structures.

Therapy, therefore, has to always take into account the political framework under which the traumatisation took place and the current political situation in which the therapeutic encounter is conducted.

In psychological evaluations, admission notes and other clinical documents, one needs to name the psychological sufferings of the client and the causes for the inner pain. In working in areas of conflict or with political refugees, this often seems rather odd to me. Does it really take an academically educated expert to deliver an opinion that can be summed up as something like: 'After the murder and "disappearance" of multiple family members, abuse and displacement, it would be detrimental to the client's mental health to again have to go through losing his or her apartment, access to food and health care'. I wonder whether an inkling of empathy and common sense would not lead anybody to the same conclusions (Preitler 2004a).

In addition to the awareness of the political situation, awareness of differences between cultures is necessary in order to understand how traumata were induced, what additional forms of suffering they might entail and how they can be overcome as individuals or in groups. Special care needs to be taken, if the therapist and the client are from different cultural backgrounds or social strata. The symbolisation of pain and suffering can differ significantly, and, thereby, become a source of misunderstandings.

## Safe Counselling Relationship

The most important tool in the therapeutic/counselling work with traumatised clients is the safe counselling relationship. In developing it, it is necessary for the therapist/counsellor to permit himself or herself to be tested by the client: Can the therapist/counsellor bear it all; can he or she take becoming witness to all this suffering?

Severely traumatised people often suffer from the idea that what has happened to them is so terrible that no one else can be expected to face it. And it is true that it is extremely difficult to open yourself up to such immense human suffering. But this is exactly what a good trauma therapy or trauma counselling offers.

How such a safe counselling relationship can be established is shown to us by a young trauma counsellor working in North Sri Lanka after the tsunami. In a workshop for 'trauma counselling', she relates her impressive success in bridging the gap between herself and her client, thereby establishing the basis for a safe and long-lasting relationship:

> She told about her difficulties in dealing with a widow who has lost her husband and one of her three children in the Tsunami. The house had been destroyed and now she was living a very difficult life in a refugee camp. Other people in the camp had identified her as a person in need of counselling, but when the counsellor introduced herself, the woman refused to speak to her.... The widow wanted to show how bad the food for the refugees was and asked the counsellor to share the meal with her. It was old, cooked,

already rotten rice. The counsellor accepted the invitation—even though she normally would not even touch rotten food like the one being offered to her. This shared meal was the beginning for the counselling relationship—in eating a little bit of this rotten rice together with the refugee woman the counsellor had built the basis for the necessary healing relationship.

Educated in psychoanalysis, I was deeply impressed by this story of the young counsellor: in sharing a little bit of the food the refugee had to eat, she was showing her willingness to be really on the side of this woman who has suffered so much and had now to live the stressful life as widow in a refugee camp.

Rice is in a Hindu context 'pure' food and the preparation and consumption follow specific rules. Only fresh prepared rice will be offered to guests. Now the refugees face their low social status also by being given old rotten rice of low quality, thus hurting their dignity.

What helped most in developing the relationship between the two women was the gesture of the counsellor to share with her even the 'bad taste', suggesting the meaning of being a tsunami victim and a refugee.

We were moved by hearing this episode which has become a wonderful symbol for the spirit of offering psychological assistance for trauma victims. I think we have to share with the survivors at least a little bit the 'rotten rice' and its bad taste, to be able to understand the past and the present situation of our traumatized clients. (Preitler 2009: 51f.)

In order for such a safe counselling relationship to develop, we, as therapists or counsellors, need to be willing to be tested. Our empathy as well as our strength are called into question and put to the test.

## Cooperation between Medicine and Psychotherapy

In the psychological and psychotherapeutic work with victims of human rights violations, a close cooperation with doctors is absolutely necessary. It is best to have the results of a thorough physical examination and, if necessary, a corresponding treatment plan, before beginning psychotherapy. Physical symptoms almost always play a major role in people's desire for psychotherapeutic support. Therefore, it is important to clarify whether any of the experienced pain has an underlying physical cause in addition to the psychological non-coping.

> One of my clients complained about severe back pains. His history suggests the possibility of long-term physical damage in that area. Thorough medical examinations showed no causes for the pain, though, and physiotherapy

brought no relief. In our psychotherapeutic sessions, we were able to determine that he perceives the experiences in his past as a burden weighing heavily upon his shoulders, 'bending his back'. Slowly, he begins to name these burdens during therapy and dares to open his eyes to them, even if this is connected with renewed bouts of pain and grief.

It is always important, though, to clarify on a medical level, whether physical changes, even if brought on by psychological pain, make it necessary to have physical treatment. This can also be seen in the remarkable case history of a young woman who was introduced to me during a supervision session in Sri Lanka:

13-year-old K. is referred to the psychological counselling centre by the hospital, because no physical causes for her symptoms could be found. Since her father's death, K. cannot walk anymore, and has fallen unconscious repeatedly. In the beginning, her counsellor is at a loss as to how to help young K.

I ask about the circumstances of her father's death. I am told that he was riding his bicycle when he suddenly had a heart attack. The image of her father's feet not being able to operate the pedals and breaks on the bike, and him dropping to the ground dead (unconscious), help us understand the symptoms the girl exhibits.

In the next session, K.'s grief for her father and her wish to keep up the connection with him are addressed. It can be hoped that in her grief for the lost father—and, possibly, also in a revision of the conflicts in the father–daughter relationship they had had—she can slowly find a way towards resolving her problem and also give up her physical symptoms.

If K. keeps up her physical symptoms, she will be in need of physiotherapy anyway, in order to regain her physical strength and abilities.

## Psychological Therapy and Counselling with Interpreters

In order to even get into contact with the client, counsellors, in their work with traumatised people, commonly work together with interpreters. This constitutes a significant change from the usual setting of a psychotherapeutic session. The relationship restricted to client and therapist/counsellor that usually characterises individual therapy is extended to include a third person. The client, therefore, needs to relate to two people (Van der Veer 1992; Vesti 1992).

The problems that can arise out of this setting can relate to the utterances of client and therapist/counsellor (shortening or changing) and the relationship not only between client and therapist/counsellor, but also that between client and interpreter.

At the very beginning of such an interpreter-aided therapy, the roles of all participants have to be clearly defined with respect to the client as well as the interpreter. If the client or the therapist talks in first person, this is how the utterance should be translated. Everything the client says needs to be translated. It is important for the interpreter to have such a clearly defined role, otherwise the position of therapist and translator can be confused.

Essentials for the choice of interpreter are: The interpreter should not be related or acquainted with the client, and their contact should be limited to the therapeutic sessions for the duration of the entire therapeutic treatment process. This is necessary in order to ensure that the interpreter can remain unbiased. Also, the client is then not inhibited by the presence of an attachment figure in talking about the traumatisation. Simultaneously, the interpreter, who often shares the client's cultural background, is protected from becoming involved in the personal life story of the client.

Despite the problems that can arise when working with interpreters, the positive experiences with the setting show that the benefits outweigh the drawbacks (Vesti 1992; Preitler 1998/99). In many cases, it is this form of communication that enables the establishment of a client–therapist relationship in the first place. The knowledge about the specific culture and region the interpreter can contribute to the sessions can also be a real asset to the therapy.

## The Psychotherapeutic Process

### Aims of Psychotherapy

Healing, in the sense of literally making everything well again, is usually impossible after severe psychological suffering has been endured. What is done cannot be undone. The deceased family members and friends are irretrievably lost, the 'disappeared' usually remain untraceable, scars and physical mutilations remain visible. The violation of one's human rights and one's dignity become monumental parts of one's life story.

The aim of psychological and psychotherapeutic interventions can be, however, to set right the temporal dimensions of the experience. The torture does not have to be relived in nightmares every night, or suffered through again and again in recurring flashes of memory each day.

What has been lost—and most especially the people who have been lost—can be grieved for, but life—nevertheless—must go on.

## Beginning Therapy

The room for the psychotherapeutic sessions is often the very first place in which somebody—the therapist—makes time for this person exclusively for a whole hour. In this safe frame established by psychotherapy it is possible, for the first time after weeks, months and sometimes years of extreme stress put on them by terror, war or having to flee, to find a certain measure of peace. Here, there is room for a bit of regression. The tears, held back for so long, and the suppressed anger with the structures that had denied the client the safety needed have found their place.

In this room, one's own perception of reality can be tested. The events in the past are experienced as something outrageous. Often, those who had to suffer through them had started to doubt their reality. Having the reassurance of the therapist that they can talk freely about what has happened to them and their relatives, and being assured that they will be believed, the clients can begin to trust their own memories again.

As long as the situation is still dangerous and the threat of further traumatic experiences is looming, the psychotherapeutic intervention usually stays within these limits. Looking at the painful memories of the traumatic experience and the corresponding psychological processing of and coping with it become possible only once the client feels secure on a physical and social level. Only then can he or she mobilise the energy necessary to undertake coping with and overcoming the trauma.

## Grief Counselling

Traumatised people are almost always people in grief—there are deaths to mourn, 'disappeared' persons to grieve for, but the same is true, for the loss of safety, of physical integrity and of one's home. In many cases, there was no opportunity for saying goodbye or for other rituals that might have made the separation easier.

In order to make up for this, we spend large stretches of time during therapy on talking about the rituals and ceremonies that would have been conducted in the culture of the homeland in the case of bereavement. I encourage my clients to tell me what these would have looked like in the specific case of their lost relative. The clients draft obituaries and epitaphs. Often remembering the dead is difficult for them, as the way he or she died dominates all memories. If it is possible to win back some of the memories of the time before this traumatic event, then one small part of the grief work is done. Two things that are especially difficult to bear are the memory of having had to watch, to witness the murder(s) of one or more relatives, and—the other extreme—the ever-present feeling of uncertainty with regards to the fate of a beloved person in the cases of 'enforced disappearances'. During the therapeutic sessions, careful attempts are made to remember the time before the traumatic event. These memories can be set against the horror of the murder or the 'disappearance'. If, for example, the mother can be remembered not only in the hour of her death, but also as the cheerful woman caring for her children, then an important step in the grief work has been taken. The memory of the deceased gradually regains some of its positive connotations; the loss of the relationship can be mourned. The grief that had been frozen due to the violent circumstances of the death can thaw and then be processed.

The grief counselling in the case of a 'disappeared' family member or friend presents a very special task for therapists. This had been addressed in previous chapters and will be discussed in more detail in the following ones.

## Dealing with Traumatisation through Violations of Human Rights

Severe violations of human rights, such as torture, are such flagrant events that all the coping strategies people may have developed in their everyday lives prove ineffective for dealing with them. Amery (1988: 40), in his reflections on the torture he had to endure under the NS regime, writes: 'The shame of destruction cannot be erased. ... It blocks the view into a world in which the principle of hope rules. One who was martyred is a defenceless prisoner of fear.'

Psychotherapeutic work begins with 'nevertheless'. It is about gradually beginning to cope with the fear, to hand back the shame to those who brought it upon the client, to those who aired themselves as lords over life and death in such a destructive manner.

The safe room in which the therapy/counselling takes place is of importance, as it is often the first one in which the client can come to rest. There, for the first time, fear is not allowed in. Starting from this place, the path to a present without fear can be won back. The counselling relationship becomes a model for how a person hurt so deeply by other human beings can learn to trust again. Building up this relationship can sometimes take whole months and often demands some unconventional measures. One step along the way is to give the client the opportunity to ask the therapist/counsellor (and, if present, also the interpreter) questions in the first session. Only rarely do clients take their interlocutors up on this offer, and if they do, they usually inquire about political affiliations. This step still seems important to me in order to provide our clients with as much safety as possible. Another step towards this is letting the clients choose their own place within the room, and even letting them make—moderate—changes to the room itself. A young man, for example, found the sunlight unbearable and, therefore, closed the curtains so that we sat in twilight. One of the women I have worked with wanted to sit as close to the door as possible—at least until she could completely trust her therapist. Another client had severe troubles with his back and wanted to sit on a stool, which we then got from another room.

Severe traumatisation means absolute loss of control. Therefore, it is a necessary part of trauma work to supply the clients with as much autonomy and means of controlling the situation as possible.

## Concluding the Therapy

The psychological and psychotherapeutic work can be concluded when the people and living situations lost have been mourned, when relationships have been renewed and new ones have been established, and when strategies for a new life after the trauma have already been put into practice.

Boulanger (2007: 189) describes this as follows: 'My goal is to enable the patient to live her life in spite of the trauma, not to be lived by the trauma.'

Since re-traumatisation can always occur, upon leaving, clients are given the assurance of further contact if desired, intervention in times of crisis or, if needed, brief strategic psychotherapy in the future.

## Transference and Countertransference

The reason why severely traumatised people ask for help can often be found in their desire for a quick and effective anaesthesia. All suffering should be over and forgotten. This is true for relatives of 'disappeared' as well. They want to overcome the loss and the corresponding feelings of grief. The sheer impossibility of dealing with this kind of loss is an ever-present traumatisation that leaves the clients hopeless. The wish to resolve this impossible situation is projected onto psychotherapy or various forms of medical care. What is wanted is a form of anaesthetic pill, the effects of which should last until the 'disappeared' returns, at which point the normal life together can be picked up right where it was interrupted by the 'enforced disappearance'. The traumatic event should be 'undone' in some way. A very understandable wish, but impossible to fulfil, it forms part of the beginning of almost every therapy. Becker (1992: 261) describes similar experiences with severely traumatised people, summing up the client's expectations as wanting to be the sound and safe, well-integrated persons they had been in the past, which means forgetting all the destruction that has happened since.

It is the job of the therapist to endure, grieve about and deal with the conflict between the desire to forget everything as quickly as possible and the necessity of accepting the traumatic experience. In this, psychotherapy again and again reaches its limits. As Becker (1992) rightly states, the psychological recovery is often misunderstood as the literal, total recovery of a prior state. If one takes into account the magnitude of the destruction these clients had had to face, then it becomes clear that reparation can only occur in connection with the acceptance that there will not be any literal return to health (Becker 1992: 260).

Especially in this situation of helplessness, where grieving for the lost relative is made difficult by the uncertainty surrounding his or her fate, it is necessary to pay attention to the client's possible transference reactions and the countertransference reactions of the therapist, respectively. Durst (1999) raises the issue that we often ask ourselves whether our clients can bear certain things, while we fail to question our own capacities and limits as psychotherapists. Durst cites commonly pondered questions such as 'Will the surviving relative have the inner strength to undertake this journey into the past' and suggests that instead the therapists should carefully consider whether they are truly ready for their own confrontation with death (Durst 1999: 111).

The reason for my addressing this topic was my personal form of countertransference in my therapeutic work with relatives of victims of 'enforced disappearances'. The 'disappearance' of one or more important attachment figures leaves one helpless, out of ideas, with no data or knowledge to go on. I—the educated expert meant to support the relatives—know no more than my clients. I share in the not-knowing of those who come to me expecting support. Thanks to the theoretical concepts I have studied and my personal experience with other clients, I have concrete ideas about the goals and the processes of psychotherapeutic trauma work and grief counselling. When it comes to situations where persons have 'disappeared', however, I have no more information than the relatives I am counselling. For me as a therapist, this creates an uncomfortable situation in which I myself know neither help nor advice. I am not firmly grounded by my knowledge and experience.

Sometimes, 'disappeared' relatives do 'reappear'. Therefore, it would be a serious therapeutic mistake to initiate the mourning of the lost family member as dead. The continuous waiting for the return of the 'disappeared', however, seemed to have a gruelling effect and hindered all further development.

New trends in trauma therapy pointed strongly towards the importance of memories. Making use of neurological concepts, attempts are made to change the memory of the traumatic experience, reducing the emotions involved and, therefore, making it less painful to remember. These attempts, though, characterised by clear forms and techniques for the psychotherapeutic work with severely traumatised people, which go as far as formulating instructions about the steps to be taken in each therapy session, do little but illustrate the defensive reaction of scientists and treatment advisors to frightening issues such as trauma, death and 'enforced disappearances'.

According to Devereux (1984), when faced with the kind of fear that is found in behavioural scientific data, which could lead to a subjective distortion and, therefore, influence the results, we tend to try to distance ourselves from it via scientific tools, such as tests, interviews and technical equipment, trying to use them as filters.

The psychotherapeutic work with severely traumatised people who had to suffer difficult losses can take a very long time. It takes a lot of patience to make it through phases of stagnation together with the clients.

Fleeing into intellectualisations appears to be one of the most common forms of defence in those giving treatment to people who have been traumatised. Ottomeyer and Peltzer (2002) mock this kind of behaviour,

## 124  Grief and Disappearance

calling entering such personal and dynamic data into tables with orthogonally meeting columns and rows or the use of a four-sides model a 'crucifixion'. They see the main purpose of such pseudo-objectifications in being able to project an image during a peer-conference. Another kind of objectivist defence they name is that of being overzealous in one's diagnostic precision (Ottomeyer & Peltzer 2002: 142).

Another form of defence against the traumatic experiences of the clients can be the denial of the person's suffering and pain. It is astounding how long it took until trauma disorders were recognised as an independent set of symptoms. At the same time, this diagnosis provides the possibility of denying the social and political dimension. In declaring the person ill, the problem is reduced to that of an individual. It is then enough to cure the individual from his or her defect (meaning from PTSD). Ottomeyer and Peltzer see the possibility of avoiding the horror of the client's traumatisation in a distorted perception of the dynamic of the trauma (Ottomeyer & Peltzer 2002: 142).

Butollo et al. (1998) point out another danger, namely that of wrongly or prematurely forcing the client into relating the traumatic event, not because of the client's but of the therapist's need. They describe how therapists can struggle with their own feelings of inadequacy. The therapists, in the face of the slow or non-existent progress in the therapy, worry about the effectiveness of his/her own work. Unable to bear the feeling of impotency, the therapists defends him or herself by hurrying on the client. If the client is unwilling or unable, then the lack of success at least seems to be the responsibility of the person in therapy, not that of the therapist.

Many techniques are introduced that claim to achieve a fast processing of the trauma through targeted enforcing of the recount of the traumatic experience. The need to talk about the traumatic event is an individual one, though, and can vary significantly, depending on the specific situation. Attempts to find one unified strategy for all survivors stem from the wish of the medical and psychological personnel for a kind of handbook against their own helplessness, rather than from the psychological abilities of the clients.

How dangerous such therapeutic actions can be for the clients involved, since they pose a massive threat to the safe counselling relationship, is summed up astutely by Boulanger (2007: 117): 'Forcing survivors to relive their experience against their will is never therapeutic, nor will it encourage them to seek treatment when they are ready to do so.'

Methods of exposure to the traumatic event provide no answers, neither to the issue of the 'disappearance' of a person, which is, in fact, a non-event, nor, consequently, to the resulting continually traumatic situation in everyday life. At the most, there is one traumatic situation that can really be described, namely that in which the relative has initially been taken away. But the forceful separation was followed by a time of searching, waiting, hoping and despairing that has stretched over days, weeks, months and sometimes entire lifetimes. None of the government agencies seem to have even heard of the name, so all inquiries come to nothing. It seems as if this person had never existed, as if the earth had opened and swallowed the person up. Henceforth, life is characterised by a feeling of uncertainty that must most definitely be seen as traumatising. There are no traumatising events as such to be described, though.

The established methods as well as the recently developed ones can be of assistance in overcoming the effects of an isolated traumatic event. When it comes to the grieving processes characterised by frozen or prolonged grief, as is typical for the relatives of victims of 'enforced disappearances', I have found no indication that such methods can be of help.

There is a tendency to pay rather little attention to the experiences of loss that all people who have been traumatised by war or torture have had to suffer through. One possible reason for this lies in the feeling of helplessness the psychotherapists experience in these cases. For isolated cases of bereavement—no matter how dramatic the circumstances of the death might have been—answers to many questions can be found in the literature on grief studies. When it comes to the 'disappearance' of an attachment figure, the state of affairs becomes foggy and unclear. It is rather difficult to engage in a kind of theory building that is actually helpful for those working in curative professions. Our possibilities are limited when it comes to helping and curing. Psychotherapists reach their own limits and become—like their clients—helpless. Becker (1992) writes about the dilemma therapists working with severely traumatised people find themselves in. For one thing he names the seemingly inherent contradiction of the therapist needing to surrender to a certain degree to an illusion of being omnipotent in order to even involve him or herself in a therapeutic process with a severely traumatised client, while at the same time having to accept a loss of omnipotence from the very beginning if the therapy should be successful in the end. For another, Becker describes the related issue of both, the client and the therapist, tricking themselves into a feigned success born out of the fantasies of omnipotence the therapist lives and the client's desire for harmony. An alliance between these two feelings can ultimately lead to a complete failure of the treatment (Becker 1992: 260).

A possible consequence of such a failure can be the turning of the feeling of omnipotence into its complete opposite. Severely traumatised clients have always been experiencing helplessness, and the feeling usually continues. If the fate of a family member or friend is still unknown, and it is feared that they are being terrorised and tortured, or have been killed already, then the feeling of helplessness increases. There are no means of getting information, let alone getting into contact with the 'disappeared'. During psychotherapy, this condensed accumulation of feelings of helplessness can lead to severe countertransference:

> The therapist also empathically shares the patient's experience of helplessness. This may lead the therapist to underestimate the value of her own knowledge and skill, or to lose sight of the patient's strengths and resources. Under the sway of countertransference helplessness, the therapist may also lose confidence in the power of the psychotherapy relationship. It is not uncommon for experienced therapists to feel suddenly incompetent and hopeless in the face of a traumatized patient. (Herman 1992: 141)

Thus, psychotherapy with severely traumatised people always means facing one's own feelings of helplessness and disempowerment, as well as one's feelings of horror at atrocities such as torture, death and 'enforced disappearances' (for further discussions on this, see Chapter 9).

In conclusion of this chapter, I would like to cite Nathan Durst in his paper on his work with Holocaust survivors living in Israel. The people he encounters in his psychotherapeutic work have all suffered numerous losses. Very often there is no grave and no certainty about the circumstances of the 'disappearances' or deaths of the beloved persons.

> Our excuse for refusing to work with the survivors and to expose ourselves to their pain and suffering is that we do not want to follow them on their journey into the past; because we are afraid of the contents of Pandora's box. In my experience, however, Pandora's box is filled with nothing but tears; with tears that have never fallen in the presence of a witness, a person of significance to them, someone with whom they have a real, stable interpersonal relationship, a person that could offer closeness and solace. We know that time does not heal this kind of wounds and that the sadness will return like the wave of the ocean. Grief is the emotional expression of a relationship to a human being that has been lost, and it remains with us forever. The question we as therapists have to ask is: Can we let the survivors live this moment of sadness together with us, or do we leave them alone in it. This is what loss means: being left all alone.

In summary it can be said that we need to be modest in our expectations when it comes to our therapeutic work with survivors and other traumatised people. We cannot change their reality. But sometimes we can help to ease the pain. (Durst 1999: 111)[1]

# Note

1. Translation from the German edition.

# 5
# Individual Reactions to 'Enforced Disappearances'

In psychological and psychotherapeutic programmes that support people who have been traumatised by structural violence, war and torture, 'disappearances' are a recurring issue. In my research I started out with the assumption that during the first interview most clients list other problems, such as physical or psychological hurts or problems of dealing with everyday life as reasons for their wish to start therapy. I assumed that the issue of 'disappeared' relatives is not often addressed at that stage, and only comes up at a later point.

In order to test this hypothesis, I analysed the minutes of all the first interviews held at Hemayat in Vienna in June 2012, extracting the personal reasons the clients give for coming to psychotherapy. Hemayat is the leading organisation that specialises in supporting survivors of torture and war traumata in Austria. All interview partners came to Europe from abroad (mainly from Asia and Africa). I am aware of the fact that this analysis is based on a small and rather arbitrarily compiled sample. Nevertheless, I found it to be not insignificant in size, since I was able to attain a total number of 147 reports. The result of my analysis came as a surprise: The minutes of 57 of these first interviews (38.7 per cent) contained reference to the 'disappearance' of a relative. Statements such as 'lost the children' and 'stayed in the home country' were not included in this count. The other 90 reports held no direct indication for a 'disappearance'; however, this merely means that the issue was not raised during the first interview, not that there are no 'disappeared' relatives.

My surprise relates to the difference to my own perception, and, in that, to my countertransference: Despite having put great emphasis on this issue in my work for more than a decade now, it had so far escaped my notice that the desperation regarding the loss of a relative in this particular way is given such priority at such an early stage in therapy.

In the reports on my own clients mention of 'disappeared' relatives is even more frequent. Of the 20 patients who I worked with in psychotherapeutic sessions in the final months of 2012, 14 (70 per cent) have relatives who have 'disappeared'. Their home countries are Afghanistan, Chechnya, Somalia, Iraq and Turkey.

Five of these clients have lost contact with their relatives in the course of fleeing their home countries and now have no way of getting in touch. The reasons for this are varied: lack of education, which bars them from access to written forms of communication, their chaotic escape routes having led them into different directions, and also their fear of bad news. At this point in time the uncertainty is easier to bear than the possible news of somebody's death.

In four of the 20 cases, mothers do not know the whereabouts of one or more of their children. The feelings of uncertainty result in strong forms of dissociation in all—otherwise very different—cases. These include blanking out the very existence of the child, transferring the grievance to everyday life in the country of exile and aimless wanderings through the city.

Five of the 20 clients have lost a brother, sister, cousin or brother-in-law through an 'enforced disappearance'. In all these cases the 'disappearance' was clearly an act of terror: The entire family is affected by the 'disappearance' of this person. As possible reasons the clients name feuds between rivalling clans and the unwelcome political activities of the then 'disappeared' person, or at least the suspicion of the person having been involved in such activities.

In two of the cases the 'disappearance' lay more than 10 years in the past; for the other clients the situation is more acute: In three cases the therapeutic contact had already been established when the news about the 'disappearance' of the brother, the sister, the son reached them.

This brief overview of the cases I have worked with in a professional context is, of course, not representative. It does give an idea of how intrinsically connected 'disappearances' and structural violence, war, torture and fleeing a country are.

Boss (2006) is one of the few authors who deal with this subject matter. In her 'Ambiguous Loss Model' she describes the omnipresence of the 'disappearance' in the lives of the relatives:

> Without proof of death, family members don't know whether to close out the missing person or keep the door open for him or her to return. Family processes freeze and boundaries are unclear. People become preoccupied with the lost person and may think of little else. As a result, they may no longer function in their usual roles and relationships. (Boss 2006: 7f.)

For the following sections I draw on my extensive experience as a psychotherapist, which consists of years of working with survivors of torture and war, and, most of all, with relatives of victims of 'enforced disappearances' and of many encounters in my work as a supervisor and trainer in Austria and Asia. Despite the differences between the individual cases, certain similarities and patterns can be recognised.

## Caught between Searching, Despair and Resignation

At first, the search for the 'disappeared' is a central issue. In many cases the drive for it levels out with time, turning into resignation. Certain factors occur again and again though, that reactivate the search.

> One day Mrs F. comes to therapy looking thoroughly dejected, but at first she cannot talk about the reason for her state of mind. It takes 10 minutes for her to be able to talk about the news she received the day before. She tells me that there have been mass executions in the prisons of her home country. Ever since the news has reached her she is plagued by images and night mares of her husband having been executed. She starts to ponder ways of getting information about his situation again.

Sometimes the desire to keep searching has to be sacrificed in the interest of the needs of other family members.

> Mr S. has accepted the 'disappearance' of the two eldest of his seven children as now unalterable. His futile investigations had only resulted in threats to the remaining family members. Mr S. felt forced to abandon his search for the two 'disappeared' children in order to protect the rest of the family. He fled his home country together with his wife and their five remaining children.

The inability to actively search for missing relatives is generally experienced as extremely difficult and strenuous by those affected, and results in intense feelings of helplessness.

However, the means of searching available are treated in an ambivalent manner. Many relatives cannot bring themselves to register a tracing request.

There are many different ways of searching for 'disappeared' relatives. Probably the most well-known tracing service is that of the International

Red Cross. Online media opens up new means of searching that cross great distances and borders in an effortless way. Social networks can serve the attempt to find the relatives themselves, or at least a trusted person who lives in the vicinity and can, therefore, be asked for information. In the virtual reality of the worldwide web it is possible to make inquiries without revealing one's own geographic location—which is especially important for those who have fled from political repression, threats or persecution. In some cases religious communities or political groups can help in the search on an international level.

All these means of searching are discussed in the therapy/counselling sessions. Striking, though, is how often the eagerly expected tracing request is then not filled in or handed in to the tracing service. The page on the social network site gets set up but is never opened again, leaving it open whether or not anyone ever tried to get in through that way.

One of my clients, a young man from an Asian country currently at war, explained his point of view to me. 'I would have no reason to live, if they were all dead. I couldn't bear this news'.

Avoidance strategies that might protect one from bad news can also lead to good news about the fate of a relative not getting through.

Mr J. decides to actively make use of all available means of searching for his relatives. It is important for him to re-establish the contact with his mother and his brother. His many letters to their home address remain unanswered. Once his own psychological state has stabilised, the search for his relatives takes a central position in his life. A number of therapy sessions are spent on discussing hitherto unexplored ways tracing them. The conversation focuses on whether certain measures are indeed practicable, and whether or not they might endanger the family. Mr J. decides to register a tracing request with the Red Cross, but he also wants to find other means of searching.

For a long time he weighs the option of trying the fax number of one of the friends of the family as a way of maybe getting in contact with his mother. Finally, he decides to risk it. A week later he comes to therapy beaming with joy: In his hand he has a piece of fax paper that has four handwritten lines on it—a message written by his mother.

## Longing for the 'Disappeared' Person— the Desire to Be Reunited Again

The inner longing for a reunion with the 'disappeared' person is understandably a very strong one. While awake, people tend to suppress this desire, dismissing it as unrealistic or judging it to be too painful to think of, but in their dreams it is expressed in powerful ways.

A dream sequence related to me by N., a young African woman who has no contact with her family at all, shows this desire clearly:

> N. is in a dark forest that seems eerie to her. She is holding a very small baby. Her brother is with her, which makes her happy. At the same time she is worried, because in this dream her brother is deaf-mute. She peppers him with questions, but he only smiles at her.
>
> It feels like somebody is following them. There are three soldiers behind them. N. tells them to leave her brother alone. He is deaf, so he cannot have overheard anything and he also cannot reveal any information. Nevertheless a solder steps closer in a threatening way. N. develops enormous powers, fights with the soldier and—in her dream—cuts his throat.

While dreaming and after she has woken up, N. is shocked by the fact that she was capable of killing this soldier in her dream. Even three days later, when talking about the dream in therapy, she is obviously distressed. She is aghast by her violent actions, but it is also the thought of her brother being deaf-mute that pains her. Since she has not heard from her family in two years, she takes the dream literally. She is extremely scared that her brother might really have become a deaf-mute.

In our interpretation of the dream I try to confirm the truths that can be found in her dream. It is true that she cannot communicate with her brother—Her words cannot reach him (deaf); she cannot hear anything from him (mute). However, that does not mean that he has, in fact, become a deaf-mute. The dream sequence refers to the inability of the siblings to communicate with each other. What also finds expression in the dream is her urgent desire to protect the younger brother—using violence, if necessary.

N. has herself been imprisoned and tortured more than once; her father has been killed by soldiers. Her aggression towards the soldier who threatens her brother and her refers back to real-life events that she and her family have been subjected to.

What the baby that N. carries in her dream stands for has her dumbfounded in the beginning. In the course of our conversation, though, she identifies it as representing the new chances for self-development Europe holds for her, all of which are still in the earliest stages, in their infancy, so to speak. She would be willing to give them all up for her brother and the rest of her family.

Mrs C. is from Africa as well. Her father was in all likelihood killed by military men. In the process of fleeing the country she lost all contact to the rest of her family. C. dreamt of her mother:

> C. is back home, in her mother's house. Mother and daughter walk to church together, as it is a Sunday. On their way, they meet a friend of C.'s. The mother continues to walk to the church on her own. C. follows her, together with her friend. As the distance to the mother increases C. becomes anxious. The friend points out another path, saying that this is a shortcut. C. can see the mother in the distance front of her, but cannot reach her. She can see the mother praying in the church. It frightens C. with what fervour her mother is praying. C. tries to get to her, but cannot reach her.

N., who was separated from her siblings, tells about a dream that is similar in its dynamics:

> She is walking along a street that runs along a canal. Suddenly she discovers her siblings walking on the other side of the canal. She desperately wants to get to them, she calls out, and they react to her calls, but do not respond to the questions she shouts at them. They smile and gesture for her to come over. N. tries to find a way to cross the canal, but the canal widens and widens, with the siblings disappearing in the distance until she cannot see them anymore.

In both dreams the fulfilment of their wishes constitutes the beginning—they are reunited with their 'disappeared' relatives. But on their way they gradually lose contact. With increasing effort, their fears rising, they try to reach them but fail in their attempts. A piece of reality intrudes on the dream and prevents the desired reunion.

N. and C. are both very shaken when relating their dreams, and both talk about experiencing intense feelings of longing for their families after having woken up.

Such dreams are characteristic for relatives of 'disappeared' persons. They express the longing for the beloved person, as well as the slow and painful detachment from them (Irmler 2001).

D. tells me about having had a dream in which she could talk to her mother. When she comes to therapy a few days after that particular dream, she wears her hair differently. She tells me that she dreamt of her mother.

> She met her mother, who behaved very caringly towards her. Responding to her mother's questions, D. tells her of all that has happened since their separation, and of how she is feeling. Before that her mother had asked why she was doing her hair differently than she had before.
> In the dream, D. asks her mother how she is and what has happened to her in the past years. After having asked this question, D. wakes up.

D. is saddened by the dream. She would have liked to hear her mother's answer. She hopes to soon have another dream like this one. By changing her hairstyle—back to the one her mother knows her with—she feel more connected to her mother. By this change in appearance she makes herself look the way her mother must remember her. For five weeks she keeps this hairstyle, then she changes back to her usual—new—hairdo. The hairstyle becomes a transitional object that makes it possible for D. to feel close to her mother for some time, and thereby better control her fears regarding her mother's fate.

Being a European therapist I offer a European kind of dream interpretation: The fears and hopes that find expression in a dream are very real—but they are woven into stories and, therefore, require analysis and interpretation. The separation and the fear for the relatives are real, even if they get pushed away during the waking hours. If they manifest as symbols in dreams we can try to understand them in our conversations about these dreams.

If these symbolisations that come up in the dreams are understood as feelings we are not conscious of, then this can reduce the clients' fears and can make it possible to see these dreams as chances for further self-development.

## Avoidance

One way of reacting to the 'disappearance' of a relative is to avoid the topic as such.

> 13-year-old C. is not ready to talk about the 'disappearance' of his father and his sister. Whenever I bring up this issue, he wards off

the topic and seeks escape into somatic ailments. 'I get a headache when you ask me about this.'

A similar situation is that of Mr V., who lost his entire family in the turmoil of the civil war that was raging in his home country when he was a teenager.

The closest we get to the events surrounding the 'disappearances' and deaths of his family members is his recount of his grandfather's death and, another time, of his aunt and her family being killed. He is not able to talk about the 'disappearance' of his parents and his siblings. He only mentioned it in bullet-point fashion during the first interview. At that time he talked so fast that it was impossible to ask for details. His many ailments hint at his sufferings and losses, though.

He also lives in mortal fear of fire and is constantly afraid that one of the other inhabitants of the residential home he lives in might set the house on fire. It takes some time for him to finally tell me that some of his relatives have died in a fire.

Even in the course of the long psychotherapeutic process, it is not possible to put into words the deep wounds of the traumatisation. Sometimes it takes a very long time for a discussion of these wounds to become possible.

In this, it is necessary to maintain a balance between respecting the pain and the silence of the client and forcing the trauma narrative. The therapist has to face the question whether his/her own feelings and needs are influencing the situation: Would it primarily help the therapist to get a clear picture of the events, or is it necessary for the client to verbally express the traumata? Or is it, in fact, the therapist who avoids the confrontation with the traumatic events and the emotions that come with it, and therefore fails to create a situation in which the client can address this matter during therapy?

The individual needs and abilities of the person who is looking for help in psychotherapy need to remain in the centre of attention. For some people, putting the terrible experiences into words will be helpful, for others doing this would be too painful an experience that then is itself an event that overwhelms them, becoming a traumatic experience in its own right.

As in the case of Mr V., the lone survivor of an entire family, it might be necessary to accept the lasting unspeakability of the traumatisation and grief. When Mr V. was finally able to talk about the horrible tidings, this had a liberating effect on him. His physical symptoms and his panic-like fear, which he had been projecting on his housemates, abated.

An avoidance strategy that is particularly hard to understand for many helpers is the refusal to make use of the various ways of searching for relatives. For a long time, young N. declined our offer to get into contact with the Red Cross and ask them to trace her missing relatives. This reaction, at first very incomprehensible, even disconcerting, became understandable in the course of the therapy:

> Once already somebody from her family—her mother—had 'disappeared'. After a year of waiting, worrying and hoping, the devastating news of the mother's death arrives. In order to avoid a repetition of this terrible news, the uncertainty of not knowing is given preference. As long as she has no information to the contrary, her 'disappeared' siblings, to her at least, are alive.

To directly address the apprehension that the 'disappeared' relative might be dead, is often the equivalent to a flat-out breach of a taboo. It is not only the client him/herself who tries to avoid certain issues, as a situation described by the psychotherapist B. Abdallah-Steinkopff shows: One of her Afghan clients lost her son in the course of fleeing their home country. The boat, which they had to use for part of the way capsized, and the client fell unconscious. When she awoke after the accident, her son, who had been on the boat with her, was gone. The client's worry for her child was the main topic of the therapy. When the therapist wanted to address the possibility of the son's death, she encountered resistance on the part of the interpreter. Abdallah-Steinkopff (2003: 5) describes how the interpreter refused outright to translate this sentence as to assume that the son might be dead constitutes a sin. No matter how strong the evidence, a mother may not put into words the possibility of her son's death, in his opinion.

This behaviour corresponds with the presence of 'psychological barriers', as described by Madariaga (1992). Such psychological barriers can help to protect the mental health of a client, but they also serve as avoidance strategies. In this case, the very real possibility of the son's death is consistently blocked out. Even the slimmest hopes for his survival are clung to. It is—as described above—a sin to even consider the possibility of the relative's death, let alone to articulate such a thought. Through this, the impossibility of the death is solidified and chronified. The search has to go on forever, just as for the wives of Sri Lankan soldiers listed as MIA (De Soysa 2001; see also '"Enforced Disappearances" through War and Terror'). One's life may not be open for new chances or relationships.

In counselling and therapy, we need to stay by our client's side. Our job is it to not leave them alone with the uncertainty and concomitant despair and to, against all odds, develop ways of living on in a good, positive way.

## Aggression and Anger

N.'s anger in her dream described earlier is focused on the soldiers of her home country. It was soldiers who attacked her personally, who in all likelihood killed her father, and whom she perceives as the most prominent threat against her relatives still living in her home country. Her aggression and her wish for revenge, which comes to the forefront in the dream, are, therefore, clearly understandable. It is not always possible to arrive at such clear correlations between the provocateur and the target of the relative's aggressions. Sometimes the aggression is directed directly or indirectly at themselves in especially painful ways.

Very memorable in this context I found a dream of Mr A.:

> In his dream he sees the dictator who is in power in his home country, and whom Mr A. makes responsible for the persecution of his family and the torture he himself had to endure. The hitherto suppressed aggression comes out in the dream. Mr A. ties the dictator down, pulls a bag over his head and beats him over and over again until the body before him is bathed in blood and does not move anymore. At this point in the dream, Mr A. experiences a feeling of great power and relief—finally he was able to avenge his wife's death and his own torture. The face of the dictator is covered by the bag. When Mr A. pulls off the bag of the now lifeless body, it is not the dictator who he sees, but—to his extreme shock—his own mother.

To me, this dream seems very dense in its imagery and so fitting to the life story and the sufferings of the client. At the time of this dream, his mother has been gone for five months. She has 'disappeared', and he does not think that she is still alive. Imagining her alive means imagining her suffering—but her death is too terrible an option.

He feels responsible for her 'disappearance'. Maybe she might have been spared that fate, had he not, after years of imprisonment and cruel and brutal torture, fled the country. His powerlessness and anger become visible in the dream: The hated dictator should die, and he should die in terrible ways, like all the people whom Mr A. has watched die in prison. This is his desire for justice and also for revenge. In his dream he can fulfil this wish.

But then his fear for his family and his gnawing feeling of guilt towards his family come in: The small triumph of having successfully fled and thereby evaded the dictator and survived is contrasted by his simultaneous impotency when it comes to protecting his family. In his dream the fulfilment of his wish suddenly turns against his family, and it is thereby marked by his feelings of grief and guilt. The dream contains another element though: In this dream his mother dies by his hand. Worst for him would be, if she is being held in the same prison in which he was treated in the most inhuman of ways. Compared to this it would be better if she were dead. But can he really wish one of his closest relatives dead? The aggression he feels towards the dictator and his tormentors turns into a boomerang reaction against himself. But maybe the guilt and anger are easier to bear than the feeling of being totally helpless and powerless against the supremacy of the inhuman dictatorship.

For Mr A. it was a relief to be able to speak aloud about this distressing dream in a therapy session. It needed the neutral space and the professional setting in connection with the secure counselling relationship to be able to do so. It would have been impossible for Mr A. to tell his friends, let alone his relatives, about this dream.

Therefore, it is very important to offer this safe space in counselling/therapy, vital to create a place where issues that are so intrinsically connected with feelings of confusion, shame and guilt can nevertheless be addressed.

After discussing and interpreting the dream together, Mr A. is relieved. His feelings are now comprehensible for him and, therefore, not as threatening anymore.

Yes, it is okay for him to be angry and aggressive after all that he has gone through. Yes, it is reasonable to be very worried for his 'disappeared' mother. In the therapeutic supervision, he is not left alone with these feelings. The next step we take is the discussion of how he can transform the energy that comes with his anger into something meaningful and useful; Mr A. wants to become involved in the support of young people living as refugees and wants to help them towards a good education. A couple of months later he becomes a member of an organisation of exiled, which advocated a peaceful political change in their home country.

## *Auto-aggression*

Relatives of victims of 'enforced disappearances' often long for death. Attempted suicides and auto-aggressive behaviour in the form of self-injury are common. The pressure and the strain of not being able to do anything about the situation, of having to endure the uncertainty can become so great that physical pain presents a form of relief.

Mr S. has extinguished his burning cigarette 10 times on the back of his hands. If he had had a knife that evening, he would have cut off his arm, he explains in the next therapy session.

Mr D.'s arms are covered in scars from the cuts he himself has made. The urge to hurt himself becomes especially strong when, once again, bombs have rained down on the area of his home, and he does not know whether any of his family members have been hurt or killed.

Thoughts or fantasies of suicide are mentioned by the majority of clients who have relatives that have 'disappeared'. They are characterised by a certain longing. Maybe there are answers to the 'disappearances' to be found on the other side, and maybe there is a place there, where one is reunited with the beloved person. It is not so much a desire to be dead, but rather a manifestation of the wish to have a life together with the 'disappeared' relative, that lies at the bottom of these suicidal ideations.

Thoughts of suicide are taken very seriously in the psychotherapeutic process, and they are analysed in detail: What lies behind this idea? If, as it is mostly the case, it is the dream of a better life without pain and desperation, then the next step in the psychosocial counselling/therapy is to try to find ways of realising this dream at least to some extent in this world already. Sometimes the auto-aggression needs to be controlled from the outside in order that the brunt of the current onslaught of despair be absorbed to some degree. At the end of the session, an agreement is made that until the next session (which is usually in a week) there will be no aggressive or auto-aggressive behaviour. This is either signed, or the therapist and client shake hands on it. By having the therapist/counsellor take over the control over this, the suffering client, overwhelmed by his/her situation, is relieved of some of the burden. By limiting the agreement to a week, the time span remains manageable. It is, of course, important in this phase to renew the agreement every week, until self-control and the will to live have sufficiently been restored for the client to autonomously choose life again.

## Aggression towards Others

In the work after the tsunami in different parts of Sri Lanka together with a number of teams of psychosocial workers, we all noticed a surprising number of parents who behaved aggressively towards their healthy surviving children. This corresponds with the general experiences in psychotherapeutic settings after traumatic situations. Mr S. was not capable of controlling his aggressions:

> I suggest Mr S. to immediately commit himself to a psychiatric hospital, as at this point he had no control over himself of his actions towards his son. He tells me that on the previous evening he beat up his son. Before that he had never laid hands on any of his children. He was horrified by his actions: He had caused harm to the only child still left to him.
>
> Mr S. was able to agree to the hospitalisation because we made sure that his son would be put into family-based childcare and there be protected from violence. This was important for the father. He felt that at this point this arrangement would surely be better for the son, since he as father could not control himself.

When it comes to aggressive behaviour towards children or other weaker members of the community it is vital to quickly establish ways of controlling the aggression—even more so than it is when dealing with auto-aggression. The aggression in and of itself is understandable in the light of the traumatisation and must be seen as a normal reaction—nevertheless rules need to be laid down as to how this aggression is dealt with. This external control of aggressions is necessary to make it possible to get out of this downward spiral of violence.

External control of aggressions here means having a clear agreement of non-violence that is accepted as being in force till the next meeting (see above).

Others, less harmful outlets for the aggression, can be found:

1. Sports can help to release the built-up energy. Many types of sport actually require a certain degree of aggression (one team wants exactly what the other one is trying to prevent). Ideally external control of aggression is ensured by the presence of a referee.
2. Screaming can be helpful. There are few places, however, where our society permits adults to really shout out loud. Some clients have found it helpful to go to places that are loud by nature, such as waterfalls or railway bridges, and there scream into the existing deafening noise. Parents can turn that into a game with their children.
3. Hitting is allowed—as long as it is not a living being that receives the blow. But beating a pillow or other soft object is okay. Sometimes it is

helpful to have a specific anger-pillow or ball. Sponge balls find application here: These balls, made of soft foam material, can be thrown to the floor or against the wall, can be crunched up, torn apart, etc.

A bit more violent, but still definitely preferable to hurting a child, is the smashing of dishes by throwing them against the wall or floor. In the counselling or therapy sessions all these ways of channelling the aggression can be discussed, and the client can take stock of their feelings towards them. In the days following the session, the client can try out those that felt to be the best. If the strategy is effective, it is maintained. If not, then another form of controlling the aggression is searched for.

4. Women from more traditionally oriented cultural backgrounds often do not do sports at all, so we tried to come up with an outlet for their aggression that comes from their own sphere of living. Almost all cultures have recipes for simple dough to make bread or strudel from. These mixtures of flour and water need to be worked with quite a lot of force in order to turn out well. We make use of this kneading and beating to relieve the pent-up aggressions—although it should be said that it is better if this dough, full of anger and despair, are thrown out afterwards, and not baked into bread for the family.

This list of possible outlets for aggression is by no means extensive and can be supplemented in all creativity. What is important is that the clients understand that their aggressions are a normal reaction to the sufferings they have been put through. It is just the expression of the aggression that needs to be controlled so that it does not then in turn cause more suffering and pain.

## The Difficulty of Entering into New Relationships

For the relatives or 'disappeared' people, entering into a new relationship is very challenging. For one thing, the loyalty and devotion to the 'disappeared' needs to stay intact, and a new relationship might pose a threat to it. For another, a new relationship brings with it the danger of another loss.

A new man has entered Mrs F.'s life a couple of months ago. He invites her and her daughter to his home. He cooks for them, picks the daughter up from school, helps her with her homework, accompanies Mrs F. to various government agencies and gives her advice on social issues. To his wish for a more intimate relationship Mrs F. reacts with excuses and stalling words.

When he suddenly proposes to her, Mrs F. is greatly distressed and irritated. Despite having entered into a life partnership with him, she is by no means willing to call it that. After all, she is a faithful wife to her 'disappeared' husband.

Her inner ambivalence becomes apparent in this: She keeps idealising her husband and wants to remain in close connection with him. At the same time she is glad about the friendship and help she is receiving from her new male friend. As long as this friendship has no label, she can manage the balancing act between her loyalty to her 'disappeared' husband and the partnership with the new man. Once she is required to give this partnership a certain status (marriage), the ambivalent balance can no longer be maintained. Mrs F. breaks off all contact with the man, which results in an enormous amount of additional stress for the working single mother. She feels lost and abandoned during this time, despite her assurances in the therapy sessions that she could not have acted in any other way.

When the friend relents after a couple of weeks, she is more than willing to accept his renewed friendship. Both act as if the proposal had never happened. In the therapy sessions, Mrs F. tries to hide the fact that she and the friend have reconciled. When it comes up nevertheless, she tries to trivialise it and justify it as being for the good of her daughter. 'He wanted to see my daughter again, and the child needs someone to help her with her homework, after all.'

None of my clients whose partners have 'disappeared' have a new partner. Most of them live alone and are not even willing to permit questions about the possible wish for a new relationship. All new potential partners are measured against the idealised image of the 'disappeared' spouse, which they can, of course, never live up to, being real human beings of flesh and bone.

Clients whose parents and/or siblings have 'disappeared' also find it difficult to enter into new relationships. It seems as if the experience of having a beloved person suddenly 'disappear' is such a shattering one that any deep forms of emotional attachment are henceforth to be feared. In order to make sure to never have to experience such pain again, close relationships are avoided from the start.

Relationships that have a clearly defined form, like that between the therapist and the client, can serve as the stable secure frame that makes it possible to relearn having a secure relationship and to develop anew the trust in the fact that people do not generally 'disappear' but show up at the time and place agreed upon. Keeping the intervals between the sessions regular is, therefore, a factor that can increase the feeling of security.

Every Wednesday, young B. comes to therapy on time. He sits down in his chair and waits for the therapist to speak. Mostly, he answers question only in brief. 'I don't feel like talking' is what he says again and again. To the question whether we should conclude the therapy, or have longer intervals between the sessions he reacts alarmed. No, he really wants to come every week. He looks forward to Wednesdays for days, as this is when he will see the therapist again. 'It makes me feel less sad', he says.

Before a break in the routine of the sessions because of, for example, a holiday or a journey, the fear of once again losing a person who one has grown familiar to is often addressed. I tell my clients who have lost a relative because of a 'disappearance' why I will not be there for some time, and also, if I go on a trip, where this trip will take me. Sometimes we have a look at the globe and pinpoint exactly where I will be. Through this, we establish that, despite me not being in the familiar place, I am nevertheless in a real geographic location in this world. If at all possible, I write postcards from that place, in order to underline my presence there.

After the therapist has been absent for a couple of weeks, an interesting phenomenon can be observed: All clients keep the first appointment we have. The week after, though, is characterised by an unusual number of cancellations. This seems like reclamation of autonomy in a relationship. After having assured themselves that the other has returned safely, the clients show that they have the freedom to cancel an appointment as well.

Ideally, the relationship between the client and the counsellor/therapist can serve as a model for the safety and stability of relationships between people in general which can then be transferred onto other relationships and partnerships as well.

## Blocking out the Unbearable

Mrs K. comes to the fifth therapy session. She talks about the events of last week, spent in her new home, and about her feelings about the goings on in her life. Only when I ask about her relatives does she mention her son, who is still in the home country. She tells me that he 'disappeared' five days ago and that she is worried that he might have been taken by a certain militant group. This particular group is said to be especially cruel and is known to torture and kill their hostages. The fate of most of those taken by this group remains forever uncertain, they remain 'disappeared'.

I, the therapist, am still processing this information and, therefore, say nothing at that time. Before I can respond, Mrs K. starts talking about her living situation in Austria again, peppering me with questions and asking me to help her in these social problems. My attempts to stir the conversation back towards her son are blatantly ignored; she sticks to the issue of the problems with the flat in Austria, the country of asylum.

Only in my analysis of the therapy session do I realise how willingly I followed Mrs K. back to the topic of everyday life in Austria: I, the helper, who does not even know Mrs K.'s son personally, did also not want to be confronted with the magnitude of helplessness that comes with the 'disappearance' of the son. Additionally, I tried to evade feeling how powerless I am to help Mrs K. in this. Not by chance the substitute topic was one where clear interventions on my part are possible. With regards to her housing situation I can support her in an immediately apparent way through a couple of phone calls—here neither the client nor I am helpless—quite contrary to situation of the 'disappearance' of her son.

This example case shows a pattern that is well known in the work with relatives of 'disappeared' people: The client's helplessness is noticeable to everyone; the helper is not exempt from it. This situation cannot be softened by means of therapeutic theories or techniques. The tension is more often than not diffused by the client him/herself—he/she looks for another topic to talk about in order to break through the feeling of helplessness.

This might have been the only form in which Mrs K., and the therapist as well, could cope with the sheer incomprehensibility of the information. Sometimes it seems to be enough to have someone to confide the terrible news to. What is important is for the therapist to reflect on the therapeutic relationship. Consequently, from then on, very consciously I started to ask Mrs K. about her 'disappeared' son at the end of each session, if she had not mentioned him before. Most of the times, she would only state in brief that there was no news about his whereabouts, sometimes she expanded a bit on the topic.

After about a month, we have a longer talk about the son, in which she tells me of the boy's gentleness, and of how much it had hurt having to separate from him. At the end of the session we sum up how the mother is feeling, now that she has talked about the son. She feels sad and worried, but also a bit relieved. We open the window and finish the session by doing some breathing exercises.

The room in which the therapy is held is a place where both, talking and silence about the 'disappeared' relative are possible. The therapist/counsellor creates the secure frame for both.

## Psychosomatics as Symbols and Forms of Connectedness

During the first interview, Mrs J. gave an account of the deaths of her elder children and the 'disappearance' of her younger son. Ever since, however, she has not been willing to talk about them. But she comes to every session in severe pain: at one time she feels like her head is going to burst, the next time her back hurts terribly and then she has severe abdominal pains. Really, her entire body is just one big accumulation of pain. Her desperate search for the right doctor, the one who will understand what is going on with her, the one that will give her the right medicine against all that pain, remains without success. The visits to the doctors are important to her, though: they keep her busy and determine her everyday life. Therefore, they help her to focus on her own situation in the here and now, and not on the pain that comes with confronting herself with the children she has lost. By constantly being in severe pain, she shows her solidarity to her 'disappeared' son, who might be suffering at that time as well.

In this situation of acute grief and uncertainty, psychotherapy constitutes only a part of the medical system for the client. Even the most tentative of remarks that she must be feeling the grief and fear for her children has to be blocked by her at this stage in the therapy. Nevertheless, the sessions do her good; she thanks me after every session for the relief she has experienced.

Psychotherapy plays an important part in this situation, as it provides someone who, in a sense, 'co-endures' and 'co-perseveres', who is there with the clients as they are hanging on, and also someone who is there to bear witness.

In my own countertransference I can often feel the severity of these personal sufferings, the heaviness of their lot. I can observe myself breathing a sigh of relief when such sessions are cancelled, and also when one of them is over. But precisely here we can see the importance of consistently keeping up these therapy/counselling sessions: At least for a while the sheer unbearable burden is eased a little, as there is someone who is willing to help carry it.

Mrs I. has had a certain medical treatment, but is very much unsatisfied by the result. She still suffers from severe pain; she must have been poorly cared for by the doctors. She shows her anger and frustration with the, to her mind, incompetent doctors. When I carefully point out her abilities of self-healing, and tentatively address that she herself plays a major part in the experience of her pain, she rejects this, explaining that previous treatments had led to much better results. At a later point in the therapy session, the subject of her family comes up. Mrs I. tells me that Tuesday was a very hard day, as it was the seventh anniversary of her sister's 'disappearance'. Mrs I. blames herself for her sister being taken away. My client feels that she, as the oldest, had been responsible for her younger siblings.

For the therapist, the mentioning of this terrible anniversary makes the connection that had previously been unclear suddenly evident. The intensification of the pain is closely connected to the feelings of guilt, fear and the loss of control. At the same time, the pain is a way of showing solidarity with the 'disappeared' person.

This strategy of avoiding grief comes up in cases where a particularly traumatic death needs to be blocked out, as well as in cases of 'disappeared' relatives. An often bizarre symptom plagues the relative and all medical examinations remain inconclusive. No doctor can find the underlying cause for the physical problems. The psychotherapeutic process takes a long time as well until it leads the participants to an understanding of the symptoms.

In the case of Mrs I., the connection between the acute pain and the 'disappearance' of a beloved person could be made after a number of inquiries on the part of the therapist. The pain, which was the focus of the particular session, did not have to be symbolised in physical symptoms anymore, but could, by talking about the anniversary, be identified as the grief for the sister who was no longer present in Mrs I.'s life.

## *Eating Disorders*

Eating disorders stand in close connection with psychosomatic symptoms. They often occur in adolescents, such as the 17-year-old client of mine named N.

Young N. often really forgets to eat something. In order to get to the bottom of this matter, I change the setting of our psychotherapeutic sessions. Before each session I put a plate of cookies on the table and offer them to N. She eats like a normal—actually really hungry—teenager; by the end of the session not one cookie is left on the plate.

I interpret her behaviour as a form of regression. N. wants to be cooked for, wants to be fed. This not-eating is also a form of mourning for her; shared family meals were a central element in the family life she has lost. I make use of the situation to help strengthen her memories and her resources. N. is able to draw up a vivid picture of a family dinner. In this exercise of imagination I invite her to remember the room in all its details: the smells and the sounds as well as the images. N. is very relaxed during this session. She can describe exactly what the mother had prepared, how the family gathered around the table, etc.

The care of the two maternal figures present—the therapist and the interpreter—quite obviously does her good. With the help of a diary, N. begins to record her eating habits, making sure that she eats at least one hot meal and one small snack every day. Through this, she also grows up a little bit—she herself takes responsibility for her wellbeing.

## Fear and Worry as Forms of Connectedness

Mrs L. is mortally afraid that something might happen to her children. Leaving them at the kindergarten and school every day is a real effort for her. She uses even the smallest indispositions as an excuse to keep the children home for the day. She does think the teachers are capable of taking good care of her children, but the strange fear, as Mrs L. describes it, does simply not let go of her.

About a year into the psychotherapeutic treatment it becomes clear where this extreme fear stems from: Mrs L.'s first child 'disappeared' 12 years ago. This fact comes up in therapy quite by accident and not via any conscious effort on the client's part.

From then on, the therapy is often about giving this fear a clear name and a clear place: This fear cannot help to save her first child. Therefore, Mrs L. needs to learn to accept the factuality of the 'disappearance'. Gradually, the grieving process begins: The terrible loss of the child needs to be addressed as such, it needs to be mourned and accepted, in order to free the relationship with the younger children from the burdens of the past.

Calling the terrible events by their names proves to bring relief to the client: The 'disappearance' of the son in the middle of the turmoil of war lies so far in the past that his death must be assumed as almost certain. The relationship between the mother and the child has been broken in any case.

The relationship with her younger children on the other hand is real and certain. It has never been under such a threat as that with the first child had been: Mrs L. lives in a different time in different country, and this country is not in a state of war. She is encouraged by the therapist to tell the other children about their big brother. It takes a while until she decides to do so. It turns out that she can take pleasure in answering her younger children's question about their brother and about the times she had spent with him. In telling about his life and their shared experiences, her positive memories are reactivated.

In the course of a time-intensive therapeutic process, Mrs L. learns to mourn the loss of her eldest child, and through this to also let go of it. At the same time she manages to see her younger children as the autonomous young persons they are. By now the youngest child is older than her oldest son had been at the time of his 'disappearance'.

When it comes to symptoms that apparently have no medical cause and sometimes even strike us as bizarre, it is often necessary to learn more about the client's history. As was the case with Mrs L., the underlying cause for great pain can be a traumatic experience that has been split off from the rest and completely suppressed.

## Delayed Rituals

The significance of rituals for the relatives of the 'disappeared' plays a major role in the psychotherapeutic work.

After an attempted suicide, Mr V. is committed to a psychiatric hospital. The next two years consist of frequent alternations between the psychiatry ward and a residential home for men. He can no longer imagine a life without sedatives and sleeping pills. At the same time he sees himself as stigmatised and debased because of his dependence on the medication. His studies, which he had pursued with much success, belong to another world now; for Mr V. they are no longer real. His desired aim for the therapy is to be able to get by without the medication. It takes a very long time until he feels safe enough in the therapeutic relationship to be able to talk about the news of his family's deaths. He does not know the details of what exactly happened in his remote home country, but the fantasies of what might have happened regularly come to haunt him. His recurring nightmares become the focus of our sessions. It seems to me as if every night brings him the same suffering and mortal pain that he has to live through together with his relatives.

Since I do not know the mourning rituals of his home country, I ask Mr V. about the traditions of the country. At first he ignores the question. After some more careful nudges, however, he does seem willing to talk about them. When I address the topic anew, Mr V. responds and paints a vivid image of the Buddhist burial rituals in the immediate vicinity of his home. For once, his words are not marred by despair and hopelessness in the way I see so often when he describes of the recurring images in his dreams, but are characterised by his gratitude towards the relative and by the hope for a better life after death. From this time onwards, the nightmares dwindle and the fear of dying in a similar manner decreases significantly.

Rituals can be created and performed in the context of the therapy. Another option is to work in an encouraging way towards the clients turning to their own religious or cultural communities and asking for the performance of the appropriate ritual.

In the case of Mr V., I first tried to gain access to the ethnological information about the traditional forms of burial typical for Mr V.'s home country. Later I realised, however, that the individual memories of such a ritual and, based on them, the symbolic image of the burial and with it the act of saying goodbye are much more important than any ethnological authenticity.

While Mr V. talked about the traditional rituals in general, the process became much more concrete in the case of young N.:

> In the therapy work with N., we try to, in our thoughts, hold the funeral for her mother and father. N. has written obituaries and epitaphs for her parents. She reads them out and explains why she has chosen to write the text for her father the way she did. When she reads out what her mother's obituary should say, she starts to cry. Afterwards she calms down though. She tells me what the funeral would have been like: Who would have come, what prayers

would have been said, who would have prepared what dishes, etc. This makes it possible for her to cry for her parents and to, at least symbolically, erect a headstone for them. This therapy session is characterised by intense sadness and seriousness. Nevertheless, in the end we all experience a feeling of relief. As she says goodbye, N. even smiles.

Sometimes the right ritual for a 'disappeared' relative can arise in an intercultural, interreligious setting.

> Mr T. is fascinated, when he sees a Pietà, a statue of Maria, cradling the dead Jesus in her lap, in a Catholic hospital. The mother in pain, holding her dead son, embodies his own pain and his longing for his own mother. In his conversation with the hospital's pastor he asks for details about the background of this image, and talks about his family. The priest invites him to join them for mass as a guest. There, he prays specially for all the deceased and 'disappeared' relatives of T.'s family. Despite this religion not being his own, Mr T. feels understood, accepted and comforted by this.

Rituals are psychologically of immense importance. They help to accept deaths, losses and 'disappearances'. They mark the transition from the time together with the beloved person to the time without him or her. Therefore, the rituals should be performed at any rate, ideally in the familiar way intended by the respective social community. If this is impossible, then the rituals should be made up for at a later point in time. For 'disappearances' specifically there are no known rituals. Therefore, new forms need to be created. In many cases, slight modifications are enough; elements from other traditions or religions can be adapted, or a completely new ritual may be invented.

# 6
# The Family and 'Enforced Disappearances'

Boss (2006: 76) aptly describes the chaos that characterises the family structure after a 'disappearance': 'With ambiguous loss, the family's identity becomes confused because one of its members is neither in nor out of the system....'

This chapter mainly deals with the difficulties that arise within a family in response to the 'enforced disappearance' of one of its members, and with how they can be supported through psychosocial counselling.

## Taking Over Roles

In times of crisis, children are especially focused on the parent or parents who are with them. How their parents react has a strong influence on the children's social and especially their psychological means of coping with the situation:

> ... children tend to reflect the affects and deepest expressions of stress and loss within the family and are highly sensitive to the conflict and distress, as well as coping abilities and dysfunctions of their parents. Children with parents who are able to be supportive and capable, even in the midst of profound devastation and chaos, are tied to the resourcefulness of their parents and are thus less vulnerable to the negative impact of trauma.... Unfortunately, in a family where a parent has been killed, the surviving parent or caretaker may be experiencing deep bereavement, making him or her emotionally unavailable to their children. (Straussner & Phillips 2004: 27)

Parents can be so singularly focused on the 'disappeared' or deceased family member that they become oblivious to the presence of their healthy child. The resulting negligence can naturally be understood as a form of aggression, but it usually has its origins in the parents being overwhelmed emotionally by the severe traumatisation and grief. During psychosocial counselling or therapy, a father or mother can address the desperation and distress and regress a little bit for a restricted period of time. There, they can permit themselves to show their own helplessness and cry, and be comforted in a mothering way by the counsellor/therapist. This helps many parents to then fulfil their part of the responsible adult, the father or mother. Individual therapy sessions with traumatised fathers or mothers, therefore, always benefit the child as well.

If the family has lost the father or mother, or both parents, because of an 'enforced disappearance', other family members tend to take on the role of the 'disappeared' person in a similar manner as after the death of a parent.

Often, it is the eldest daughter or son who takes on the part of the parent. Not only do they feel responsible for their siblings, but they also try to be a substitute partner for the remaining parent. This, of course, places an excessive demand on the child, which can manifest itself in different ways.

In the case of 13-year-old C., this kind of overburdening shows itself in strong aggression.

> When his mother gets into an argument with one of the male neighbours about a minor issue, C. gets hold of a knife and threatens the man. Little C., looking even younger than he is, knew no other way of protecting his mother. In the residential home they live at a commotion ensues which the resident advisor informs me about.
>
> During our next therapy session, I ask C. whether anything noteworthy has been going on. He declines. Only when I tell him about having received a phone call from the residential home, he begins to relate the event. On the one hand he is embarrassed about what has happened, and about the stir he has caused, on the other hand he defends his actions as having been necessary—after all, he needs to take care of his mother.

For young E., the consequences of this confusion arising from the change in roles were especially dramatic and destructive.

> After the 'disappearance' of his father, the then 13-year-old E. took on the task of standing by his mother, even making decisions regarding his four younger siblings. He was encouraged in this by his uncles and aunts, who praised him for his mature behaviour. The shock of the adults is great when, at the age of 16, he is arrested for a series of robberies he has committed together with a gang of youths. A couple of months earlier, his mother has met a man and married him—without really talking about it with E. E. is angry at his mother, who, in E.'s opinion, is abandoning the father and reverting to treating E. like a child again after years of him acting the

part of the substitute partner. E. has so lost his place in the family. Unfortunately the safety and security that he finds in the gang is of a very destructive nature.

The psychosocial work with E. is made difficult by his prison sentence. In his case it is of vital importance that the family is involved in the work. The mother needs to acknowledge what E. has done for his family over the last years, and talk with him about what special place he still has in the structure of the family. It is also necessary that the stepfather is perceptive regarding E.'s needs and pays attention to when and where the adolescent feels threatened or pushed to the side because there is a new man in the house. He needs to see where he can take some of the load off the boy's shoulders. The mother and the stepfather need to create a space for E. where he can catch up on some of the time of being a child unburdened by adult responsibilities, which he had left prematurely.

It is not only the immediate change in the roles of the family members that provides challenges and difficulties to the relatives of the 'disappeared', but also the overburdening situation can show its agonising effects for years to come, as the case of N. shows.

N. had to act as surrogate mother for her siblings. Her dreams of a high-school degree and subsequent studies at the university had come to an abrupt end. She could not completely live up to this new role though, and is consequently plagued by guilt. She is afraid to find her siblings again, only to be blamed for having left them. She also feels guilty with regards to her mother, to whom N. had promised to look after the younger children.

N. is haunted by this guilt in her dreams, one of which she found particularly upsetting. Her mother came to her. First she acted in a loving, motherly fashion, but then she asked about the whereabouts of the other children. Since N. does not know, she could not answer her mother.

To the therapist's assurance that N. has fulfilled the promise she had given to her mother, that she has done nothing wrong, N. reacts with relief. It is not sufficient, however, to hear this only once. Again and again throughout the therapy N. asks me, the therapist, if I think that she should have done more for her younger siblings, and is relieved to always receive the same answer.

As a therapist, I slip into a mother-like role for N., relieving her of some of the responsibility she feels burdened with. This way, N. is allowed to assume a role with regards to her feelings towards her siblings that is more adequate for her age.

## Children as Carriers of Symptoms

The strain the entire family is under because of the 'disappearance' of one of its members leads to tensions in the individual relationships. Important matters are not discussed anymore; everyday problems seem too banal to be solved and consequently grow into insurmountable barriers.

Sometimes, the communicative channels are reactivated if the family is faced with a problem that concerns all its members and, therefore, reunites them. In many cases, this problem takes the form of the ostentatious behaviour of a child, or a child's sudden illness. It can be the case that the most sensitive family member 'sacrifices' himself or herself for the family. By displaying severe physical symptoms or behavioural abnormalities, which necessitate that all family members take care of the child, the family is pushed towards becoming a communicative, functional entity again.

During therapy or counselling it is, therefore, necessary to be aware of the entire family and understand their situation. Is the alleged patient really the ill person who needs treatment, or is he/she merely the carrier of symptoms for a vulnerable, compromised family system? Following this, a decision can be made if the situation calls for individual therapy and/or support for the entire family unit (Becker 1992).

## Regressive Behaviour

The stress a 'disappearance' of one of its own puts on the family is often answered with regressive behaviour by the children affected.

> In Sri Lanka, a woman talks about the great problems she has with her niece. The 10-year-old girl has been living with her ever since her mother passed away half-a-year ago. The father of the girl had 'disappeared' one and a half years before the mother's death. The woman tells us that her niece is a well-behaved, obedient child, but the situation becomes difficult whenever the aunt leaves her. The girl clutches to her and desperately implores her aunt to stay or to take her with her. Every separation from her new attachment figure, no matter how short, throws the girl into panic.

In light of the girl's previous experiences, her behaviour is quite understandable. Twice already she has had to go through the experience of a beloved person suddenly not being there anymore. Her fear of losing her aunt as well is an unbearable one. Therefore, her dramatically regressive, infant-like behaviour needs to be understood and respected. At the same time it is necessary to get through to her and give her the necessary feeling of safety and restore her trust in human relationships as quickly as possible and in a way that is suitable for her age.

The girl need to be given a lot of information: Where does the aunt go, what does she do there, who is responsible for her during the duration of her aunt's absence and who will respond to her needs. It is especially vital to establish the time of the aunt's return. This should be done with a buffer for possible delays in mind, so that the child gets to experience the joy of an early reunion rather than the fear of a belated return.

'Clinging' to an attachment figure is one of the most common forms of regressive behaviour in traumatised children, especially if one or both parents have died or 'disappeared'. Other typical forms of behaviour are enuresis (bed-wetting), eating disorders (see also Chapter 5), mutism and incessant crying. In the therapy or psychosocial counselling, one has to try to find the purpose of the respective symptom and accept the child in its distress, and together with the child come up with a plan for future actions and behaviour. Adult attachment figures need to be coached in this direction as well: Scolding the child or making it feel ashamed only increase the child's psychological stress. This will only result in a relocation of symptoms, not in an improvement or normalisation. Even if punishment results in the symptom to subside, it is usually replaced by another one.

Adults should show understanding for the child and its ways of expressing its desperation, and try to improve the situation in cooperation with the child.

Psychosocial interventions and therapies not only have the afflicted child at its centre of attention but also involve the parents and other attachment figures.

## The Desire to Protect the Children

In situations where all feelings of security collapse with the 'disappearance' of a family member, where one's whole world is suddenly called into question, many would like to protect their children from the terrible changes. Consequentially, the children are either lied to, or their questions are left unanswered. These well-intentioned measures often result in the complete opposite: Left all alone with their questions and fears the children are at the mercy of their feelings of uncertainty much more than if they were made privy to the scraps of information available. At the same time, the formerly secure relationship to the adult attachment figure is drastically called into question, since the person is obviously giving them answers that are untrue.

> Mrs M. has told her children that her father is just hiding out at his comrades' place, and that he will rejoin them soon. Yet the truth is that he has 'disappeared' shortly after having arranged for his family to flee the country. Mrs M. is hurt by the aggressive behaviour of her son, who accuses her of not taking care of the family as well as the father would have had. During one of their arguments, the son even blames the mother for the father's absence. Mrs M. is deeply hurt by this. She feels abandoned by her husband and misunderstood by her children.
>
> To my question, whether it might not be better to tell the children the truth she reacts with consternation. She states that she does not want to encumber her children even further. I explain that it is likely that the children are already aware of the fact that there is something wrong with their father. Therefore, the lack of information is an additional burden that heightens their feelings of insecurity.
>
> Mrs M. promises to think about it. I offer one of our therapy sessions as the time and place for the talk with the children, should this make Mrs M. feel a bit more secure.
>
> For six weeks Mrs M. struggles with the decision whether or not to share what little she knows about the current whereabouts of her husband. Then she tells me almost in passing that her youngest child has calmed down a bit. Only upon my enquiry as to a possible reason for this change does she tell me that she has talked with the children about the 'disappearance' of their father.

Bittenbinder (2000) describes a similar situation that arose in the course of a therapy. A woman from Iran feared that her husband might have been executed, since she had not heard from him in a whole year. The woman felt that she could not talk to her eight-year-old son about this, because she wanted to protect him. In this case it did become possible, after long talks with the mother, to provide the son with this important information. Bittenbinder describes the eventual conversation with the son. She tells us that it started out with a dialogue between the son and the therapist, which helped the mother realise how hard the uncertainty was on her son, and how many thoughts about his father's situation have been weighting on the boy's mind. It became clear to her that suspecting terrible things to have happened but not knowing for certain was putting a lot of stress on him. This realisation led to the mother gradually involving herself in the conversation and talking to her son. In words appropriate to the boy's age, the mother explained about the events in their home country and carefully confronted the boy with her worries about the possibility of the father's death (Bittenbinder 2000: 43).

These kinds of worries taking place in the mind of a young child became apparent in my own psychotherapeutic work as well. In a case, my client's husband had died at the local hospital of a severe chronic illness.

> For months, the widow tells her 5-year-old daughter that her father is still extremely ill and, therefore, in hospital. The excuses for the impossibility of the daughter visiting her father become more and more intricate. After about half a year, the mother overhears a conversation the daughter has with a child of her own age. To the question where her father is, the daughter of Mrs Z. answers that he is dead. The mother is surprised and confused. When she talks to her daughter, the girl's questions and the way she talks imply that she thinks her father to be still alive.

The five-year-old seems to have learned to protect her mother. By asking questions about the father, both of them can retain the illusion of the father still being alive. In the same way that the mother keeps the father's death a secret, the little daughter keeps her knowledge of the father's death from her mother.

In this case, there is clear proof of the father's death. But this example shows especially clearly, how tempting it is in cases of 'enforced disappearances', where no such evidence exists, to lose oneself in hopeful fantasies and illusion. For adults, these stories they tell their children, in which they themselves start to believe more and more, become islands of hope. For the children, though, they are a source of great confusion. They can feel the ambivalence between the appeasing words and the adult's behaviour together with the time of waiting that gets longer and longer. Consequently, the children are no longer able to talk with these trusted persons about their own fears.

In some cases, the fate of the family is so turbulent and dramatic that this kind of 'protection' of the child, constructed and retained through immense effort, breaks apart. In the case of Mr S., it becomes possible for him to talk with his eight-year-old son before being admitted to a hospital.

Mr S. talks in our presence—that of both, a therapist and an interpreter—about the 'disappearances' in their family. He tries to explain in simple terms what he knows, and why the family has reached such a low point and is in urgent need of help. This conversation between father and son takes place shortly before Mr S. is committed to a hospital. The boy, who already has had to live through the 'disappearance' of two siblings in their home country, the family's escape from there, the separation from the mother and the remaining siblings, now has to say goodbye to his last remaining family member, his father.

Although this goes far beyond the scope of our sessions, we make lots of room and time for this goodbye—at least this time the family members should know of each other's situation. We set all wheels in motion to make sure that both know where the other will be, and that they can always get in touch with each other by phone. The son walks his father to the ambulance where the two say their goodbyes. Afterwards, the therapist and the interpreter together bring the eight-year-old to an assisted living community for children in times of crisis. There, they have a long talk with the pedagogue on duty, giving the boy time to have a look around and get to know some of the others living there, while lending him safety through their familiar presence.

The surviving family members are oftentimes not able to communicate about what has happened. They do not share their pain and despair. The belief that in their silence they are protecting the other results in a family life characterised by isolation and loneliness.

It takes a professional from outside the family—like a psychological counsellor—to make it possible to talk about one's emotions.

## Aggression towards Weaker Family Members

Clients who have survived flagrant violations of human rights are often perceived as silent and passive when in public. Since we strongly sympathise with them, we tend to dismiss all aspects of aggression. But where human beings have had to experience violence with no means of reacting to it in an adequate way, especially if the perpetrators were not even punished, there is a lot of pent-up aggression to be found. The targets of this aggression are often the weaker members of the family. If addictive substances like alcohol are used as a means of self-medication, the result is often not the intended calming of the nerves, but a bout of aggression that breaks through to the surface—and hits those who happen to be nearest. In families with severely traumatic experiences, domestic violence is common.

> Mrs W., a single mother, has, through sessions with her counsellor and talks with her children's teachers, learned to control her aggressive tendencies. In the course of the psychotherapy, her dismay and her shame regarding her behaviour come up. She is extremely troubled by having hit her then very young children. By now she has learned to keep herself under control. Sometimes she still yells at the children, but then she is brought up short by the fear she can see in their faces.

In our therapy sessions, Mrs W. receives recognition for having been able to stop her aggressive behaviour towards her children. She has every right to experience anger due to all the traumatic experiences she has had to suffer through. But, as she rightly realised, it was not her children who brought about this aggression. Under no circumstances must they become the target of her aggression. She is confirmed in her new treatment of the children and encouraged to keep it up. As a further way of reducing her aggressive tendency, Mrs W. selects one of her pillows to be the one she can hit, ball up or throw on the ground in those moments when her anger needs an outlet. Since she has this pillow, she actually hardly needs to use it though, as Mrs W. tells me in one of our sessions.

Attempts of suicide or vocalised suicidal ideations on the part of a parent are experienced as extreme threats by the children. Being confronted with them constitutes an extreme form of aggression towards the child.

> We are hosting a small party for our clients and their families. The atmosphere is good, the adults and children present seem to be happy and are enjoying themselves. Suddenly, the 11-year-old daughter of one of my clients comes up to me and asks to talk to me in the adjacent room. She does not seem happy at all, but scared and distraught. From her pocket she takes a small scrap of paper. It turns out to be the label of an insecticide. She tells me that during a quarrel with the father on the previous evening her mother threatened to drink this. Little J. consequently hid the insecticide and all cleaning products that seemed potentially harmful. She is still plagued by fear

though. I promise J. to talk to her mother immediately, and ask the woman to come to join me in the room we had withdrawn to. I sum up what J. has told me and tell the mother about her daughter's fear. The mother is shocked, but also embarrassed about me finding out about this. At the same time she is also relieved that I as a therapist am now involved in the process of finding a solution to the problem. In the presence of the therapist, Mrs W. promises her daughter that she will not kill herself, and also that she will not threaten to do so anymore. If she does not feel well, then she will talk about this with her therapist. J. is assured that she can also call me any time, if she is scared. This way the responsibility is handed over to a therapist, relieving the child of this burden.

In some, even more dramatic, cases, the suicidal intentions and ideations are extended to include the children. If parents see no place for themselves in this world, they often feel that they need to 'take their children along with them'.

A client considered a murder-suicide when one of her children damaged a library book. She feels like she failed in the way she reared her children. She feels that the family honour has been tainted by this act of damaging public property. The solving of this kind of problem was to be her husband's responsibility. My client feels completely overwhelmed by the task. She wants to repair the family honour and make sure it is never endangered again. At the same time she wants to punish her husband for having transferred all his responsibilities to her by 'disappearing'. All this leads to a small mishap almost bringing about the complete eradication of an entire family.

The problem of the library book, incidentally, was easily solved. The attendant in charge at the residential home was able to sort out the issue with the library saving the mother from having to confront herself with the situation. In the next therapy session her longing for death is addressed, as well as the needs of her children. The client becomes aware of her children's strong desire for life and their great hopes and expectations for the future.

In cases such as this one, psychosocial intervention can prevent clients from such panic-driven, sudden, irrational acts. With the help of therapy or counselling, clients can quickly regain control over their own aggressions by establishing anchorage in life through focusing on future prospects.

After the incident described above, the client had begun to gradually trust in her social network, and later in her own abilities. Suicide had ceased to be an option.

## Children Supporting Children

Halpern and Tramontin (2007) point out that the peer group represents an important resource for the re-establishment of normality in the lives of older children and teenagers. Therefore, these children/adolescents should be allowed to have contact with their friends. They also need to be permitted to talk about difficult issues with their peers. Children should not be forced into silence by family taboos, nor should they be burdened by their conscience after having talked about such a tabooed topic with their friends. If the political circumstances make it necessary to keep certain information a secret, then the children need to know that. They still need to have room to talk about these facts with people of their own age (specific friends, cousins).

Especially for the growing number of unaccompanied refugee minors (URM) coming to Europe, the support they receive from their peers is their best resource. Adolescents from countries in Africa or Asia, who have often lost all contact with their families, band together during their flight, forming communities of fate that become their new family unit. It is remarkable how they care for their weaker members in this way. Nevertheless, these children and adolescents do need the support of adult advisors, since the responsibility for the care for their friends often exceeds their financial and emotional resources.

## A Challenge to the Relationship with the Partner

So far, this chapter has mainly addressed the relationship between parents or other adult attachment figures and the children in their charge. The relationship between spouses or partners, however, is also critically endangered by the 'disappearance' of a family member. It is distressing how often it becomes clear during therapy how much about the individual suffering is kept silent between spouses. A stable therapeutic relationship or counselling relationship can often facilitate the very first opportunity for an articulation of the harrowing circumstances. The therapy becomes a possibility to talk to an unbiased but empathetic person who is not part of the social network outside of the actual therapy sessions. These circumstances make it possible to speak about that which seems unspeakable. In the search for a narrative of the encumbering events, the clients sometimes succeed in understanding themselves as well as what has actually happened. Ideally, these revelations can later be shared with the partner.

The mere possibility of talking about the fears and hardships in the context of a therapeutic setting can have a disburdening effect on couples and families. Relatives often report that after the therapeutic sessions the client is calmer and more relaxed and, consequently, the whole family atmosphere is improved.

Psychotherapy and psychological counselling can also, as has been described earlier for the situation of parents and children, open up the floor for conversations about those things that otherwise would have been kept silent between the spouses.

> Mrs P. repeatedly talks about her immense worries regarding her husband. I ask her whether he might want to come along for a joint session one day. For the next appointment they arrive together. They voice the accusations they have harboured for each other. I chairing the session moderate the speed of the exchange, working in breaks that force the two to go slowly. I also insists on the use of respectful language. In this setting, Mr and Mrs P. can actually listen to what the other says. Mr P. relents and shares his feelings of guilt for not being able to take better care of his family, and also his admiration for his wife's vigour and her zest for action. After that, she can in turn tell him how glad she is about his loving caring manner in dealing with their children—something which can by far not be taken for granted considering the patriarchal traditions practiced in his family. Building on this appreciative basis, the two can now also address the grief for the two brothers of Mrs P. who have 'disappeared'. Mr P. can listen to his wife's intense worry for her brothers and to how sad their absence makes her.

The strength of the couple's relationship has been severely shaken by the 'disappearance' of two relatives. Spouses should be able to support each other during such trying times. They need to find ways to bolster as well as comfort each other, if need be with the help of a therapist, counsellor or spiritual director.

## Psychosocial Work with Affected Families

The ability to remain neutral and to avoid over-identification with only one family member is essential to the trauma specialist. Following traumatic events, each family member may have different psychological agendas according to pre-existing relationships, exposure, and subsequent impact. When there is work with individual children and parents after a traumatic event, these different agendas must be appreciated. (Nader 1994: 196)

In our experience, this means to, apart from supporting those family members who are quite obviously suffering, also pay special attention to those family members who behave in a quiet, apparently well-adjusted manner. In many cases the helpers focus on those people who are able to express their pain. But children, especially, often show no outward signs of struggling; they do not behave in any particularly noteworthy way, but seem calm and composed. However, it is important to understand their inner plight in order to help them cope.

If sufficient human resources are available, it is evident that it would be beneficial to all to have a separate counsellor/therapist for each family member. In this setting, there is room for the individual feelings of distress, as well as those of anger, shame and those of guilt projected onto the other family members. These feelings can be addressed, analysed and, by talking about them, understood. The family system is, thus, relieved of some of its burdens, which leaves room for positive interactions between its members.

In those cases where a support system relying on such a large amount of manpower is impossible, psychosocial work can still be of much assistance to the family. In the work with counselling teams operating after the tsunami catastrophe, four major points were identified and used in the training programmes:

1. *The family members should share their opinions and beliefs with each other*: After a certain amount of time has passed since the 'disappearance', all family members will have arrived at their own opinions and beliefs as to what has happened to the 'disappeared'. In many cases though, the family members do not talk about these but assume that the others have gone through the same thought processes and must, therefore, have arrived at the same conclusions. This, of course, is a source of many misunderstandings.
    Psychosocial counselling can provide the space for the family members to talk about their respective beliefs. In many families

one family member (often one of the children) clutches to the idea that the 'disappeared' is still alive and accuses the others of not being sufficiently invested in the search. It is necessary for the family members to talk about their opinions and beliefs and how they have arrived at them, without being judgemental about the positions the others take in this matter. The presence of a counsellor makes it possible to neutralise the accusations and aggression that might come up, and have a constructive conversation. The aim of this kind of intervention lies in having all family members know where the others stand on the situation of the 'disappearance' and their relationship to the 'disappeared', and in developing a respectful acceptance for the stances of the others. It is essential for them to understand though that this information constitutes a snapshot in time. Changes in the member's inner processes can occur at any point in time. It is advantageous to repeatedly have such family talks over a course of time, in order for the family members to notice and accept such changes in themselves as well as in the others.

2. *Supporting families in (re)building the new family structure*: The casualty counts after natural disasters such as the tsunami in December 2004 are enormous. Entire families were obliterated. In many cases, only a very small number of members of the extended family have survived.

In these families, torn apart by disaster, the survivors feel isolated and alone. Rarely do the family members talk about their losses. The grief and longing for those who are gone often overlay the worry for those who have survived. Again and again situations are described in which mothers treated their surviving children badly, in which fathers cannot deal with their new role as a single parent, in which parents put all their energies into searching for the 'disappeared' child, becoming apparently oblivious to the surviving children that are with them.

In these situations it is absolutely paramount to have professional help that comes from outside the family structure. A large part of our time during the workshop was spent on analysing such broken families and developing approaches for how and where counselling must start out in such situations: It has to start out with the family unit as a whole as well as with the individual family members.

The goal of such interventions is for the broken family to learn to function as a family unit again, i.e., to support each other and be there for the other members. The surviving parents need psychological as well as advisory support, in order to be able to care for themselves as well as their children. For the children, it often helps to reduce the strain put on them if they can express their worries, their confusion and their anger in verbal or non-verbal ways, and be understood in their words and actions by an adult. Children also need to be allowed to be cheerful, despite the catastrophe. The shared grief, characterised by shared rituals, can redefine and strengthen the relationships between the surviving family members.

3. *Helping single parents to take on their new parenting roles*: The tsunami catastrophe brought about a new phenomenon in Sri Lanka. Those who had had the muscle power to run away fast, climb to safety or clutch to something had much better chances of surviving the flood wave. Consequently, the number of older people, women and children who perished in it was disproportionally high.

As a result, it is often the father who survived and is now alone with the children that made it through. But, generally, fathers in Sri Lanka are rarely or not at all prepared to care for children. Previously, in the case of the mother being lost for some reason, there were grandmothers or aunts who would assume the larger part of the parenting duties. But a large part of the older population died in the tsunami.

Reports about children living in orphanages despite one of their parents still being alive are common. Widows, but especially widowers, feel overwhelmed by the burden of caring for a child and opt for the apparently easy way out and put them into the care of strangers—an option that is strongly promoted by the international disaster relief organisations. The fathers—and mothers—have fallen into such deep despair over the loss of the partner and, in many cases, that of other children, that the care for the surviving children seems an impossible task. On top of the loss of the mother and siblings, these children then have to deal with the loss of the father as well.

It is of immense importance that the surviving parents are supported in their struggle to be 'good enough' as parents, meaning that they can provide for their children financially as well as on an emotional level. In part, they need practical advice, but most of all they need emotional support in order to be able to rise to this important task. In succouring children after catastrophes, a large part of the money intended for orphanages should be reallocated to be spent on psychosocial support of mothers and fathers. Counsellors should be educated in advance in order to be able to coordinate the psychological support in the case of such an emergency situation and to be capable of organising further training programmes for other helpers.

4. *Supporting families in finding their own rituals*: After the tsunami, the dead were buried quickly. Often, this happened at a time when close relatives were still hospitalised or had not yet been able to journey there. In these families, different stances towards the deaths are taken. Those who had not been able to take part in the funeral have more trouble accepting the death. It seems important to have a ceremony all can take part in—a ceremony which can also be held months (or even years) after the initial loss.

Such rituals are necessary for the surviving family members to accept and mourn their loss. Relatives of 'disappeared' should be encouraged to create their own rituals or to simply base their ceremonies on those existing in their cultural or religious circle. Counselling can initiate and further the planning, preparations and performance of such a ceremony. Children should take up a special place in this ceremony, in order for them to feel accepted in their grief and be able to say goodbye to the beloved person in the course of this ritual of commemoration.

# 7

# Interventions for Communities after 'Disappearances'

If an entire community is affected by death and 'disappearances', then it is necessary to, apart from the interventions for individuals, also have psychosocial models for the community as a whole. Chapter 3 has already in great detail described different forms of coping on a communal, national and international level. The present chapter focuses on programmes and forms of interventions that are characterised by a clearly psychological or therapeutic approach. The transition between the initiatives started by the people affected and the psychological/therapeutic interventions is a fluent one.

## Psychological Support in the Middle of Crisis—a Short Manual

Most of the concepts discussed here apply to the situation 'after' the traumatic event has taken place; we speak about 'post-traumatic' intervention. But there are many people, and this also means many children, who are caught in the middle of violence, in need of support.

The short manual presented in here was drawn up in cooperation with colleagues from various countries in Europe and Asia. I developed it in response to the need to help children and adolescents during the conflict situation in Sri Lanka in 2008. Its purpose lies in providing clear, easy-to-follow guidelines for those working in the situation of acute crisis. Since then, the manual has proven its worth in the hands of counsellors and social workers working in a number of different situations, like, after the earthquake in Haiti or in the conflict-ridden regions of East Africa.

This manual is intended for helpers on site, who often do not have a specialised psychological or therapeutic education to fall back on. The interventions suggested here are all to be seen under the central premise that we need to, *first, do no harm*. This might also mean that children might not be able to let themselves participate in the exercises described here.

## Supporting Children by Supporting Their Adult Caregivers

### SUPPORTING CHILDREN ALSO MEANS STRENGTHENING THEIR PARENTS, TEACHERS AND CARE TAKERS

War is scaring for everybody—generally speaking, adults usually have a more concrete idea about how dangerous a war situation is. They might have already survived traumatic situations. Their fear is based on past experience. In many cases, the current situation might even constitute a 're-traumatisation' for them. From this it follows that many adults will connect the ongoing dangerous situation with overwhelming experiences from their past or, in other words, old psychological wounds are reopened and become painful again. This can be related to many symptoms commonly occurring in such situations, such as sleeplessness, panic, easy startling, a number of avoidance mechanisms, feelings of nervousness or high tension or sensitivity to all forms of noise (including noises children make).

In such a situation, it is very difficult for adults to deal with the questions and fears the children develop. Therefore, it is of crucial importance to give assistance to adults in order to support them in assisting the children.

### Basic Psychological Education: Explaining the Impact of Psychological Traumata to Parents and Teachers

An important step in supporting care giving adults is helping them to understand that some of the emotions and feelings of the ongoing situation might be related to pre-existing post-traumatic feelings.

Another is explaining the situation the children are in: Children in a chaotic situation orient their behaviour in relation to that of their caretakers. If their parents are overwhelmed by feelings of helplessness, the children are just as lost in this feeling. If, however, the parents/teachers, while expressing their honest concerns about the current situation, do not give into their feelings of vulnerability and lack of power, but discuss the situation as openly as possible, devoting attention to their children's fears, listening to them and comforting them, then the children can still feel safe and well-protected by their caregivers.

### Training Adults—in Order to Then Help the Children

It is not easy for adults to control such feelings of fear and helplessness in an overwhelming situation of crisis like that of a war. Here are some techniques that can help to keep a level head and heart during such difficult times:

1. *Short Relaxation Exercises*: If there are already known relaxation techniques, encourage people to practise these. Find short exercises which can take only a few seconds or minutes, which is sometimes all one has, in a situation of crisis.

    - *Breathing*: Just take time to breathe out. Make sure that both your feet are firmly planted on the ground. Consciously step on your right and then on your left foot, feeling its respective contact with the floor. Take a deep breath. Breathe in and out. Breathing out should take twice as long as breathing in took. Repeat this three times.
    - *Muscle relaxation*: Clench your hands into fists as tightly as you can. Hold your breath for two seconds. Breathe out and at the same time open your hands. Repeat this three times.

    This is the simplest of the relaxation exercises taken from Jacobson's Progressive Relaxation Techniques, which can be done in virtually any situation. A more complex form involves consecutively tensing all muscle groups in your body individually and then letting go.

    - *Count down*: Take a deep breath and count down from 10 to 1.
    - *Small prayers and mantras*: Religious people often draw strength from small prayers or mantras. Regular practise can help them make use of that influx of strength in situations of crisis.

2. *Inner Safe Place*: This exercise works with people's imagination (Reddemann 2011). It has to be trained in a safe situation (do not conduct these training sessions during stressful times or when those participating are in fear because of already ongoing fights or *Hartal*s [strike-actions], etc.!).

    *Procedure*: Make sure that the participants are comfortable (sitting or lying on the floor).

    - Start by instructing them to take some deep breaths.
    - Invite them to close their eyes, or—if closing the eyes feels unsafe—to fix their sight on a specific spot on the floor or wall.
    - Once everybody is silent, all they should do is listen to your voice.
    - Now you invite them to, in their imagination, visit their own, special, safe place. This can be a real, existing place, a place they

## 170  Grief and Disappearance

have been to in the past time or even a place that only exists in their mind. This place belongs only to them and it is totally safe; nothing they do not want there is allowed to enter this place.
- Help to create this place with instructions like:
Look around—what is the climate like in your safe place? What time of day is it? Are you alone there, or are there other people in this place with you? What does it smell like? What colours can you see? Is there any sound? Find a place to rest somewhere in your safe haven. Make yourself comfortable there.
- Allow your participants to stay there for a while: 'Enjoy your safe place for a little while' Keep the room silent for that time.
- After a few minutes invite them to come back: 'It is time to leave your safe place for now. Get up, look around and say "Good bye" and "I can come back here" and slowly begin your journey back to the room we started out from. When you have arrived back here, open your eyes.'
- Invite the participants to stretch like after a good night's sleep.

It might be useful to repeat this exercise under the guidance of a counsellor. When it is well established, you can tell the participants that this inner safe place is always there with them and nobody can take it away from them. They are always allowed to visit this place. People can even have more than one 'inner safe place'.

When you do this exercise make sure that everybody feels safe in this situation. During their visit to the safe place, check if everybody is relaxed and concentrated on his/her inner world. If this should not be the case, lead them as soon as possible back to the present situation.

These are just some ideas to help adults in dealing with situations of crisis. Different people will find different techniques helpful. What they use themselves they can share with others and with their children as well.

## Direct Support of Children in Times of Crisis

### ALLOW FOR REGRESSION TO SOME EXTENT

In situations of crisis, children are often expected to behave especially mature. While this is what the situation demands, they should also be allowed to have certain 'islands' where they are allowed to be children or even behave in a particularly childish manner.

If the burden of constant fear becomes too heavy to bear, it is a psychological form of self-protection to regress to an earlier stage of development, back to a time where life was stable and the child's small world, safe and secure.

Such regression can be seen in different forms of behaviour. Some examples are listed here:

- In times of crisis, some children need physical contact to an extreme extent, sometimes to that of the needs of a baby, to feel safe. This is a real need that should be fulfilled at least for the time being. Parents/teachers/caretakers should allow children to stay close to them if this is what they want.
- Some children might start to wet the bed again. It is important to understand this as a normal, psychological reaction the child should not be blamed for. Instead, it has shown itself as helpful to ask the child if something is bothering him or her. Find practical solutions if the problem continues without making the child feel ashamed for something he or she has no control over.
- Even older children (girls and boys!) will cry if the experience of horror and fear becomes too much to bear. Allow the children to express their feelings. Make it clear that strong people can also cry for some time, and that this often helps them to gather the strength to move on.
- Children might experience especially strong feelings of anxiety when separated from their parents during a time of crisis. Explain to them as well as possible why this has to happen and when they will get to see their parents again. Make sure that you keep any promises you make. (If you tell the child, for example, that you will pick her/him up at 12—make sure that you are there a few minutes before 12!)

Take people's fears seriously—do not blame anybody for being scared; especially not a child. Try to give comfort to the children living through such trying times.

### Preserve Normality as Much as Possible

If at all possible, the children should continue with their routines and duties: going to school, doing homework, assisting their parents with housework, etc.

Directly after a traumatic event, a certain period of time might be necessary to overcome the initial shock, during which the routines of everyday life may be suspended. But once a couple of days have passed, it is generally beneficial to return to one's state of normality as much as possible.

Normality supports the children in overcoming traumatic situations and helps them to understand that a normal life still exists. If their parents are too overwhelmed by a certain traumatic event, then teachers, relatives or social workers can assist in establishing the routines of normality for the children for some time.

### SAFE ISLANDS

Especially in the middle of a crisis situation it can help children if you create safe islands for them, situations in which, despite the general instability surrounding them, they can feel safe at least once a day. For example:

1. *Games*: Play with them—The best games to play during such difficult times involve all children at the same time without creating a competition between them. (Where there is a winner there is a loser as well—and these children have to deal with enough loss as it is, there is no need for them to face it in games as well!)

    Here are some examples for such games:

    - Hand clapping: All participants stand in a circle and pass a clap along the circle. First, you start out slowly, then, gradually, the clap travels faster and faster from one child to the next. The children have the choice between clapping only once—then the clap keeps on getting passed along in the same direction—or clapping twice—then the clap changes direction
    - Movement around the circle: One child starts out with a specific movement of their choice. One child after the other repeats the movement, letting it pass through the circle like a wave. Then the next child presents a move that gets passed along through the circle, until all children have had a chance.
    - One child starts by saying a single word that could be the beginning of a sentence. The next person repeats this word and adds a second word and so on. The words should follow grammatical rules to build a sentence. Let's see what sentence the group will create.
    - We can do a similar exercise on a black board as well: One child starts out with one line, the next continue by adding another line—each child can draw once or twice. In the end we have a picture created by the group. Now we can ask somebody to be an art expert and explain what we can see.

And there are many more you also can create yourself.
These kinds of games need little to no materials and can be played in the span of a few minutes, or for longer, if desired. Encourage children to play! Give them space for their games!
2. *Story telling*: All children like to listen to stories. Through the power of their imagination, they can travel to the places in the stories. Stories work so well as 'islands' in days of stress, because the children get a chance to sit down for a while and listen to a story where the world is in order and where everything eventually leads to a happy ending. It might be good to tell positive stories before going to bed to calm the children's minds and set them at ease.

TRANSITIONAL OBJECTS

Children might need objects representing their loved ones to help them handle their fears and situations of separation. Therefore, children should have such 'transitional objects', like a little toy given to them by their father, or a picture of their mother, etc. They should be allowed to keep these objects with them wherever they go, even to school.

Younger children especially might only feel safe if their doll or teddy or even a specific piece of cloth is with them. Allow this! Children that do not have such a transitional object to help them yet can even be invited to choose such an object.

RITUALS

Rituals can help to control fear by creating a routine, a state of normality. Rituals performed as a group also create a feeling of belonging together for the members of this group, which helps to reduce the ever-threatening feelings of loneliness and helplessness.

Families can perform rituals on a regular basis, such as, every morning and evening (for some families, this might be done in a religious context). School classes or children's clubs can perform rituals as well—existing, traditional ones or rituals created specially for this group. All these rituals can help in re-establishing a feeling of safety and stability, of being protected by the group.

FORMS OF SELF-EXPRESSION

1. *Speaking and Listening*
Children should have an adult to whom they can turn to, to speak about their fears and problems. Encourage parents to ask their

children about their well-being. Encourage teachers as well to give their charges room to, within the class community, talk about their experiences and feelings. (Especially right after the region has been hit by disaster.) Elder people in the community or distant relatives can also take this role. Sometimes it might be easier for a child to speak to somebody who is not a close relative.

Children need room to speak about the horrors they have experienced. Offer children a space to share their opinion on the terrible situation they have had to face. But do not force them to speak out, just invite them.

Permit questions and give serious answers! Children need to be allowed to ask questions. It is important to listen to them, take them seriously and answer honestly! Keeping unpleasant answers away from a child is not a form of protecting them! If a family member has died, the child needs to know the truth. Accept that the child might cry.

While a lie might be easier in the moment, it creates the serious risk of an emotional separation of the child from the rest of the family. All other family members are in the know, only the child is left alone with his or her own, often terrible, fantasies about why the relative is not there anymore.

Even if the circumstances are unclear, share the truth that you know and explain to the child that you also do not know any more than that. The child then has a chance to mourn with the family and the shared knowledge will bring the surviving family members closer to each other; they can be supportive (and even a little child can be a great resource!) in situations of confusion and crisis.

Of course, it is important to answer the question a child poses to you in words children can understand. Giving an honest explanation might require some time. Sometimes children reach a point where they have heard enough; then they might interrupt your explanations. Answer their questions as honestly and directly as possible. Normally children stop asking when they have the impression that it is enough. Respect their needs.

Children will develop their own forms of coping. Especially in school, it might be helpful for the class to share different forms of coping—then children can learn from each other how to handle situations of fear and crisis better. This can include: religious services, playing music, singing, being with friends, going to a specific place, etc.

Children aged 4–6 might even have an imaginary friend. In their imagination, they might choose to have a strong and powerful figure that protects them and is by their side at all times during such unsafe situations. Permit such fantastic forms of protection. Once they are not needed anymore, the fantasies will also stop.

2. *Role Play*
Some children will not speak about what has happened to them. In their games, however, they will often reveal what weighs heavily on their minds by re-enacting their experiences in role plays—together with other children or with figurines, dolls or stuffed animals.

These role plays can help to integrate the situation and the feelings connected to it. Sometimes, children even find helpful ways of handling fear and grief in their games.

3. *Drawing and Painting*
Many children—whether they can talk about what has happened or not—will express their bad experience as soon as you give them a piece of paper and some pens. Allow children to create such little pieces of art. You can try to talk with individual children about their pictures—but do not force them. Sometimes drawing is the only possible form of expression the child has.

Especially if a child draws the same scene over and over again, it might be important and helpful to pay special attention to the situation the picture depicts.

4. *Diary*
Older children often find that they can express themselves through writing. Children should be encouraged to keep a diary—to such a companion they can tell everything they want at any time. Maybe some of them will even write very serious reports on the ongoing situation.

## CHILDREN AND GRIEF

If a family member is killed, somebody is seriously injured or has 'disappeared', surviving parents might be too overwhelmed to give their child the care it needs. Other less-affected family members like an aunt or a cousin should take special care of the children and meet their needs in this time of grief.

Again, it is of vital importance to answer the questions of the child seriously and honestly. Never deny the fact of death. Priests, monks and nuns can often help in such situations as well—religions generally have their own hopes for and understanding of life after death.

In the particularly difficult situation of having lost a child, help parents to still be good caregivers to their surviving children. (It often seems to be the case that in the initial phase of grief, parents feel such a close connection to their deceased child that they need outside assistance in the care for their surviving children until they themselves can be good caregivers to them again.)

TAKE CARE OF YOURSELF!

Last but not least, being a support to the children and adults around you in such difficult times means a lot to them and to the whole community! But please, do not forget your own needs. Make sure that you have some time to rest, to say your own prayers and replenish your energy. Also, find somebody to whom you can talk about the burdens you bear and the difficult situations you yourself experience.

A number of tried and tested international standards exist specifically for situations of crisis. One of them, for example, refers to how local, national and international relief organisations can provide psychosocial support immediately after a catastrophe. The Inter-Agency Standing Committee (IASC) was founded with the purpose of optimising the cooperation between the UN and other aid agencies. A large number of organisations have contributed to the development of an important standard work that can be used effectively in situations of crisis: the IASC Guidelines on Mental Health and Psychosocial Support in Emergency Settings (2007).[1] One group that is identified there as being especially at risk and, therefore, in need of being paid particular attention to by the aid agencies are children that have been separated from their families.

## Long-term Communal Programmes

There are a number of programmes that have been developed to help entire communities after large catastrophes. As examples for these, three are introduced here.

### Psycho Education after the Genocide in Ruanda

Staub and Pearlman (2006) worked with the survivors of the genocide in Ruanda that cost almost a million people their lives in the summer of 1994.

Their community-based interventions, developed in cooperation with local NGOs, are built around five central subject areas:

1. *Understanding the effects of trauma and victimisation and avenues to healing:*
   In all situations of war and crisis it has proven helpful if the people affected know about the impact and the psychological consequences of traumata. This helps them in their understanding of their own suffering and relieves them of some of their feelings of helplessness. This kind of general information can be presented to the group of village community as a whole, in the form of advanced education sessions.

   Although there is some disagreement about the need for survivors to talk about their traumatic experiences ... the preponderance of clinical and empirical evidence suggests that doing so is helpful for many survivors. Survivors of sudden, traumatic loss also require a framework for understanding traumatic grief and the need for mourning. (Staub & Pearlman 2006: 219)

   This is in accord with my own experiences in South Asia and with refugees from different continents. Often, the people affected experience their own symptoms as an additional problem. They fear to now 'become crazy', on top of all else. If they are given information on the psychological reactions to severe traumatisation, they can better understand themselves as well as their family members. The situation becomes assessable and thereby controllable.

2. *Understanding genocide*
   'People also often see their own suffering as unique. Learning about similar ways that others have suffered and examining the psychological and social roots of such violence can help people see their common humanity with others' (Staub & Pearlman 2006: 219).

   Severely traumatised people often feel cut off from the rest of the world. They cannot communicate their terrible experiences to anybody. In information sessions that also open up the floor for contributions by the participants, it becomes possible for them to share their experiences, compare them with those of the others, put them into perspective, and, most of all, acknowledge and accept them.

3. *Understanding basic psychological needs*
   Apart from the information on the consequences of massive traumata and the concept of grieving, the community also needs information on how the suffering can be alleviated to some degree: What can be

done for one's own psychological well-being and how can the other members of one's family and community be supported.

It is always helpful to ask about the kind of strategies that are already well established within the group and have proven themselves before. Here, one can make use of pre-existing resources to the benefit of all.

4. *Writing, drawing and discussions in small groups*
Ways are created to express the injustice suffered, the grief and the worry for those who were killed or have 'disappeared'. There is room for drawing, painting, text composition, pieces can be read out and the events can be discussed in small groups.

As mentioned earlier in the section on the different forms of coping in the middle of the crisis or in between traumatic events, non-verbal forms of expressions such as art present a way for people to express that which is unspeakable. Verbal forms such as the writing of poems, fairy tales or other texts can help to find one's own narrative, one's own tale of the unfathomable.

This is also a way to create a place where those who have been killed or have 'disappeared' can be remembered.

5. *Vicarious traumatisation*
Staub and Pealman (2006) point out an important aspect: It is not only the people immediately affected by a crisis who can suffer from post-traumatic complications, but also the witnesses and helpers. In their programme in Ruanda, they mostly worked with journalists and community leaders. It was important to not only reflect on the people the programme was intended for, but also on their own feelings when listening to the related experiences and on the relationships to the people they work with. Forms of mental hygiene had to be developed (see also Chapter 9).

## *Psychological Group Therapy in a Village in Chile*

While the other models introduced here are intended for general situations of crisis, for situations where people often 'disappear' and their relatives need a special kind of support, the following programme was explicitly devised for the family members of 'disappeared' people.

Madariaga (1992) describes the work of the team of CINTRAS, an organisation based in the Chilean village Parral. Twenty-nine inhabitants of the village, mostly farmers, 'disappeared' in the time of terror that constituted Pinochet's regime. Seventeen years after the men's 'disappearance', psychosocial help was sought for the village. Once a week a psychiatrist and a social worker went out to Parral for three hours of individual therapy, two hours of working with group and two hours of social support for families.

As in other countries, it was again mainly the mothers who were most actively involved in the search for the 'disappeared' relatives, and who suffered the most under the uncertainty. And again it was the solidarity of other mothers that helped the individual women. Madariaga and his team observed that the family members of the same generation as the 'disappeared' were very little involved in the search or in the demands for certainty and justice. They mostly showed forms of denial or rationalisation of the traumatic events. The consequence was often an alienation from the rest of the family, who kept on searching. Sometimes it even led to identification with the perpetrators. Madariaga sees the reason for the latter in the fear to be associated with the political ideologies of the victims. It is a fact that the 'disappeared' men are repeatedly accused of criminal activities. Many of the perpetrators were still well-respected members of the community at the time of the programme.

This is the atmosphere into which the CINTRAS programme entered. An average of 18 people took part in the group therapy sessions. Madariaga describes the process in the group in four phases.

The first phase focuses on the building of trust and security. All fear and mistrust could be expressed on this basis. In this, verbal as well as non-verbal techniques were used.

Once a sufficient level of security had been established, the group decided to travel to the neighbouring city and make an official statement in front of the truth commission and raise charges with regards to the 'disappearances' of their relatives.

In the second phase, the team of counsellors asked for detailed information on the psychological suffering, which had been further encumbered by the privatisation of the traumatic experience. Witness reports were suggested. The group members reacted positively to this. Madariaga (1992) writes about the benefits of this, describing how recognising part of one's own experience in the reports of the other group members led to the inhibitions regarding the expression of personal experiences that had been present in the beginning being replaced by feelings of solidarity and the willingness to take in the pain of others. He comments that approaching the matter in a cognitive way at this stage in the process facilitated an exchange of opinions between the group members, and a collective reflection on the events (Madariaga 1992: 15).

The most prevalent conflict that presented itself was that of the deaths being denied. According to Madariaga, this was the common denominator. All of the relatives seemed to have built up this safety barrier that they used to hide behind in their battle for the life of their 'disappeared' relative. Their fuel for this battle is made up of fantasies, hopes or 'intuitions'. Madariaga quotes the relatives as saying things such as 'I know that he is alive, somewhere. Of course it is possible that he has been killed like so many others, but something in my heart tells me that he lives, after all, I am his mother' (Madariaga 1992: 15)[2].

At this point, despite the fact that bone fragments had been found, the relative had kept up the denial for 17 years, as these could not be unambiguously identified.

The group reached third phasein a joint process. The desire to overcome the personal pain and become emotionally stable again was strong. The official enquiry conducted at that time, and the discovery of the remains of dead bodies in the area made it possible to revive the past for a while and, in the light of the new evidence, re-evaluate and accept the losses. Madariaga makes it clear that in this phase the relatives needed to arrive at a clear understanding that in present reality there was only one possibility regarding the fate of the 'disappeared': He or she is dead (Madariaga 1992: 15).

The last and probably the longest phase is the fourth phase—that of grief, and the support through the phase of grieving. Unfortunately, I know of no reports by Madariagas on this fourth phase of the process in the village of Parral, but 10 years later he does reflect on the work of CINTRAS:

> The experience of impunity in the southern cone of South America challenges us with the absence of truth and justice for the crimes committed by the dictatorship, a permanent load of stress for the victims and their families. This is a new type of continuous trauma that projects itself as endless in time, which deepens the psychic deterioration of these people. (Madariaga 2002: 9)

In spite of the pessimism that shines through this quote, which has its origins in the difficult political conditions and the open-ended group process, I see this community project as one that made a lot of development possible for the relatives of 'disappeared'. Now these relatives are not alone anymore in their search and their grief. With outside help, they have developed their own initiatives and are no longer speechless and helpless.

## Short-term and Long-term Interventions—Trauma Counselling during and after a Catastrophe

After the tsunami on 26 December 2004 devastated large parts of the coastal areas of South Asia, leaving only destructions and an incredible number of deaths in its wake, I spent the February and summer of the following year in Sri Lanka, educating the so-called 'barefoot counsellors' in various parts of the island state. The term 'barefoot counsellors' refers to young people doing psychosocial work who have little or no education in the field of psychology. They work under the tutelage of an experienced psychologist or psychological counsellor. At that time, Sri Lanka as such had a very limited psychological and psychiatric health care system. These laymen, individually trained for the job, were often the only resource available in terms of offering any kind of psychological counselling.

In cooperation with local and international NGOs and the University of Klagenfurt (Austria), we developed, together with the Centre for Psychosocial Care (CPC) in Sri Lanka, a three-year training programme for psychological counsellors. This training programme by necessity had to be an in-service training, since the practical work was of priority in the light of the magnitude of the natural disaster that came on top of the recent war in the area. In the beginning, the workshops focused on supporting the counsellors in training in their concrete everyday working life. Only in later seminars could the theoretical basis for the methods and procedures taught be discussed. We had to adapt our programme to the conditions present: Immediately after the natural disaster, in a situation of increasing political tension, we were only able to scratch the surface of central theoretical concepts, limiting the information to what was necessary for the immediate work of the team. All theory was explained by means of real-life examples.

This, of course, is contrary to all conventional curricula, but was necessary in the light of the circumstances. Even before they had entered our programme, the counsellors had worked with severe cases of traumatisation. As coaches, we saw our task in the support of these counsellors in their difficult work by giving them specific, practical information that enabled them to do their everyday work, by analysing cases with them in supervision session in which we also planned the next steps together, and by offering theoretical concepts, but only to the degree to which they were immediately relevant to the cases at hand. Only in the second year of their education could the theoretical concepts the intervention methods are based on be covered in detail.

## Guidelines for Psychological Counsellors in Their Support of Relatives of the Disappeared

The desire to help the victims of the tsunami to return to something like 'normal' lives constitutes a central issue in the workshop. To realise and accept that there is no healing in the sense of a return to the original state presents a huge challenge to the young counsellors. Often, they themselves have lost relatives and friends, and they are confronted with this issue every day. In the group work and the discussion it becomes clear how important the support of the relatives of the disappeared is, precisely because of this ever-present uncertainty.

What psychological counselling can accomplish?

1. *Continuous support of relatives of the disappeared*
   In the case of a 'normal' death, the many different social circles and religions of South Asia all have their own rituals for the situation, which have a helpful and supportive function: After a death, relatives, neighbours and friends get together. There are clear roles for everyone, and rules as to who supports the bereaved in what way. Even beyond the tie of initial mourning, there are established ways of supporting the relatives, which ease the way towards the new life without the beloved person. If a person disappears, however, none of these rules or rituals applies. Then the kind of support that comes from outside the social circle, which psychological counselling offers, is often the only kind of help the relatives of the disappeared receive.

   By means of professional guidance, counsellors can supplement the support given by family members and friends, or even substitute it where it is completely absent due to the difficult circumstances. Often, the despair in the face of the absence of the beloved person is extremely strong, and the social support system of their community does not extend to the relatives of the disappeared. Therefore, it may be that it falls to the psychological counsellor to, through regular meetings, return to the relative a small piece of the feeling of stability and security that has been lost because of the disappearance of the beloved person.

2. *Listening actively—supporting the positive memories*
   Many of the relatives want to talk about the person who has disappeared, even if it takes time for them to arrive at that point. Through careful and sensitive questions, the positive memories of the beloved person—before disaster struck—can be brought to the

forefront. The memories of the traumatic last moments (such as, right before the beloved person was hit by a wave) should be balanced out and eventually outweighed by these positive memories, making it possible to recall the relationship as a whole and not only the traumatic last sequence of the disappearance.

It can be helpful to look at a picture showing the person who has disappeared. Then one can ask questions about the circumstances surrounding this picture being taken, the age of the person and his or her life situation at that time, the other people depicted in the picture, etc. Often, photos are taken because of happy occasions, which, ideally, will spark off positive memories, so the counsellor's questions lead to a happy time coming back to life.

3. *Enquiring about the beliefs regarding the fate of the person who has disappeared*
In response to carefully posed questions by the counsellor, relatives can gradually become aware of their beliefs regarding the fate of the disappeared. These beliefs can change over time. Therefore, it can prove useful to ask these questions again and again. Sometimes it becomes possible for the relatives of a disappeared person to become aware of their inner process towards the acceptance of their loss, and to, in turn, accept the said process.

The counsellor does not comment on this, let alone evaluate it. The counsellor's task lies rather in repeating and summing up what has been said, thereby mirroring the information given. Through this, the relatives get a chance to observe their own inner processes and conflicts, and process and deal with these consequences of the disappearance.

4. *The relatives' beliefs must be accepted*
Months after the tsunami, the chances of a disappeared person having survived are slim to none. If the relatives believe, though, that their beloved is still alive, then this needs to be accepted. For many of the victims of the tsunami disaster, the continual clinging to this hope is all that keeps them going and makes it possible to cope with everyday life. Especially those survivors who have lost more than one relative, maybe even their entire family, see the conviction that at least one of their family members must for sure be still alive as the only remaining meaning in their lives.

5. *Support through networking*
The search for disappeared relatives can be aided by establishing communication with existing networks. Organisations such as the tracing service of the Red Cross/Red Crescent have developed

means of helping relatives in their search for missing or 'disappeared' relatives. In those cases where the death of the disappeared relative is most likely, it takes an especially long time for this step to be undertaken. Only once the possible news of the beloved person's death seems bearable can an active search begin.

6. *Rituals help*
Counselling can help to find the right forms of rituals for the specific loss, can aid in the preparations and can conduct them. This can be done on an individual, family-based or communal level.

In our training programme in Sri Lanka, we introduced a number of central concepts regarding the mourning process as well as forms of complicated mourning.

At first it was strictly these Western concepts that our students were interested in learning and applying. However as the concepts began to take on actual meaning for the participants, they found that they recalled other ways of understanding. Slowly, the students reached into their own history, culture, and ideas to introduce and to integrate profoundly meaningful processes that they had known all along. 'Trauma counseling' gave way to a more complex, meaningful and integrative process.

All the members of our group had several stories of multiple losses under terrible circumstances in which young people had died suddenly and violently. Some were confronted with dead bodies, while others had to cope with loss without evidence. Often, relationships were interrupted and the loss occurred without any possibility of farewell. All of the members of the training programme had clients who suffered from multiple losses; sometimes even people who lost their entire extended family. (Preitler 2012: 239)

**Through this process of learning and raising self-awareness, the team developed a communal mourning ritual for a village that had been attacked seven years ago in the course of the war. Of the village's inhabitants, 44 died in this attack; the appropriate rituals to mourn their deaths had never been performed. Therefore, a ritual was prepared to commemorate the seventh anniversary of their deaths, the preparations for which were a half-a-year-long process:**

The village people, monks, and the team of CPC decided on services for two days and one night in the main Buddhist temple of Gonagola.

The ceremony began with cooking. The community members, along with our students, came together on one side of the temple to prepare special meals for all participants in the ritual. Cleaning vegetables and fish in groups gave them the opportunity to talk to each other.

At dawn everyone went to change their attire. White is the color used to symbolize grief. We all dressed accordingly in white and other light colors. The female members of our training team wore traditional saris as a sign of respect. After sunset the ritual started with what is called Bodhi Puja and continued later with preaching (Dhamma Discussion). The night service ended with a meal for all the participants. Some participants remained in prayer and meditation all night in the temple. The next morning began with a small ceremony and continued with more cooking. At noon the prayer and alms giving began. This was to be the essential portion of the two day program. Alms were given to poor children and medicine was handed over to the local pharmacy, in the name of the 44 victims. The community meal marked the end of the ritual. The whole ceremony was held in a mournful but peaceful atmosphere. The CPC team was warmly welcomed by the community and well accepted as assistants and supervisors.

Months later our students from the area reported the positive impact that the ritual had in village life. People now felt freer to talk about the deceased and their own ideas and feelings about what happened. In September 2007, the community members themselves organized rituals for the eighth anniversary of the massacre. (Preitler 2012: 244f.)

## Notes

1. http://www.humanitarianinfo.org/iasc/pageloader.aspx?page=content-subsidi-common-default&sb=72 (last accessed on 26 February 2015).
2. Translation from the German edition.

# 8
# If a 'Disappeared' Person Comes Back

## Stages of Hidden Mourning

In the work with psychological counsellors, teachers and social workers, and in the reflection on and analysis of case histories of relatives of 'disappeared' persons, a number of common elements have emerged. From these, a five-stage model that represents the process many of the relatives of 'disappeared' persons go through was developed.

Some of these phases can overlap, and not all relatives go through the entire set of stages. Nevertheless, I think that this model can be helpful in understanding the reactions to the 'disappearance' of a relative.

Stage 1: *Chaos and confusion*
In the first hours or days after the 'disappearance', most people are preoccupied with the chaos the catastrophe has thrown them into. They attempt to bring in structure and order and try to organise the bare necessities essential for them and the family members currently with them. In some cases, especially after natural disasters or military conflicts, the tending of one's own wounds and the medical care of injured relatives take up a lot of time and attention. During this time, the hope is strong that 'disappeared' relatives will show up again on their own accord, or at least that reassuring proofs of life will eventually reach the family. Soon after, though, the search begins. In some cases, this first stage is over after a matter of hours; in others, it takes days or weeks.

Stage 2: *The search*
In most cases the search begins as soon as the relatives' physical and psychological state permits this, once the initial shock reaction has been overcome and basic structure and orientation are re-established. However, after a larger catastrophe has struck that affected an entire region, often it takes time for the people there to become aware of the magnitude of the disaster and the many different dimensions on which life has changed. These realisations demand time, energy and attention in order to be processed.

In the first weeks, hospitals, the places where bodies are assembled and tents in which pictures of deceased victims are put up become focal points for relatives. This is the time for collecting and gathering together all available evidence, and testing its value in terms of information about one's own 'disappeared' relative. The search for the 'disappeared' person becomes the centre of the survivors' lives and dictates the everyday life.

Stage 3: *Caught between hope and despair—about the impossibility of considering death*

Even the slightest evidence that the missing relative might still be alive gets a lot of careful attention and serves as a reason to pick up the search again. Often, vague and imprecise bits of information become the centre of hope.

For weeks or months on end, the families persist in this stage of energy-consuming search. They are not able to even consider the possibility of death. A lot of energy as well as financial resources are invested into the search for the 'disappeared'. The reunion with the 'disappeared' seems to become the one single goal in life. Nevertheless, life moves on; decisions about everyday life have to be made that concern only those family members present at the time. Experiences are made that the 'disappeared' has no part in.

Stage 4: *Clinging to hope*

Many people are physically, mentally and financially exhausted by the search. Some become angry and aggressive. They feel abandoned by the government agencies and their neighbours and families. They feel that they are all alone in their search. If only there were more willingness to cooperate with each other, they feel, then the 'disappeared' would be found for sure. Again and again, the inner fight is replaced by times of deep sadness and despair, and the desire to experience a semblance of normality again. The desire to come to an end, however, often results in a renewed search effort.

All mentions that the 'disappeared' might be dead have to be violently rejected or answered with aggressive behaviour. If doubts about the survival of the 'disappeared' arise at this stage, then they also typically result in a doubling of the search efforts.

Stage 5: *Hidden mourning versus lifelong hope*

Months, sometimes years, after the 'disappearance', a slow and complicated form of grieving begins. The process is a difficult one, as it remains unclear whether the loss is a final one. The fact remains, though, that the 'disappeared' is not there with the relatives at that time, and has not been there for a while. The relationship has been interrupted; the 'disappeared' does not share in the everyday life of the remaining family.

When it becomes possible to accept the loss of one or more missing persons, and when they can give themselves permission to lead a life without the beloved 'disappeared' depends on the kind of relationship a relative has had with the 'disappeared', on the last times spent together and on the plans that had been made for the future. It is necessary, though, to accept that some of the people whose relatives have 'disappeared' will be pained by the loss for the remainder of their lives.

If grieving is possible though, then this process needs to be supported by the environment, so that this difficult step of acceptance of the permanency of the loss is not marred by feelings of guilt. This hidden mourning process takes significantly longer than a grieving process that is clearly evident after a loss.

Many relatives experience this long, difficult process, which is often interrupted by renewed bouts of hope. Some relatives will never grief, but wait for the rest of their lives for the return of the 'disappeared'. If a 'disappeared' relative does indeed return, then the immediate reaction, the reunion as such and the resumption of the relationship depends to large parts on the progression through this grieving progress so far.

## Renewed Injury Induced by the Return

In rare cases, a 'disappeared' person is indeed found alive and returns to his or her relatives. Psychologically, this is, of course, a very lucky and positive event, but the difficulties involved in this may not be overlooked.

The relationship has to be matched up with and adjusted to the experiences of both, the 'disappeared' and the relatives who have had to live through all that time without the person. There needs to be space and time for both sides to share their stories. A prerequisite for this is that both have the psychological capacity to really listen, understand and accept what the other experienced and did during the time apart.

Odysseus massacred the suitors of his wife upon his return. How Penelope felt about that is not told as part of the Greek mythology. Did she agree to these murders? She had, after all, stalled them rather than turning them away. Did she maybe take some of them as lovers for a while, or even fall in love with one of the men? Might this have been part of the reason why Odysseus dealt so brutally with his competitors? His time of 'disappearance' was not spent in constant thought about his beloved wife; he did enter into intimacies with women. The traditional power relation between the different genders is re-established by Odysseus' act of violence.

In military conflicts, women are time and again misused and exploited as 'spoils of war'. In the course of the partition of India and Pakistan, for example, about 33,000 Hindu and Sikh women were abducted by Muslims, and circa 50,000 women were, in turn, taken by Hindus or Sikhs (cf. Das 2002). When the two countries eventually struck an agreement about the return of these women, this was done without consulting the women concerned. They became political objects twice; in both acts, their feelings and needs were completely disregarded. Butalia (1997: 103) recounts:

> As is well know by now, many family who had earlier reported their women missing, now refused to take them back because they have been 'polluted' through sexual contact with men of the other race. Worse, even some had children, living symbols of the pollution which made it difficult for families to now take them in.

Women were faced with the impossible choice of giving up their children in order to again be accepted by their own families of origin. Some had built up a good relationship with their new husbands and families. These relationships were torn apart, just as the first ones had been, without consulting the women about their wishes and needs.

In psychotherapy the choices to be made when a 'disappeared' relative returns are generally not quite that dramatic. But nevertheless, such a situation is not always easy and, therefore, requires the guidance and counsel of an external professional.

## Relationships Lost and Ended

In some cases, the relationship to the 'disappeared' person has effectively been ended and cannot be picked up again. The therapist's/counsellor's task is again to be supportive and to help the client to reach a positive decision and make plans for the future that build on this choice.

Mrs K. has been in therapy for two and a half years, when she is informed in a phone call with relatives still living in her home country that her husband has 'reappeared'. He had been imprisoned and, as far as could be gathered from the phone call, is now suffering from severe physical and mental illnesses. Mrs K. is very distraught by this news.

She started therapy after attempting to kill herself two and half years ago. Back then, she felt that she could not live on without her husband. Only her children kept her going. If it had not been for them, she would have rather returned to her homeland and searched for her husband than remain without him, even if that had meant putting her own life at risk.

During the first phase of therapy, she presented her husband as the ideal partner. Only after some time had passed did it become possible for her to articulate her anger towards her husband, who had put his political work first, neglecting his family. During this time, Mrs K. is very distressed by this betrayal. Once she starts to gradually remember the good parts about the relationship, her grief becomes less desperate. She begins to accept the separation as permanent. Linked to this is her ability to permit herself to take part in certain entertainments again. While in the beginning she denied herself the right to join into festivities ('Only once my husband returns will we celebrate'), she now starts accepting invitations, even if she justifies doing so in terms of the well-being of her children ('The children need to experience something nice'). She can admit, though, that she enjoys the invitations by and conversations with the other women. She also begins to be interested in Austria and starts feeling more and more at home.

That it turns out that her husband is still alive changes nothing about the relationship having been severed and already mourned. Mrs K. is not willing to take over the care for her husband. Of course, she had compunctions about this, and sees herself as egoistic. 'Do you really think I am allowed to do that?' she asks repeatedly during therapy. She would like to have somebody else share in the decision, even if she can stand by her choice to not be with her husband.

Mrs K. tells her therapist about the reaction of her children. It had taken a lot of courage (and time) to talk about the 'disappearance' of their father. Now she is afraid of telling them about his 'reappearance'. It takes her a week to find it in her to start a conversation about this with her children. She declines the offer to have this talk in the presence of the therapist and talks to the children alone.

One of the children agrees with the mother and her decision to only stay in contact with the father via telephone. The second child, a son, reproaches his mother and wants to see the father at once. He begins to plan a future in which he will, as soon as he has his own income, go back to get his father and bring him to Austria.

What is interesting about this case is that despite the lingering uncertainty regarding the 'disappearance', Mrs K. has gone through a grieving process that has become irreversible. This largely complies with the stages of hidden mourning described above. Once the separation is accepted as permanent, Mrs K. permits herself to become conscious of the negative aspects of her marriage and address these in therapy. At the same time she allows herself to enjoy her new role as a woman in Europe, one that her husband had never granted her.

The clear break in the relationship came with the realisation that Mrs K. felt abandoned by her husband. She had had to start a new life with her children in a foreign country, despite the fact that her husband could have gone with them. In retrospect, this was the moment when the relationship broke apart.

Half a year after Mrs K. had learned that her husband is still alive, she still feels that not wanting to see her husband again is the right decision for her.

The feeling of helplessness that one had had to go through when the relative had 'disappeared' is irrevocable. If the 'disappearance' and the time afterwards are characterised by an experience of helplessness and impotency, then this cannot be changed by a reunion. A healthy relationship can only be built up again successfully, if both parties acknowledge this and make this fact a part of their new start into the relationship.

The grieving process that the relative has already gone through—despite all resistance and attempts to keep up the status quo—will co-determine the relationship, which needs to be defined anew. In the absence of the 'disappeared', life choices have been made, even if this happened unconsciously. So far this fact need not have been realised. The 'reappearance' confronts the relatives with the process of separation that has been undertaken, and with their own hidden mourning.

Counselling and psychotherapy again has the function of helping to sort through the confused mass of feelings and assisting in the decision-making process. Cases such as that of Mrs K., where the separation is upheld, are rare. This example shows, however, how important it can be in such situations to have psychological support in order to arrive at a clear decision.

## Learning to Accept the Time Apart

If all those involved honestly confront themselves with the situation and are seriously willing to accept the time apart and all the changes that have come with it, then it can be possible to once again become a family.

Mrs U. was in the late stages of pregnancy when she and her sister fled from their home village, trying to escape the turmoil of war in their home country. She gave birth to her child under highly dramatic circumstances and without any kind of medical care. A couple of months later, a group of men attempted to rape her little sister. Mrs U. stepped between the men and the girl. In her sister's stead she became the victim of the mass rape.

Finally, with the aid of relatives, Mrs U., together with her son and her sister, reached Europe. At that time she had practically no information about the whereabouts of many of her relatives. A couple of months after starting therapy, a message reached her, informing her of the death of her older sister, who had also fled but had died of the complications of a war injury after having reached her destination. The therapy sessions focus on her grief at that time. Suddenly, this process is interrupted by her husband contacting her from another European country. A couple of days later, he arrives in Austria. After the initial happiness, the difficulties come down on them fast and hard. The brutal rape puts special strain on the relationship between the two spouses. For one thing, Mrs U. feels wounded in her physical integrity by the physical abuse she has had to suffer through, for another, she is angry at her husband whose job it would have been to protect her in this situation. At the same time she knows, of course, that he himself was fleeing the country at that time, and that rationally no blame lies with him. The couple's sex life represents a large problem.

I offer to change the therapy setting for Mrs U. to couple therapy—either with me or with another therapist. She decides on a mixed setting: Her husband is invited to join her for every other session. In these joint sessions, it becomes possible for both of them to talk about the deep wounds inflicted by the rape. They can speak about how they would like to live their relationship as a couple in the future. They both want sexuality in their life together, but it needs to take new and gentle forms. One day, the husband says to me: 'At home, we would go to our eldest with this problem. Since this is not possible here, we are really glad that we can come to you'.

Mrs U. is pregnant again. At that time, the conversations start to move from focusing on the past to planning the future. The name the couple chooses for the newborn child reflects the hopes the family has: Translated, it means 'Dawn'.

The process this family went through was characterised by phases of grief, of anger that needed to be brought under control, and of guilt and shame, because it had not been possible to prevent what had happened; the husband had not been able to protect his wife. Another topic that needed to be addressed was that of the perceived humiliation of husband—his wife had had sexual contact with other men. That he felt that way was, in turn, mortifying for the woman. These irrational feelings on both sides pose a real threat to the fragile relationship. Supported by the therapist's mediation, the spouses can gradually learn to treat each other in an appreciative manner again. They can tell each other about their daily and nightly dreams full of longing for the other, and thereby assure each other of their loyalty.

The father also needs to build up a relationship with his already 2-year-old son, and the child to his so far unknown father. At the same time, the child often manages to diffuse the tension between his parents, caught up in their accusations, with his honesty and openness.

## A New Beginning

Counselling and psychotherapy can also play an important role in those cases where the original family lives reunited again: Then its purpose is to provide space for the family members to talk openly, listen actively, acknowledge the time spend apart, mourn this time as lost and ideally build the basis for a new, positive relationship.

Mr Q. started therapy after having been in a psychiatric hospital for a time. He cried a lot and had a hard time dealing with his new life in Austria. He appeared almost childlike. Throughout the two years of therapy, though, he grew in confidence. While in the beginning he had not talked about his young wife at all, the worry for her became a central topic of the sessions in the second year. After months of no contact, he had talked to her on the phone again. At that time she lived worryingly close to the boarder of their homeland as a refugee, which made Mr Q. fear for her safety. When the contact broke off again, and nobody could tell him what had happened to her, his worry spiked. He fell back into a regressive state similar to the one he was in at the beginning of the therapy. Slowly he was able to stabilise: Wherever his wife was, if she was in need of help he as her husband would have to be able to respond to it in an adequate manner. At this phase of stabilisation that went hand in hand with him starting a vocational education, the surprise came: His wife had arrived! An uncle had arranged for her to be able to flee and make it all the way to her husband. Mr Q. is a bit overwhelmed by the situation, but with the help of a number of social workers we manage to provide the couple with a stable basis for life in Europe. Mr Q. brings his wife along for a therapy session to introduce her to us. His bearing has changed. Now he is the one who has skills regarding the country and its language and culture. At the same time he is proud of his beautiful, intelligent young wife. A short holiday the couple goes on two months after Mrs Q.'s arrival, where they visit some of their friends, becomes something of a belated honeymoon for them, and thereby a positive start into a new future together.

From the viewpoint of the therapist, this couple's new beginning was so successful because their previous relationship had been very short and had only existed under the trying circumstances of war. The new and safe environment constitutes totally new conditions. Also, Mrs Q. arrived at a point when her husband had already been stabilised to such a degree that his behaviour was no longer determined by his psychological stress. Therefore, he was able to meet her as an equal partner.

# 9
# Self-care for Professionals

In all psychosocial and psychotherapeutic work, which has the communication with people in pain at its centre, managing the balancing act between empathy and distance present an important challenge. Too much distance prevents the building up of a secure relationship. Too much empathy brings with it the danger of the helper to be overwhelmed and being traumatised vicariously.

## Recognising the Countertransference

To become aware of one's own countertransference reactions is a central element of self-care that can prevent helpers from involving themselves in unnecessary and overtaxing activities (see also Chapter 4). 'Because a therapist feels a specific feeling, it does not follow that specific behaviour, for instance rejection of the patient, results. Indeed, it is probable that the recognition of such feelings prevents most nontherapeutic actions' (Kinzie 1994: 254).

Kinzie (1994) identifies the following feelings of countertransference, which largely correspond to my own experiences in my work with relatives of 'disappeared' persons:

- Sadness about what has happened (and is sometimes still happening) to the person asking for help and sadness about the fact that such things are possible at all, here in our world. The atrociousness of 'disappearances' and the so-often cynical way searching relatives are treated are some of the most incomprehensible horrors of this world. Occasionally, the helpers experience feelings of grief although the client is not consciously aware of this feeling. The countertransference reaction sometimes makes it possible to perceive feelings that are present but are deflected as they would overwhelm the relative if they were to come to the surface. In the course of the therapeutic process, it can become possible to slowly

and gently become aware of all the feelings and the places they stem from and, therefore, belong to.
- It is important for the self-care of the helpers to call these feelings by their names and to analyse them: Which parts of them are my own (for example, do I currently have a reason to be sad?) and which parts are really those of my clients? Those parts that belong to the client's world should remain, together with this person, in the work sphere and not impede on the (personal) life of the therapist or counsellor.
- Anger, hyperarousal and irritability are closely connected to this. The counsellor's/therapist's anger usually centres on the perpetrator, meaning, in the case of an 'enforced disappearance' an unknown person or group of persons. This lets the feelings become confused as well as defused. This makes it even more important to be aware of their originating from and functioning as a countertransference reaction. 'The fact that the anger has no clear focus, no clear enemy, often leaves the feelings vague and inchoate. Typically, such feelings last long after the patient has left, spilling over into other activities and into the therapist's personal life' (Kinzie 1994: 255).

In organisations working with victims of violence, employees should be made aware of this. Many a conflict within the team contains feelings of countertransference such as anger and aggression. If these are not recognised and understood as such, then this can result in people resigning, teams splitting up or the organisation falling apart entirely! Regular supervision sessions can help to establish a good basis for communication beforehand, and pave the way towards clarifying talks and pragmatism in situations of burgeoning conflict.

The uniqueness of the shared experience often leads to an increased feeling of responsibility on the part of the helper. Since the helper often assumes and even knows for certain that no one else has ever been told this story, the pressure to do more and more to help and support the client increases. If the traumatic situation is ongoing, as is the case if a relative has 'disappeared', then the psychological strain the helper is under can reach extreme levels.
- Excessive identification: There is a certain risk of making the experiences of the client one's own, of becoming too involved. Oftentimes it takes an outside perspective to become aware of this countertransference. Supervision and intervision led by

experienced colleagues and sometimes people from one's private sphere can draw one's attention to the fact that the boarders between the problems of the client and those of the helper are dissolving. In such cases, these need to be re-established. In supervision sessions, an analysis of the situation can become the basis for changes that have the protection of the therapist or counsellor at their centre. These newly established protective mechanisms enable the helper to become capable of clear actions again, and thereby serve to improve the psychotherapeutic or psychological intervention as well.

- Intolerance of other clients: This form of countertransference is almost an adversary counterpart of that of excessive identification. The immense impact the suffering of relatives of 'disappeared' people can have can lead to the problems of other people being belittled, as they both are placed on a hierarchical scale and thereby compared and evaluated in terms of their difference in severity. Hence, a client, whose 'only' problem is that his sister has 'disappeared' might get empathy only to a certain degree if he comes right after a client who has, after all, lost three family members. These feelings and subconscious judgements need to always be reflected upon in order for the therapist/counsellor to be there for the client in a positive, effective way. For the therapist/counsellor, this also means to become aware of his or her own limits: After an intervention concerning a particularly difficult situation, it is necessary to take a break in order to process one's own shock over that which has been told, before again turning one's attention to other cases.

It takes time and practice to become aware of these feelings and analyse them in terms of their degree of belonging to oneself or to the client. The effort is worth it, though, in terms of one's professional work as a helper as well as in terms of one's own psychological health.

If I as a therapist am aware of my countertransference, then I can prevent myself from slipping into indiscriminate actions; then I do not have to permanently do and act, just to relieve my own inner pressure. If the task of the helper is in the field of psychosociology, then knowledge about countertransference helps to be clear and efficient in one's work and not fall back on dedicating time and energy to unnecessary and maybe overwhelming actions and deeds, which go far beyond those of the role and ability of the helper, just in order to do something.

Rothschild (2006: 21) suggests a simple exercise to test one's own countertransference. She has devised a checklist for the awareness and analysis of one's own mental state:

- Sensations you feel in your body (hot, cold, achy, prickles, etc.)
- Visual or auditory images that arise in your mind (pictures, colors, sounds, songs, etc.)
- Movements or muscular impulses in your body (head turning, sitting back, legs tensing, clenched fists, etc.)
- What you feel (angry, irritated, sad, happy, scared, turned on, disgusted, etc.)
- Any thoughts that occur to you
  Next, take a few minutes to consider which of your responses could be mirrors of your client's experience (sensations, images, behaviors, feelings, thoughts)? Which are more likely reflections from your own past?

This reflection exercise makes it possible to understand what parts originate from countertransference reactions and which really 'belong' to the helper. It provides a firm basis for further plans.

## Self-care during Acute Situations Right after Traumatic Events

If an intervention is conducted right after a traumatic event has taken place in which people went missing or have 'disappeared', then it is especially important for the helpers to be aware of their own vulnerability. Halpern and Tramontin (2007) point to the simple, but nevertheless valuable guidelines drawn up by the American Red Cross with the purpose of helping people to remain stable in times of chaos and crisis.

1. Take breaks.
2. Eat and drink well and take simple exercises.
3. Get support from colleagues and family.
4. Stick to your shifts. It is important to take breaks and, together with colleagues, take turns in the care of those in need.
5. Take time off. If the intervention requires long-term involvement, as is the case with 'disappearances', then it is a good idea to also take a holiday after a while and completely remove oneself from the situation for some time.
6. Breathe deeply.

## Self-care in the Long-term Process

Authors, such as Pearlman and Saakvitne (1995) warn of the danger of vicarious traumatisation. Constantly hearing about terrible experiences and unresolved traumatic sequences can change one's own self-image and that of the world we live in. The clients' suffering pervades the feelings, thought processes and actions of the helper and can lead to symptoms such as nightmares, crying fits, tense muscles, somatic pains and social retreat.

In the long-term care of relatives of victims of 'enforced disappearances', it is, therefore, important to properly manage one's resources. It is helpful to be aware of one's strengths, and of what ways of recuperating and replenishing one's energy levels work best for oneself. This includes not only the small things that brighten up everyday life, but also long-term plans like annual holiday trip, a visit to relatives or friends one is close to, as well as important celebrations throughout the year. It is good to know which people can help one to feel comfortable, which activities help to relax (sports, lazing around, reading, writing, other creative ventures, cooking, etc.), and whether or not religions and rituals can also provide support in one's life.

It takes quite a degree of self-awareness, though, to know and accept one's own limits. In the style of Winnicott's (1956) 'good-enough mother', the authors Welt and Herron (1990) and Baker (2002) suggest the concept of the 'good-enough therapist', which can in fact be extended to the entire field of psychosocial work.

Winnicott describes the 'good-enough mother' as a primary attachment figure that can respond adequately to the needs of the child: The child is supplied with food, clothing, safe housing, etc., in an age-appropriate way. The mother is able to understand the child's needs and desires, be they communicated verbally or non-verbally. She can react to these, enter into an emotional relationship with the child and can provide the child with a basic experience of safety. A 'good-enough' mother will make mistakes, but these will not threaten the basis of the safe relationship between mother and child.

Parents are relieved of some of their inner stress by the concept of the 'good-enough mother' or the 'good-enough father'. In a similar manner, therapists, counsellors and social workers can relax a little bit: They do not have to be perfect. They do not have to heal all wounds. It is sufficient to be good enough. The therapeutic relationship is at the centre of the work. The therapist/counsellor supports the client, but he or she does not have to solve all the problems of a client. In the field of psychosocial work being 'good-enough' means taking a clear position and defining early-on and in a clear manner the possibilities and limitations of the support offered. '... here is a fine line between being competent enough and being perfect. The former is a reasonable goal; the latter is impossible. Our perspective on this issue can significantly affect the degree of pressure we experience at work ...' (Baker 2002: 111).

## Forms of Organised Mental Hygiene

### Intervision

In the psychological first-aid interventions right after a traumatic event, the work in teams of twos has won through. I know of no model in which on-site psychological crisis interventions are carried out by only one helper. Small teams of two or three persons make possible a more sensitive and careful approach to the chaotic situation. At the same time, the team members are supported in their self-care: The presence of a peer provides safety; in moments of great uncertainty, someone is there to consult with immediately, issues that are difficult to deal with for one team member can be taken over by another, shock and dismay can be shared and discussed immediately after the respective session. Nevertheless, it is necessary to have room for a debriefing after the intervention has been concluded, in order to return back to normality afterwards. Many of the helpers working in or after a time of crisis have come up with their own rituals for this. Some of them are simple, such as showering and changing attire, others are more complex, consisting of complex, formalised debriefing sessions with detailed documentations. There are some spiritually-oriented forms such as joint prayer meetings or meditations. Some closing rituals are very creative in nature. It is advantageous to have the option of intervision or supervision sessions to supplement these with, if an intervention has been particularly difficult.

Long-term counselling and psychotherapy take place in the more intimate atmosphere of a closed room. Colleagues of the counsellor/therapist are usually not present. Here, organised forms of intervision are of special importance. In working with severely traumatised people it can already prove helpful to simply be able to meet up with colleagues in between sessions to have a quick exchange about the situation. In my experience, even the shortest kinds of emotional statements can alleviate some of the stress and burden. A quick 'This was really difficult now' or 'It really gets to me how bad my client is feeling right now', without any further explanation, is often enough in order to remain capable of further actions and deeds. The simple fact that a colleague knows that this most recent session has been hard on me can make it possible to breathe easier.

In the long run, this is not enough, of course. Ideally, at the end of the working day the stress of the day can be talked about with colleagues. Their questions and their slightly different perspective on the situation, thanks to their emotional distance to the client, can help to significantly reduce the tensions that have built up. It is important that such meetings have their place and time within the routine of work—and that this time is remunerated. Such exchanges between colleagues should be furthered within the organisations working in this field.

## Supervision

Here, I refer to the European form of supervision: An experienced colleague who is well-versed in the particular field but does not work in the same organisation and ideally has no connection with the organisation at all offers to contribute his or her professional knowledge for the analysis of case histories and the planning of further steps in the therapy/counselling. This kind of input is especially necessary in those cases where a therapist/counsellor has become too involved. It constitutes an important form of assistance for the therapists/counsellors and is, therefore, part of every good therapeutic or psychological intervention.

The professional external viewpoint helps in the understanding of one's own countertransference reaction and makes the visibility of blind spots possible. A second professional opinion often helps in the difficult work of supporting traumatised people. It strengthens and reassures the therapist or helper.

Since feelings of isolation, helplessness and loneliness are central topics in the conversations with the relatives of 'disappeared' people, the helpers need a solid counterweight to balance these out and not be themselves overwhelmed by these feelings. Regular supervision sessions have proven themselves in this respect.

## A Positive Working Climate

Helpers who work with issues of traumatisation, first and foremost, have to offer safety to their clients. This can only be possible if they themselves feel safe. Therefore, importance needs to be attached to this in all considerations about the entire working conditions.

One thing that is needed is a safe place to work at: The rooms should be large enough, and equipped with all resources necessary to do one's work (for example, if the clients are to receive legal advice, then access to a computer and Internet are certainly necessary). It is not only work rooms that are needed, but rooms to withdraw to during breaks are equally important.

> In a workshop in South Asia, an employee of a legal aid organisation tells us that he suffers from stomach pains. On most days, he does not eat the lunch he brings to work, which is usually prepared with love by his wife. The reason for this is that the NGO basically only consists of one large room. So he would have to eat right under the eyes of his waiting clients. The recommendation he takes from the workshop is an appeal to the management team of his NGO to at least provide a small break room for the employees.

In a good team, communication takes place on three levels. It is important that some of the work time is set aside for this and is seen as an essential part of the process as a whole.

1. All employees have access to the information relevant for their work. The information exchange happens either in the course of team meeting, in e-mails sent to everyone involved, via regularly checked platforms for information, in work meetings of the small group, in the form of a telephone call, etc. If somebody takes on a task, then he or she needs to be provided with all relevant information.
2. Case reviews: These can take place in the form of intervision or supervision as discussed earlier.
3. Informal exchanges: It is not necessary for all co-workers to be best friends. The interactions between them should be characterised by a generous form of understanding and sympathy, especially in such a difficult field of work. Conversations with each other, and mutual appreciation should be furthered. It takes space and time to talk about everyday worries and joys. Congratulating each other on occasions such as birthdays for once puts the employees at the centre of attention. Everybody enjoys positive feedback—and most especially those who are willing to give so much in their support of other people.

# 10

# Conclusion

In this book, I have spanned the gamut from the theoretical bases, complicated grief and trauma to the historical dimension of 'enforced disappearances', collective forms of coping, psychotherapeutic work with severely traumatised people and the psychosocial and psychotherapeutic interventions for relatives of 'disappeared' persons.

In my almost two decades of working within the field and investing myself into this area, I have seen the deepest abyss of human behaviour when it comes to what people are prepared to do to others, but I have also been privileged to witness people showing enormous strength in situations that are hopeless and desperate. Despite their peril, they search for, and indeed find, ways to move on and keep on living.

The open question as to what has happened to the 'disappeared' remains thus—but I do hope to have been able to point out ways of coping and dealing with the problematic situation of a 'disappearance' in this book.

The grieving process after having lost an attachment figure because they have 'disappeared' (are missing, lost without a trace) is especially difficult, no matter in what circumstances. Drawing on existing works discussed in the literature review in Chapter 1 as well as on the cases described throughout the rest of the book, one can establish the following propositions, which, in turn, warrant further research into this little-explored field.

1. *Denial of loss*

    Times of doubt and denial are natural parts of all grieving processes. By the verifications of the reality of the beloved person's death—the body of the deceased, the death certificate in one's own hands, and others—the bereaved is painfully reminded of the reality of the loss. Thereby, the factuality of the person's death must be acknowledged and accepted, and so the grieving process can begin in earnest.

    Relatives of those who have 'disappeared' have no such means of verifying reality. Evidence for the beloved person's death is just as vague as that which might be interpreted as a sign of life.

    Consequently, the bereaved sometimes spend their lives clinging to the hope that the 'disappeared' relative might return after all. Particularly memorable in this context was a Jewish woman who was searching for her mother in Manhattan in 1999—a mother she had last seen at the ramp at Auschwitz.

Also to this group belong those refugees who did not dare to fill in an application form for the Red Cross Tracing Service. Even the slim possibility of getting confirmation for the death of the missing relative lets them divest themselves of the equally slight chance that they might receive a sign of life from the 'disappeared'.

Time appears to be playing an important role here. After a number of years of hope and denial, people do become ready to face reality, as could be seen in the examples of the truth commissions.

2. *Frozen phase*

Oftentimes, though, relatives deny themselves the acceptance and the mourning of their loss if a relative has 'disappeared'. With fervour, they work on retaining the status of the beloved being merely lost (the most widely known literary example of this being, of course, Penelope). The spot of the 'disappeared' has to be kept open at all cost, even if that should be detrimental to the growth and development of other living family members.

Actually taking the step of detaching oneself would be too much of an emotional burden, as it would feel like a kind of social murderer of the beloved person who has 'disappeared'.

3. *Denial of the existence of the 'disappeared' and the 'ban on mourning'*

Especially in those cases were the 'disappearance' was politically motivated, relatives often get little support from their families and friends. Oftentimes, people pretend that the 'disappeared' has, in fact, never existed at all. Consequently, no mourning rituals can be held. Sometimes, the 'disappeared' are literally kept dead quiet.

This form of avoidance can be observed in therapeutic settings as well. In order to not have to confront the overwhelming reality of the loss, relatives evade all conversations, every thought about the 'disappeared'. In this way, they also lose the positive components, that of a strong, affirmative relationship and the memories shared.

4. *A delayed grieving process is sometimes still possible*

After a period of feelings of hope, resignation and a certainty about the 'disappeared' person's death start to outweigh these feelings.

The grieving process begins in a delayed fashion and can easily be interrupted and thereby extended in time by periods of denial. Nevertheless, grieving can be possible, and the bereaved can find their bearings again and re-orient themselves.

Conclusion    205

While these propositions describe tendencies that can be seen as generally present in the reactions of relatives of victims of 'enforced disappearances', individual factors come into play as well. One needs to be aware of these in order to be able to understand the individual reactions. These include:

- *Pre-traumatic factors* such as the cultural and social background one was raised and has lived in, and the relationship one had had with the 'disappeared'.
- *Traumatic factors* such as the circumstances under which the beloved person has 'disappeared', what means the family was able to employ in their search, as well as to what extent other family members felt to be under threat too, and if they were additionally traumatised through, for example, imprisonment or torture.
- *Post-traumatic factors* which include any and all aspects of the entire process of dealing with the loss of the 'disappeared' person. Individual, family-specific and socio-political components come into play here.

In working in a therapeutic setting with relatives of victims of 'enforced disappearances', the central element is support throughout the time of dealing with this ambivalent kind of loss and grief.

At the beginning of the therapeutic process, I try to explain to my patients, who come from various cultural backgrounds and often have only the vaguest idea as to what psychotherapy entails, what our work is about. For this, I make use of the following image.

My work is similar to that of a mountain guide who offers to accompany a hiker on his or her way. The path that is to be travelled starts out in a dark and desolate place, but should lead to better, lighter, more fertile lands. As a companion, I will walk with the hikers, but not for them. I have walked the mountains with others before and have watched them overcome similarly difficult passages, but the very road we are taking now is new to me as well. I know the terrain, however, and can therefore point out possible surface irregularities and warn of dangers. I can spot safe places to rest and have a general idea as to where the end of the journey may lie. Thanks to my experience, I can sometimes tell what we will face behind the next turn, even if my clients cannot see it yet themselves. Sometimes—if the path leads through particularly treacherous lands—I will take care of part of the burdens the client has to bear. As a good guide, I will naturally not only take good care of my client, but also of myself, of my safety.

Throughout the years that I have done psychotherapeutic work with survivors of war and torture, many of who had lost relatives because these had 'disappeared', I was able to accompany many people on this path and support them throughout their complicated grieving process. These people were able to arrive at a point where their grief was no longer that desperate and immediate, were psychological safety had become a reality once more, where hope for, as well as a trust in human relationships had once again become possible.

Many of the experiences my clients related to me have found their way into this book. Without the openness of these clients and their willingness to share not only their experiences and their despair but also their hope I would have had little to say. I, therefore, see this book also as a means of giving voice to all the relatives of 'disappeared' persons in this world who have no information about the whereabouts of a beloved family member.

I want to encourage people to support the relatives of 'disappeared' persons and stand by them, be it in the professional capacity of a psychologist, legal advisor, social worker, minister, school staff or therapist, or as a friend or relative.

'Disappearances' make us all helpless and thereby speechless. What we need to understand is that neither the professional helper nor the caring friend needs to always have all the answers. What is important is that they be there for the relatives of the 'disappeared', stay by their side and support them through the difficult process of dealing with the loss.

Pauline Boss has found the right words to describe this kind of work in which we, the helpers, have no answers or solutions to offer to our clients, and to explain one's own role in it, and with it a way of staying psychologically healthy in the midst of the storm:

> Paradoxically, knowing we can live with not knowing provides us with the resiliency we need to be effective when treating ambiguous loss....
> I learned with each onslaught that 'getting over it' was not possible. I now walk with the tension of imperfect solutions and balance them with the joys and passions in my daily life. (Boss 1999: 209f.)

# Bibliography

Abdallah-Steinkopff, B. (2003). Psychotherapie und Beratung mit Dolmetschern. *Refugio Report November*, 4–5.
Acuna, J. E. (1987). *Children of the storm. Experiences of the children's rehabilitation center.* Manila: Eigenverlag.
Agosin, M. (1992). *Circles of madness. Mothers of the Plaza de Maya.* New York: White Pine Press.
———. (1993). Surviving beyond fear. Women, children and human rights. In M. Agosin (Ed.), *Latin America* (pp. 98–125). New York: White Pine Press.
Ainsworth, M., Waters, E., & Wall, S.(1978). *Patterns of attachment.* Hillsdale: Erlbaum.
Alic, A. (2003). Srebrenica denial continues. Retrieved from www.ceed.com/aspx/search-articles.aspx (accessed on 26 February 2015).
American Psychiatric Association. (1980/1994). *Diagnostic and statistical manual of mental disorders.* Washington, D.C.: APA.
Améry, Jean. (1989). *At the mind's limits: Contemplations by a survivor on Auschwitz and its realities.* Bloomington: Indiana University Press.
Amnesty International. (1982). *...nicht die Erde hat sie verschluckt.* Bonn: Amnesty International.
———. (1993a). *Getting away with murder. Political killings and 'disappearances' in the 1990s.* London: Amnesty International Publications.
———. (1993b, February). *14-Point program for the prevention of 'disappearances'.* Retrieved from http://www.amnesty.org/en/library/info/POL36/001/1993 (accessed on 19 January 2015).
———. (1996). *Latin America crime without punishment: Impunity in Latin America.* London: Amnesty International Publications.
———. (1997). *Sri Lanka. Government's response to widespread 'disappearances' in Jaffna* (ASA 37/24/97).
———. (2002, May). *Amnesty International Report 2002: Russian Federation.* Retrieved from http://www.refworld.org/docid/3cf4bc12c.html (accessed on 19 January 2015).
———. (2010). Ein Leben in Angst und Ungewissheit. Verschleppung, Geheimhaft und politischer Mord. Retrieved from http://www.amnesty.at/informiert_sein/ein_leben_in_angst_und_ungewissheit/ (accessed on 10 July 2013).
———. (2012). Jetzt Gerechtigkeit für die Familie Matanovic fordern. Retrieved from http://www.amnesty.at/index.php?id=1827 (accessed on 4 September 2012).
Ansary, M. (2003). *Flieh, bevor der Morgen graut. Die Geschichte einer iranischen Frau.* Bergisch Gladbach: Ehrenwirth.
Antonovsky, A. (1987). *Unraveling the mystery of health: How people manage stress and stay well.* San Francisco: Jossey-Bass.
———. (1979). *Salutogenese. Zur Entmystifizierung der Gesundheit* [*Health, Stress and Coping*]. Tübingen: dgvt Verlag [San Francisco: Jossey-Bass].

Arcel, L. T., Folnegović-Šmalc V., Kozarić-Kovačić D., & Marušić, A. (1995). *Psycho-social help to war victims: Women refugees and their families from Bosnia and Herzegovina and Croatia.* Copenhagen: IRCT.
Ashenberg Straussner, S., & Kolko Phillips, N. (2004). *Understanding mass violence. A social work perspective.* Boston: Pearson.
Asian Human Rights Commission. (1999). *Sri Lanka: Disappearances and the collapse of the police system.* Hongkong: AHRC Eigenverlag.
Asian Human Right Group (AHRC). (2006). Sri Lanka: 20 forced disappearances reported in December 2005 (Urgent Action 017-2005). Hongkong: Asian Human Right Commission.
———. (2013). *Sri Lanka: Whose remains are in the mass grave at Matale* (AHRC-STM-083-2013). Hongkong: Asian Human Right Group.
Auerhahn, N. C., & Laub, D. (1984). Annihilation and restoration: Post-traumatic memory as pathway and obstacle to recovery. *International Review Psycho-Analysis, 11*, 327–343.
———. (1988). Intergenerational memory of the Holocaust. In Y. Danieli (Ed.), *International handbook of multigenerational legacies of trauma* (pp. 21–42). New York: Plenum Press.
Baker, E. K. (2002). *Crying for ourselves. A therapist's guide to personal and professional well-being.* Washington, D.C.: American Psychological Association.
Ball, P. (2005, January 7). Mass graves are not necessary for tsunami victims. *Nature: International Weekly Journal of Science.* Online. Retrieved from http://www.nature.com/news/2005/050103/full/news050103-10.html (accessed on 19 January 2015).
Baradaran, Monireh. (1998). *Erwachen aus dem Alptraum.* Zürich: Unionsverlag.
Baron, N. (2002). Community based psychosocial and mental health services for southern Sudanese refugees in long term exile in Uganda. In J. De Jong (Ed.), *Trauma, war, and violence. Public mental health in socio-cultural context* (pp. 157–203). New York: Kluwer Academic.
Bayer, O. (2001). Die Schatten der Verschwundenen. Die Diktatur in Argentinien und ihre Folgen. In J. Müller-Hohagen (Ed.), *Stacheldraht und heile Welt.* Tübingen: Edition Diskord.
BBC. (2004). *Hidden graves.* Retrieved from http://news.bc.co.uk/1/hi/world/south_asia/125691.stm (accessed on 19 January 2015).
Becker, D. (1992). *Ohne Haß keine Versöhnung. Das Trauma der Verfolgten.* Feiburg i.Br.: Kore.
———. (2006). *Die Erfindung des Traumas—Verflochtene Geschichten.* Berlin: Freitag.
Becker, D., & Weyermann, B. (2006). *Gender, Konflikttransformation & psychosozialer Ansatz [Gender, Conflict Transformation & The Psychosocial Approach. Toolkit].* Retrieved from http://www.deza.admin.ch/ressources/resource_en_91135.pdf;http://opsiconsult.com/wp-content/uploads/92880853292022.pdf (last accessed on 19 January 2015).
Becker, E. (1973). *The denial of death.* New York: Simon and Schuster.
Beckermann, R. (1989). *Unzugehörig. Österreicher und Juden nach 1945.* Wien: Löcker Verlag.
Belic, M., & Kesic V. (1994). Center for women. War victims/survivors (Zagreb): Wer wir sind und was wir tun. *Werkblatt, 32*, 108–118.
Benedek, E. D. (1985). Children and disaster: Emerging issues. *Psychiatric Annuals, 15*(3), 168–172.
Benson, D., McCubbln, H.I., Dahl, B. B., & Hunter E. (1975). Waiting: The dilemma of the MIA wife. In I. Mccubbin Hamilton et al. (Eds), *Family separation and reunion. Families of prisoners of war and servicemen missing in action* (pp. 157–168). Washington, D.C.: U.S. Government Printing Office.
Benz, W. (1995). *Der Holocaust.* München: Beck.

# Bibliography

Abdallah-Steinkopff, B. (2003). Psychotherapie und Beratung mit Dolmetschern. *Refugio Report November*, 4–5.
Acuna, J. E. (1987). *Children of the storm. Experiences of the children's rehabilitation center.* Manila: Eigenverlag.
Agosin, M. (1992). *Circles of madness. Mothers of the Plaza de Maya.* New York: White Pine Press.
———. (1993). Surviving beyond fear. Women, children and human rights. In M. Agosin (Ed.), *Latin America* (pp. 98–125). New York: White Pine Press.
Ainsworth, M., Waters, E., & Wall, S.(1978). *Patterns of attachment.* Hillsdale: Erlbaum.
Alic, A. (2003). Srebrenica denial continues. Retrieved from www.ceed.com/aspx/searcharticles.aspx (accessed on 26 February 2015).
American Psychiatric Association. (1980/1994). *Diagnostic and statistical manual of mental disorders.* Washington, D.C.: APA.
Améry, Jean. (1989). *At the mind's limits: Contemplations by a survivor on Auschwitz and its realities.* Bloomington: Indiana University Press.
Amnesty International. (1982). *...nicht die Erde hat sie verschluckt.* Bonn: Amnesty International.
———. (1993a). *Getting away with murder. Political killings and 'disappearances' in the 1990s.* London: Amnesty International Publications.
———. (1993b, February). *14-Point program for the prevention of 'disappearances'.* Retrieved from http://www.amnesty.org/en/library/info/POL36/001/1993 (accessed on 19 January 2015).
———. (1996). *Latin America crime without punishment: Impunity in Latin America.* London: Amnesty International Publications.
———. (1997). *Sri Lanka. Government's response to widespread 'disappearances' in Jaffna* (ASA 37/24/97).
———. (2002, May). *Amnesty International Report 2002: Russian Federation.* Retrieved from http://www.refworld.org/docid/3cf4bc12c.html (accessed on 19 January 2015).
———. (2010). Ein Leben in Angst und Ungewissheit. Verschleppung, Geheimhaft und politischer Mord. Retrieved from http://www.amnesty.at/informiert_sein/ein_leben_in_angst_und_ungewissheit/ (accessed on 10 July 2013).
———. (2012). Jetzt Gerechtigkeit für die Familie Matanovic fordern. Retrieved from http://www.amnesty.at/index.php?id=1827 (accessed on 4 September 2012).
Ansary, M. (2003). *Flieh, bevor der Morgen graut. Die Geschichte einer iranischen Frau.* Bergisch Gladbach: Ehrenwirth.
Antonovsky, A. (1987). *Unraveling the mystery of health: How people manage stress and stay well.* San Francisco: Jossey-Bass.
———. (1979). *Salutogenese. Zur Entmystifizierung der Gesundheit* [*Health, Stress and Coping*]. Tübingen: dgvt Verlag [San Francisco: Jossey-Bass].

Arcel, L. T., Folnegović-Šmalc V., Kozarić-Kovačić D., & Marušić, A. (1995). *Psycho-social help to war victims: Women refugees and their families from Bosnia and Herzegovina and Croatia.* Copenhagen: IRCT.

Ashenberg Straussner, S., & Kolko Phillips, N. (2004). *Understanding mass violence. A social work perspective.* Boston: Pearson.

Asian Human Rights Commission. (1999). *Sri Lanka: Disappearances and the collapse of the police system.* Hongkong: AHRC Eigenverlag.

Asian Human Right Group (AHRC). (2006). Sri Lanka: 20 forced disappearances reported in December 2005 (Urgent Action 017-2005). Hongkong: Asian Human Right Commission.

———. (2013). *Sri Lanka: Whose remains are in the mass grave at Matale* (AHRC-STM-083-2013). Hongkong: Asian Human Right Group.

Auerhahn, N. C., & Laub, D. (1984). Annihilation and restoration: Post-traumatic memory as pathway and obstacle to recovery. *International Review Psycho-Analysis, 11,* 327–343.

———. (1988). Intergenerational memory of the Holocaust. In Y. Danieli (Ed.), *International handbook of multigenerational legacies of trauma* (pp. 21–42). New York: Plenum Press.

Baker, E. K. (2002). *Crying for ourselves. A therapist's guide to personal and professional well-being.* Washington, D.C.: American Psychological Association.

Ball, P. (2005, January 7). Mass graves are not necessary for tsunami victims. *Nature: International Weekly Journal of Science.* Online. Retrieved from http://www.nature.com/news/2005/050103/full/news050103-10.html (accessed on 19 January 2015).

Baradaran, Monireh. (1998). *Erwachen aus dem Alptraum.* Zürich: Unionsverlag.

Baron, N. (2002). Community based psychosocial and mental health services for southern Sudanese refugees in long term exile in Uganda. In J. De Jong (Ed.), *Trauma, war, and violence. Public mental health in socio-cultural context* (pp. 157–203). New York: Kluwer Academic.

Bayer, O. (2001). Die Schatten der Verschwundenen. Die Diktatur in Argentinien und ihre Folgen. In J. Müller-Hohagen (Ed.), *Stacheldraht und heile Welt.* Tübingen: Edition Diskord.

BBC. (2004). *Hidden graves.* Retrieved from http://news.bc.co.uk/1/hi/world/south_asia/125691.stm (accessed on 19 January 2015).

Becker, D. (1992). *Ohne Haß keine Versöhnung. Das Trauma der Verfolgten.* Feiburg i.Br.: Kore.

———. (2006). *Die Erfindung des Traumas—Verflochtene Geschichten.* Berlin: Freitag.

Becker, D., & Weyermann, B. (2006). *Gender, Konflikttransformation & psychosozialer Ansatz [Gender, Conflict Transformation & The Psychosocial Approach. Toolkit].* Retrieved from http://www.deza.admin.ch/ressources/resource_en_91135.pdf;http://opsiconsult.com/wp-content/uploads/92880853292022.pdf (last accessed on 19 January 2015).

Becker, E. (1973). *The denial of death.* New York: Simon and Schuster.

Beckermann, R. (1989). *Unzugehörig. Österreicher und Juden nach 1945.* Wien: Löcker Verlag.

Belic, M., & Kesic V. (1994). Center for women. War victims/survivors (Zagreb): Wer wir sind und was wir tun. *Werkblatt, 32,* 108–118.

Benedek, E. D. (1985). Children and disaster: Emerging issues. *Psychiatric Annuals, 15*(3), 168–172.

Benson, D., McCubbln, H.I., Dahl, B. B., & Hunter E. (1975). Waiting: The dilemma of the MIA wife. In I. Mccubbin Hamilton et al. (Eds), *Family separation and reunion. Families of prisoners of war and servicemen missing in action* (pp. 157–168). Washington, D.C.: U.S. Government Printing Office.

Benz, W. (1995). *Der Holocaust.* München: Beck.

Berk, J. H. (1998). Trauma and resilience during war: A look at the children and humanitarian aid workers of Bosnia. *Psychoanalytic Review, 85*(4), 639–658.
Bettelheim, B. (1980). *Erziehung zum Überleben. Zur Psychologie von Extremsituationen.* Stuttgart [*Surviving and Other Essays*]: Deutscher Taschenbuchverlag [New York: Alfred.A. Knopf].
Bittenbinder, E. (2000). Trauma und extreme Gewalt—Systemische Psychotherapie mit Überlebenden von Folter und die Bedeutung 'innerer Bilder'. *Psychotherapie im Dialog, 1,* 38–44.
Black, L. (1999). Forced disappearances in Sri Lanka constitute a crime against humanity. Retrieved from www.disappearances.org/mainfile.php/articles_srilanka/9/?print=yes
Blos, P. (1979). *Adolescent passage.* New York: International Universities Press.
Böhme, K. W. (1965). *Gesucht wird.... Die dramatische Geschichte des Suchdienstes.* München: Süddeutscher Verlag.
Boss, P. (1999). *Ambiguous loss. Learning to live with unresolved grief.* Cambridge: Harvard University Press.
———. (2006). *Loss, trauma and resilience: Therapeutic work with ambiguous loss.* New York: Norton.
Boss, P., Beaulieu, L., Wieling E., Turner, W., & LaCruz, S. (2003). Healing loss, ambiguity, and trauma: A community-based intervention with families of union workers missing after the 9/11 attack in New York City. *Journal of Marital and Family Therapy, 29,* 455–467.
Boulanger, G. (2007). *Wounded by reality. Understanding and treating adult onset trauma.* Mahwah: The Analytic Press.
Bouvard, M. G. (1994). *Revolutionizing motherhood. The mothers of the Plaza de Maya.* Wilmington, DE: Scholarly Resources Inc.
Bowlby, J. (1958). The nature of the child's tie to his mother. *International Journal of Psychoanalysis, 38,* 350–373.
———. (1961). Childhood mourning and its implications for psychiatry. *American Journal of Psychiatry, 118,* 481–498.
———. (1969). *Attachment and loss.* New York: Basic Books.
———. (1980). *Loss, sadness and depression.* New York: Basic Books.
———. (1983). *Verlust: Trauer und depression.* Frankfurt am Main: Fischer.
Bracken, P. J., & Petty, C. (1998). *Rethinking the trauma of war.* New York: Free Association Books.
Brenner, I. (1988). Multisensory bridges in response to object loss during the Holocaust. *Psychoanalytic Review, 75,* 573–587.
———. (1996). Child survivors as parents and grandparents. In J. Kestenberg & I. Brenner (Eds), *The last witness: The child survivor of the Holocaust* (pp. 107–129). Washington, D.C.: American Psychiatric Press, Inc.
Brkic, C. A. (2004). Eyewitness: Unearthing Bosnia's dead. Retrieved from http://news.bbc.co.uk/1/hi/world/europe/3975599.stm (accessed on 19 January 2015).
Brune, M. (2000). Posttraumatische Störungen. In C. Haasen & Y. Oktay (Eds), *Beurteilung psychischer Störungen in einer multikulturellen Gesellschaft* (pp. 107–125). Freiburg i.Br.: Lambertus.
———. (2010). Wenn Verbrechen nicht gesühnt werden—Reflexionen zur Psychotherapie mit Opfern lateinamerikanischer Diktaturen. In K. Ottomeyer, B. Preitler & H. Spitzer (Eds), *Look I am a foreigner. Interkulturelle Begegnung und psychosoziale Praxis auf fünf Kontinenten* (pp. 49–60). Klagenfurt: Drava.

Bunster, X. (1993). Surviving beyond fear: Women and torture in Latin America. In M. Agosin (Ed.), *Surviving beyond fear. Women, children and human rights in Latin America* (pp. 98–125). New York: White Pine Press.
Butalia, U. (1997). Abducted and Widowed Women. Questions of Sexuality and Citzenship During Partition. In. Thapan M. (Ed.). *Embodiment: Essays on gender and identity/ed.* Delhi: Oxford University Press, 90–106.
Butollo, W., Krüsmann, M., & Hagl M. (1998). *Leben nach dem Trauma. Über den therapeutischen Umgang mit dem Entsetzen.* München: Pfeiffer.
Canacakis, J. (1992). Unser Leben—ein ständiges Abschiednehmen. Trauerfähigkeit als notwendige Psychohygiene. In *Goldegger Dialoge: Schmerz—Stachel des Lebens.* Goldegg: Eigenverlag.
Carlson, E. S. (1996). *I remember Julia: voices of the disappeared.* Philadelphia, PA: Temple University Press.
*Childline. Childline 1098. Night & Day.* http://www.childlineindia.org.in/missing-children-india.htm (accessed on 15 January 2015)
Comite International ICRC. (1996, May 30). *Missing persons on the territory of Bosnia and Herzegovina.* Geneve: Red Cross/Eigenverlag.
Corr, C. (1993). The day we went to Auschwitz. *Omega, 27*(2), 105–113.
Damian, S. (1987). *The psychotherapeutic approach to the psychological sequel of civil war in the district of Jaffna.* Unpublished typescript.
Daniel, E. V. (1997). Suffering nation and alienation. In A. Kleinman et al. (Eds), *Social suffering* (pp. 309–358). Berkely: University of California Press.
Danieli, Y. (1981). The aging survivors of the Holocaust. *Journal Geriatric Psychiatry, 14,* 191–210.
———. (1994). Die Konfrontation mit dem Unvorstellbaren. Reaktionen von Psychotherapeuten auf die Opfer des Nazi-Holocaust. In H. Stoffels (Ed.), *Terrorlandschaften der Seele. Beiträge zur Theorie und Therapie von Extremtraumatisierungen* (pp. 83–103). Regensburg: S. Roderer Verlag.
———. (Ed.). (1998). *International handbook of multigenerational legacies of trauma.* New York: Plenum Press.
Danieli, Y., Rodley, N. S., & Weisaeth, L. (Eds). (1996). *International responses to traumatic stress.* Amityville: Beywood Publishing Company, Inc.
Das, V. (1997). Language and body: Transactions in the construction of pain. In A. Kleinmann, V. Das & M. Lock (Eds), *Social suffering* (pp. 67–92). Berkely: University California Press.
———. (2002). Nationale Ehre und praktizierte Verwandtschaft. Unerwünschte Frauen und Kinder nach der Trennung Pakistans von Indien. In B. Duden & D. Noeres (Eds), *Auf den Spuren des Körpers in einer technogenen Welt* (pp. 77–102). Opladen: leske + budrich.
De Jong, J. (2002). *Trauma, war, and violence. Public mental health in socio-cultural context.* New York: Kluwer Academic.
De Osterheld, E. (2001). Doch in mir bleibt nichts als Schmerz. In Missionszentrale der Franziskaner (Ed.), *Verschwunden in Argentinien. Neue Wege gegen Straflosigkeit und Vergessen. Berichte, Dokumente, Kommentare Nr. 84.* Bonn: Eigenverlag.
Der Standard. (2004, January 3). Fischgerichte derzeit tabu. *Der Standard,* p. 4.
De Soysa, P. (2001). Conflict-related trauma in an Asian country: A report from Sri Lanka. *International Review of Psychiatry, 13,* 201–208.
Deutsches Rotes Kreuz. (1988). *Die Genfer Rotkreuz-Abkommen vom 12. August 1949 und die Beiden Zusatzprotokolle vom 8. Juni 1977* (8th ed.). Bonn: Schriften des Deutschen Roten Kreuzes.

Devereux, G. (1984). *Angst und Methode in den Verhaltenswissenschaften* [*From Anxiety to Method in the Behavioral Sciences*]. Frankfurt am Main: Suhrkamp Taschenbuch [The Hague: Mouton].
De Wind, E. (1968). The confrontation with death. *International Journal of Psycho-Analysis*, 49, 302–305.
De Zoysa, P. (2001). Conflict-related trauma in an Asian country: A report from Sri Lanka. *International Review of Psychiatry*, 13, 201–208.
Diner, D. (Ed.). (1988). *Zivilisationsbruch. Denken nach Auschwitz*. Frankfurt am Main: Fischer.
Domansky, E. (1997). A lost war. World War II in Postwar German Memory. In A. H. Rosenfeld (Ed.), *Thinking about the Holocaust* (pp. 233–272). Bloomington/Indianapolis: Indiana University Press..
Duras, M. (1985). *Der Liebhaber*. Frankfurt am Main: Suhrkamp.
Durst, N. (1994). Über Einsamkeit und das unendliche Trauern von alternden Überlebenden des Holocaust. In H. Stoffels (Ed.), *Terrorlandschaften der Seele. Beiträge zur Theorie und Therapie von Extremtraumatisierungen* (pp. 44–53). Regensburg: S.Roderer Verlag.
———. (1999). Psychotherapeutisches Arbeiten mit Überlebenden des Holocaust. *Zeitschrift für Politische Psychologie*, 7(1+2), 101–112.
Edelman, L., Kersner, D., Kordon, D., & Lagos, D. (2003). Psychosocial effect and treatment of mass trauma due to sociopolitical events: The Argentine experience. In S. Krippner & T. M. McIntyre (Eds), *The psychological impact of war trauma on civilians: An international perspective* (pp. 143–153). Westport: Prager Publishers.
Edelman, L., Kordon, D., & Lagos, D. (1998). Transmission of trauma. The Argentine case. In Y. Danieli (Ed.), *International Handbook of Multigenerational Legacies of Trauma* (pp. 447–463). New York: Plenum Press.
Erikson, E. H. (1968). *Identity, youth and crisis*. New York: Norton.
Extraordinary Chambers in the Courts of Cambodia (ECCC). (2012). *About (ECCC)*. Retrieved from http://www.eccc.gov.kh (accessed on 18 October 2012).
Eyer, D. E. (1992). *Mother–infant bonding*. New Haven: Yale University Press.
FEDEFAM (2004). *Fighting against forced disappearances in Latin America*. Retrieved from http://www.desaparecidos.org/fedefam/eng.html (accessed on 19 January 2015).
Fernando, B. (1998). Disappearances: A matter of survival of society and the country. *Christian Worker*, 2, 6–11.
———. (2004). *The right to speak loudly. Essays on law and human rights*. Hongkong: Asian Legal Resource Centre.
Final Draft from the Violence and Grief Work Group. (1997–1998). Document on violence and grief. *Omega*, 36(3), 259–272.
Fink, I. (1996). *Die Reise*. Frankfurt am Main: Fischer.
Fischer, G., & Riedesser, P. (2003). *Lehrbuch der Psychotraumatologie* (3rd ed.). München, Basel: Ernst Reinhardt Verlag.
Fischer, J. (1989). *Mothers of the disappeared*. Boston: South End Press.
Foa, E. B. (1998). *Treating the trauma of rape: Cognitive-behavioral therapy for PTSD*. New York: Guilford Press.
Fogelman, E. (1998). Group belonging and mourning as factors in resilience in second generation of Holocaust survivors. *Psychoanalytic Review*, 85(4), 537–549.
Fravel, D. L., & Boss, P. (1992). An in-depth interview with the parents of missing children. In J. F. Gilgun & K. Daly (Eds), *Qualitative methods in family research*. Newbury Park: SAGE Publications Inc.
Freeman, J. (2012, October 4). Khmer Rouge survivors risk prolonged grief disorder. *The Phnom Penh Post*.

Freud, S. (1914/16). *The standard edition of the complete psychological work of Sigmund Freud*. London: The Hogarth Press.

———. (1916). *Trauer und Melancholie*. G.W. Band X. Frankfurt am Main: Fischer, pp. 427–446.

———. (1918). *Reflections on war and death*. New York: Moffat, Yard and Co.

———. (1961b). *Hemmung, Symptom und Angst*. Frankfurt am Main: Fischer Taschenbuch.

———. (1961b). *Die Traumdeutung*. Frankfurt am Main: Fischer.

———. (1994). *Das Unbehagen der Kultur und andere Kulturtheoretische Schriften*. Frankfurt am Main: Fischer.

Gampel, Y. (1998). Reflections on countertransference in psychoanalytic work with child survivors of the Shoah. *Journal of the American Academy of Psychoanalysis, 26*(3), 343–368.

Garcia, S. N. (2001). Den Tod erinnern, um weiterleben zu können. In Medico International (Ed.), *Die Gewalt überleben: Psychosoziale Arbeit im Kontext von Krieg, Diktatur und Armut* (pp. 37–42). Frankfurt am Main: Mabuse.

Geiger, B. (1996). *Fathers as primary caregivers*. Westport: Greenwood Press.

Gelbin, C., Lezzi, E., Hartman, G.H., & Schoeps, J.H. (Eds). (1998). *Archiv der Erinnerung Interviews mit Überlebenden der Shoah. Band I: Videographierte Lebenserzählungen und ihre Interpretationen*. Potsdam: Verlag für Berlin-Brandenburg.

Gesellschaft für Bedrohte Völker. (2004). Auch Jugendliche 'verschwinden'. Retrieved from http://www.gfbv.de/gfbv_international.php (last accessed on 25 February 2015).

Goldmann, H., Krall, H., & Ottomeyer, K. (1992). *Jörg Haider und sein Publikum. Eine sozialpsychologische Untersuchung*. Klagenfurt: Drava.

Goldmann, J., & Guger, J. (Eds). (2006) *Vermisst & Gefunden. Ein Schicksal—viele Geschichten*. Salzburg: A&M Weltbild.

Gonzales Castaneda, O. (2013). Scarfs of hope as a warm and performative memorial for the disappeared in Peru. Critica Latinoamericana. Retrieved from http://criticalatinoamericana.com/316/ (accessed on 4 August 2013).

Götsch, B., & Preitler, B. (2006). Traum(a)insel: Die psychische Bewältigung von Bürgerkrieg und Tsunami in Sri Lanka. In H. Weinhäupl & M. Wolfsberger (Eds), *Trauminseln? Tourismus und Alltag in 'Urlaubsparadiesen'* (pp. 111–126). Münster: LIT-Verlag.

Graessner, S., Gurris, N., & Pross, C. (1996). *Folter. An der Seite der Überlebenden. Unterstützung und Therapien*. München: C.H. Beck'sche Verlagsbuchhandlung.

Greene, W. A. (1958). Role of a vicarious object in the adaptation to object loss. *Psychosomatic Medicine, XX*(5), 344–350.

Greenson, R. R. (1978). On transitional objects and transference. In S. A. Grolnick et al. (Eds), *Between reality and fantasy. Transitional objects and phenomena*. New York: Jason Aronson.

Grolnick, S. A., Barkin, L., & Muensterberger, W. (Eds). (1978). *Between reality and fantasy. Transitional objects and phenomena*. New York: Jason Aronson.

Hackl, E. (1997). *Sara und Simón. Eine endlose Geschichte*. Zürich: Diogenes.

Halpern, J., & Tramontin, M. (2007). *Disaster mental health: Theory and practice*. Belmont: Thomson.

Hamber, B. (1995, July 26). *Do sleeping dogs lie? The psychological implications of the truth and reconciliation commission in South Africa*. Paper presented at Seminar No.5; Centre for the Study of Violence and Reconciliation, Johannesburg.

Hamburger Institut für Sozialforschung. (1987). *Nie Wieder! Ein Bericht über Entführung, Folter und Mord durch die Militärdiktatur in Argentinien*. Weinheim/Basel: Beltz.

Haney, C. A., Leimer, C., & Lowery, J. et al. (1997). Spontaneous memorialization: Violent death and emerging mourning ritual. *Omega—Journal of Death and Dying, 35*(2), 159–171.

Hassel, F. (Ed.) (2003). *Der Krieg im Schatten. Russland und Tschetschenien.* Frankfurt am Main: Edition Suhrkamp.
Haviland, C. (2013). Sri Lanka Matale Mass Grave 'dates from the late 1980'. Retrieved from http://www.bbc.co.uk/news/world-asia-21964586 (accessed on 14 May 2013).
Hayes, G. (1998). We suffer our memories: Thinking about the past, healing and reconciliation. *American Imago, Southafrica, 55,* 29–50.
Heidelberger-Leonard, I. (1996). *Ruth Klüger weiter leben. Eine Jugend. Oldenbourg Interpretation.* München: Oldenbourg.
Herman, J. (1992). *Trauma and recovery. The aftermath of violence—From domestic abuse to political terror.* New York: BasicBooks.
Hernandez, V. (2012, April 28). Argentine mothers mark 35 years of marching for justice. Retrieved from http://www.bbc.co.uk/news/world-latin-america-17847134 (accessed on 19 January 2015).
Heyl, M., & Schreier, H. (Eds). (1994). *Die Gegenwart der Schoah. Zur Aktualität des Mordes an den europäischen Juden.* Hamburg: Krämer.
Homer. (1979). *Odyssee.* Reihe: Die bibliophilen Taschenbücher/Dortmund: Harenberg Kommunikation.
Horowitz, M. J. (1985). Disasters and psychological responses to stress. *Psychiatric Annals, 15*(3), 161–167.
Human Rights Correspondence School. (2004). Disappearances: Definitions of disappearance. Retrieved from http://www.hrschool.org/modules.php?name=News&file=articl e&sid=10 (accessed on 19 January 2015).
Human Rights Watch. (2004a). Other countries show possible paths on 'disappearance'. Retrieved from http://www.hrw.org/reports/2003/algeria0203/algeria0203-10.html (accessed on 19 January 2015).
———. (2004b). *The road to Abu Ghraib.* New York: Eigenverlag
Hunter-King, E. J. (1998). Children of military personnel missing in action in Southeast Asia. In Y. Danieli (Ed.), *International handbook of multigenerational legacies of trauma* (pp. 243–255). New York: Plenum Press.
ICMP. (2008). Bosnia and Herzegovina. Retrieved from http://www.ic-mp.org/icmp-worldwide/southeast-europe/bosnia-and-herzegovina/ (accessed on 9 August 2012).
———. (2012). U.S. Helsinki Commission Hearing: 'Healing the wounds of conflict and disaster: Clarifying the Fate of Missing Persons in the OSCE': Intervention by her Majesty Queen Noor, ICMP Commissioner. Retrieved form http://www.ic-mp.org/wp-content/uploads/2012/02/icmp-dg-415-4-doc.pdf (accessed on 8 August 2012).
Independent Commission on International Humanitarian Issues. (1986). *Disappeared! Technique of terror: A report.* London and New Jersey: Zed Books Ltd.
INFORM. (1993). *Annual report.* Colombo: Inform.
International Committee of the Red Cross (ICRC). (1977). Protocol Additional to the Geneva Conventions of 12 August 1949, and relating to the Protection of Victims of International Armed Conflicts (Protocol I), 8 June 1977. Retrieved from http://www. icrc.org/applic/ihl/ihl.nsf/Treaty.xsp?action=openDocument&documentId=D9E6B6 264D7723C3C12563CD002D6CE4 (accessed on 12 July 2013).
International Commission on Missing Persons. (2004). ICMP announces positive results of the Outreach Campaign intended to inform family members of missing persons. *Press Release,* 18 August 2004.
Irmler, D. (2001). 'Mein Zimmer hier heißt Schmerz.' Überleben und Leben–Systemische Therapie mit schwerst traumatisierten minderjährigen Flüchtlingen. In W. Rotthaus (Ed.),

Systemische Kinder- und Jugendlichenpsychotherapie (pp. 446-461). Heidelberg: Carl-Auer-Systeme.

Jacobson, L., & Vesti, P. (1992). *Torture survivors-a new group of patients*. Copenhagen: RCT (Eigenverlag).

Jaffe, R. (1968). Dissociative phenomena in former concentration camp inmates. *International Journal of Psycho-analysis, 49*, 310-312.

Jelin, E. (1994). The politics of memory. The human rights movement and the construction of democracy in Argentinia. *Latin American Perspectives, 81*, 38-58.

Kahne, M. J. (1967). On the persistence of transitional phenomena into adult life. *Journal for Psychoanalysis, 48*, 247-258.

Kalayjian, A., & Shahinian, S. P. (1998). Recollections of aged Armenian survivors of the Ottoman Turkish genocide: Resilience through endurance, coping, and life accomplishments. *Psychoanalytic Review, 85*(4), 489-504.

Kampusch, N. (2010). *3096 Tage*. Berlin: List

Kast V. (1982). *Trauern. Phasen und Chancen des psychischen Prozesses*. Stuttgart/Berlin: Kreuz Verlag.

Kauffman, J. (1993-1994). Dissociative functions in the normal mourning process. *Omega, 28*(1), 31-38.

Keilson, H. (1979). *Sequenzielle Traumatisierung bei Kindern*. Stuttgart: Enke.

———. (1992). *Sequential traumatisation in children: A clinical and statistical follow-up study on the fate of the Jewish war orphans in the Netherlands*. Jerusalem: The Magnes Press.

Kernberg, O. (1984). The couch at sea: Psychoanalytic studies of group and organizational leadership. *International Journal of Group Psychotherapy, 34*, 5-23.

Kernjak, F. (2002). *Trauma und Exhumierungen. Am Beispiel Guatemala*. Wien: Diplomarbeit an der Fakultät für Human- und Sozialwissenschaften.

Kestenberg, J., & Brenner, I. (1986). Children who survived the Holocaust. The role of rules and routines in the development of the superego. *International Journal of Psycho Analysis, 67*, 309-316.

———. (1996). *The last witness. The child survivor of the Holocaust*. Washington, D.C./ London: American Psychiatric Press, Inc.

Kinzie, J. D. (1994). Countertransference in the treatment of Southeast Asian refugees. In J. P. Wilson & J. D. Lindy (Eds), *countertransference in the treatment of PTSD* (pp. 249-262). New York/London: Guilford Press.

Kinzie, J. D., Boehnlien, J. K., & Sack, W. H. (1998). The effects of massive trauma on Cambodian parents and children. In Y. Danieli (Ed.), *An International handbook of mulitgenerational legacies of trauma* (pp. 211-224). New York: Plenum Press.

Klein, H., & Kogan, I. (1986). Identification processes and denial in the shadow of Nazism. *International Journal of Psycho-analysis, 67*, 45-51.

Kleinmann A., Das V., & Lock M. (1997). *Social suffering*. Berkely: University California Press.

Klüger, R. (1994). *weiter leben. Eine Jugend*. München: Deutscher Taschenbuchverlag.

———. (1996). Einführung. In I. Heidelberger-Leonard (Ed.), *Ruth Klüger weiter leben. Eine Jugend. Oldenbourg Interpretation* (pp. 109-110). München: Oldenbourg.

Koepsel, R. (2011). *Mothers of the Plaza de Mayo: First responders for human rights*. Case-specific briefing paper. Humanitarian Assistance in Complex Emergencies. University of Denver.

Kogan, I. (2011). *Mit der Trauer kämpfen. Schmerz und Trauer in der Psychotherapie traumatisierter Menschen*. Stuttgart: Klett-Cotta.

Kordon, D. R., Edelman, L. I., Lagos, D. M., Nicoletti, E., & Bozzolo, R. C.(1988). *Psychological effects of political repression.* Buenos Aires: Sudamericana/Planeta.

Kraushaar, W. (1994). Die Affäre Auerbach. Zur Virulenz des Antisemitismus in den Gründerjahren der Bundesrepublik. In H. Schreier & M. Heyl (Eds), *Die Gegenwart der Schoah. Zur Aktualität des Mordes an den europäischen Juden* (pp. 195–218). Hamburg: Krämer.

Krishner, L. A. (1994). Trauma, the good object, and the symbolic: A theoretical integration. *International Journal of Psycho-analysis, 75,* 235–242.

Krystal, H. (Ed.). (1968). *Massive psychic trauma.* New York: International University Press

———. (1981). The aging survivor of the Holocaust. Integration and self-healing in post-traumatic states. *Journal Geriatric Stress, 14,* 165–189.

Kübler-Ross, E. (1969). *On death and dying.* New York: Macmillon.

Kübler-Ross. (1983). *On children and death.* New York: Macmillan Publishing Company.

Kurier. (2004, January 1). Hunderte Zuwanderer im Meer ertrunken. *Kurier,* p. 8.

Lagos, D., Kordon, D., Edelman, L., & Kersner, D. (2005). *Argentina: Our experience in rehabilitation work with relatives of Desaparecidos and other victims of political repression.* Buenos Aires: EATIP, Eigenverlag.

Langer, L. (1997). Social suffering and Holocaust atrocity. In A. Kleinmann, V. Das & M. Lock (Eds), *Social suffering* (pp. 47–66). Berkely: University California Press.

Laub, D. (1996). The empty circle: Children of survivors and the limits of reconstruction. *Japa, 46* (2), 507–529.

———. (2000). Eros oder Thanatos? Der Kampf um die Erzählbarkeit des Traumas. *Psyche, 54,* 860–894.

Lauritsch, K., & Kernjak. F. (2011) We need the truth. Enforced disappearances in Asia. Guatemala City: Equipo de Estudios Comunitario Accion Piscosocial (ECAP).

Leahy, J. M. (1992-93). A comparison of depression in women bereaved of a spouse, child, or a parent. *Omega, 26*(3), 207–217.

Leiser, E. (1996). Ruth Klüger. In I. Heidelberger-Leonard (Ed.), *Ruth Klüger weiter leben. Eine Jugend. Oldenbourg Interpretation* (pp. 116–119). München: Oldenbourg.

Lenz, R., & Müller, M. (2011). Die verschwundenen Kinder. *Medico international Rundschreiben.* 4(11), 8–12.

Levi, Primo. (1995). *If this is a man.* New York: The Orion Press.

Lexikon der Wehrmacht. (2004). *Keitel, Wilhelm.* Retrieved from www.lexikon-der-wehrmacht.de/Personenregister/KeitelW-R.htm

Libeskind, D. (1999). Trauma/void. In E. Bronfen, B. R. Erdle & S. Weigel (Eds). *Trauma. Zwischen Psychoanalyse und kulturellem Deutungsmuster* (pp. 3–26). Köln, Weimar, Wien: Böhlau.

Lifton, R. J. (1979). *The broken connection.* New York: Basic Books Inc.

Longerich, P. (Ed.). (1989). *Die Ermordung der europäischen Juden.* München: Piper.

Lorenzer, A. (1993). *Intimität und soziales Leid. Archäologie der Psychoanalyse.* Frankfurt am Main: Fischer Taschenbuch Verlag.

Lozowick, Yaacov. (1997). Jewish memory and the Shoah. In H. Schreier & M. Heil (Eds), *Never again!: The Holocaust's challenge for educators* (pp. 109–116). Hamburg: Krämer.

Löwenthal, L. (1988). Individuum und Terror. In D. Diner (Ed.). *Zivilisationsbruch. Denken nach Auschwitz* (pp. 15–25). Frankfurt am Main: Fischer.

Luft, J. (1989). *Einführung in die Gruppendynamik.* Frankfurt am Main: Fischer.

Madariaga, C. (1992). Verschwundene in einer ländlichen Gemeinde: Psychologische und psychosoziale Leiden. Ein Behandlungsansatz auf der Grundlage einer Gruppentherapie. In IWK (Ed.). *Seelenmord—psychosoziale Aspekte der Folter. Mitteilungen des Instituts für Wissenschaft und Kunst,* 47(1), 11–17.

Maercker, A., Bonanno, G., Znoj, H., & Horowitz, M. J. (1998). Prediction of complicated grief by positive and negative themes in narratives. *Journal of Clinical Psychology*, 54(8), 1117–1136.

Mahler, M., Pine, F., & Bergman, A. (1975). *The psychological birth of the human infant: Symbiosis and individuation*. New York: Basic Books.

Main, M., Solomon, J., & Brazelton, T. B. (1986). Discovery of an insecure-disorganized/ disoriented attachment pattern. In *Affective development in Infancy* (pp. 95–124). Westport, CT: Ablex Publishing.

Mancini, M. E. (1986). Creating and therapeutically utilizing anticipatory grief in aurvivors of sudden death. In T. A. Rando (Ed.), *Loss and anticipatory grief* (pp. 145–152). Massachusetts: D.C. Heath and Company Lexington.

Marcussen, H. (1990). Auswirkungen der Folter und Behandlungsmöglichkeiten der Folteropfer–Aus der Arbeit des Rehabilitations- und Forschungszentrums für Folteropfer, Kopenhagen. In U. Rauchfleisch (Ed.), *Folter: Gewalt gegen Menschen*. Freiburg i.Br.: Paulusverlag, 67–79.

McCubbin, H.I., Dahl, B. B., & Hunter E. (Eds), (1975). *Family separation and reunion. Families of prisoners of war and servicemen missing in action*. Washington, D.C.: US Government Printing Office.

Meijide, E. F. (1987). Erinnerung eines Vaters. In Hamburger Institut für Sozialforschung (Ed.), *Nie wieder! Ein Bericht über Entführung, Folter u. Mord durch d. Militärdiktatur in Argentinien* (p. 173). Weinheim und Basel: Beltz Verlag.

Meschiany, A., & Krontal, S. (1998). Toys and games in play therapy. *Israel Journal of Psychiatry*, 35(1), 31–37.

Mittler, G. (2000). *Jean Daligault—Eine Passion*. Rede anlässlich der Eröffnung der Ausstellung des Künstlers und Nacht-und-Nebel-Häftlings am 12.8.2000. Retrieved from www.fm.rlp.de/wir_ueber_uns/Minister/Reden/PDF/Ausstellung_jean_ daligault.pdf

Mlodoch, K. (2011). Anfal überlebende Frauen in Kurdistan-Irak—Trauma, Erinnerung und Bewältigung. In L. Reddemann (Ed.), *Psychotraumatologie zwischen Stabilisierung und Konfrontation. Zeitschrift für Psychotraumatologie, Psychotherapiewissenschaft, Psychologische Medizin (ZPPM) 9/3* (pp. 33–45). Kröning: Asanger..

Mollinca, R. F., Mc Innes, K., Poole, C., & Svang, T. (1998). Dose-effect relationship of trauma to symptoms of depression and post-traumatic stress disorder among Cambodian survivors of mass violence. *British Journal of Psychiatry*, 173, 482–488.

Mommsen, H. (1992). There was no Führer Order. In D. L. Niewyk (Ed.). *The Holocaust. Problems and Perspectives of Interpretation*. Massachusetts: D.C. Heath and Company Lexington.

Munczek, D. S., & Tuber, S. (1998). Political repression and its psychological effects on Honduran children. *Social Sciences and Medicine*. 47(11), 1699–1713.

Mupinda, M. (1995). *Loss and grief among the Shona: The meaning of disappearances*. Paper presented to Seventh International Symposium on 'Torture as a challenge to the medical Profession', Cape Town.

Murphy, S. (1988). Mental distress and recovery in a high-risk bereavement sample three years after untimely death. *Nursing Research*, 37(1), 30–35.

Nachmani, G. (1995). Trauma and ignorance. *Contemporary Psychoanalysis*, 31, S. 423–450.

Nader, K. (1994) Countertransference in the treatment of acutely traumatized children. In J. P. Wilson & J. D. Lindy (Eds), *Countertransference in the Treatment of PTSD*, (pp. 179–205). New York/London: Guilford Press.

Nadia, C. S. (1991). *The last word: Women, death and divination in inner Mani*. Chicago: University of Chicago Press.

Nash, J. R. (1978). *Among the missing. An anecdotal history of missing persons from 1800 to the present*. New York: Simon and Schuster.

Neumann, Y. (1998). On the intergenerational experience—A short-term intervention with a Holocaust survivor as part of a lengthy course of therapy. *Israel Journal of Psychiatry*, 35(1), 56–67.

Nicoletti, E. (1988). Some reflexions on clinical work with relatives of missing people. A particular elaboration of loss. In D. Kordon et al. (Eds), *From psychological effects of political repression* (pp. 57–63). Buenos Aires: Sudamerikana/Planeta.

Niederland, W. (1968). Clinical observations on the 'survivor syndrome'. *International Journal of Psycho-analysis*, 49, 313–315.

Ondaatje, Michael. (2011). *Anil's ghost*. London: Bloomsbury.

Onnasch, K., & Gast, U. (2011). Trauern mit Leib und Seele. Orientierung bei schmerzlichen Verlusten. Stuttgart: Klett-Cotta.

Österreichisches Rotes Kreuz. (2012). Rotes Kreuz: Weltweit zwei Millionen Verschwundene. Retrieved from http://www.roteskreuz.at/nocache/print/berichten/news/datum/2012/08/27/rotes-kreuz-weltweit-zwei-millionen-verschwundene-22/ (accessed on 6 September 2012).

Ottomeyer, K. (1987). *Lebensdrama und Gesellschaft. Szenisch-materialistische Psychologie für soziale Arbeit und politische Kultur*. Wien: Franz Deuticke.

Ottomeyer, K. (2011). *Die Behnadlung der Opfer. Über unseren Umgang mit dem Trauma der Flüchtlinge und verfolgten*. Stuttgart: Klett-Cotta.

Ottomeyer, K., & Peltzer, K. (2002). *Überleben am Abgrund. Psychotrauma und Menschenrechte*. Klagenfurt: Drava.

PAHO. (2005). A disaster myth that just won't die—Mass burials and the dignity of disaster victims. Retrieved from http://new.paho.org/disasters/newsletter/index.php?option=com_content&view=article&id=306%3Aa-disaster-myth-that-just-wont-die-mass-burials-and-the-dignity-of-disaster-victims&catid=153%3Aissue-98-jan (accessed on 19 January 2015).

Paneerselvam, S. (2003). Background of the issues of 'Enforced Disappearance'. Paper presented at Inter-sessional Open-ended Working Group to Elaborate a Frat Legally Binding Normative Instrument for the Protection of all Persons from Enforced Disappearance. First session.

Payne, M. (1995). Understanding 'going missing': Issues for social work and social services. *British Journal of Social Work*, 3, 333–348.

Pearlman, L. A., & Saakvitne, K. W. 1995. *Trauma and the Therapist*. New York, W.W. Norton & Company.

Perera, S. (1999). *Stories of survivors. Socio-political contexts of female headed households in post-terror southern Sri Lanka*. Colombo: Vikas Publishing House.

Pines, D. (1986). Working with women survivors of the Holocaust: Affective experiences in transference and countertransference. *International Journal of Psycho-analysis*, 67, 295–307.

Preitler, B. (1996). Zwischen Angst und Hoffnung. *Südwind*, 6, 16–17.

———. (1998/99). Der/die Dritte im Bunde. Psychotherapie mit Folterüberlebenden unter Beteiligung von DolmetscherInnen (pp. S.19–29). Wien: Hemayat Eigenverlag.

———. (2002a). Wenn Kinder Opfer politischer Gewalt werden. In H. Fronek & I. Messinger (Eds), *Handbuch Unbegleitete Minderjährige Flüchtlinge. Recht, Politik, Praxis, Alltag, Projekte* (pp. 160–175). Wien: Mandelbaum.

———. (2002b). Kriegs- und Folterverletzungen der Seele. Psychotherapeutische Betreuung von Folter- und Kriegsüberlebenden bei Hemayat. In K. Ottomeyer & K. Peltzer (Eds), *Überleben am Abgrund. Psychotrauma und Menschenrechte* (pp. 171–186). Klagenfurt: Drava.

Preitler, B. (2004a). Psychologische Betreuung von Flüchtlingen in Österreich. In G. Mehta (Eds), *Die Praxis der Psychologie* (pp. 361-372). Wien New York: Springer.

———. (2004b). Folter erzeugt Hilflosigkeit—Überlegungen zu möglichen therapeutischen Konzepten wider die Hilflosigkeit. *Zeitschrift für Psychotraumatologie und Psychologische Medizin*, 2, 31-42.

———. (2005). Zur psychotherapeutischen Arbeit mit Angehörigen von „verschwundenen Personen. Dissertation an der Universität Klagenfurt.

———. (2006a). *Ohne jede Spur... Psychotherapeutische Arbeit mit Angehörigen 'verschwundener' Personen.* Gießen: Psychosozial Verlag.

———. (2006b). Trauma Counselling Programm nach Krieg und Tsunami in Ampara (Sri Lanka). In Zentrum für Friedensforschung und Friedenspädagogik (Ed.), *Jahrbuch Friedenskultur* (pp. 69-75). Klagenfurt: Drava.

———. (2008). Friedensarbeit, Krisenintervention und langfristige Entwicklungszusammenarbeit. Reflexionen über die dreijährige Ausbildung 'Trauma Counselling' im Osten Sri Lankas. In B. Gruber et al. (Eds), *Jahrbuch Friedenskultur 2008. Internationale Krisenherde und Konflikte* (pp. 228-237). Klagenfurt: Drava. S.

———. (2009). Sharing the rotten rice. Trauma counseling in Sri Lanka after war and Tsunami. In M. Rieck (Ed.), *Social interactions after massive traumatization. Was the Holocaust survivors' encounter with the post-war society conductive for generating private and collective memories?* (pp. 63-77). Berlin: Regner.

———. (with Ottomeyer, K., & Spitzer, H.) (Eds). (2010). *Look I am a foreigner. Interkulturelle Begegnung und psycho-soziale Praxis auf fünf Kontinenten.* Klagenfurt: Drava.

Prigerson, H. G., Bierhals, A.J., Kasl, S.V., Reynolds, C.F., Sher, M.K., Day, N., Beery, L.C., et. al. (1997a). Traumatic grief as a risk factor for mental and physical morbidity. *American Journal of Psychiatry*, 154(5), 616-623.

Prigerson, H. G., Sher, M.K., Frank, E., Beery, L.C., Silberman, R. & Prigerson, J. Reynolds, C.F. (1997b). Traumatic grief: A case of loss—Induced trauma. *American Journal of Psychiatry*, 154(7), 1003-1008.

Ramirez Castello, N. (2010). Die Folgen der politischen Gewalt und der Versuch einer Bewältigung: Forschungsaufenthalt im peruanischen Andendorf Santiago de Lucanamarca. In K. Ottomeyer, B. Preitler & H. Spitzer (Eds). (2010). *Look I am a foreigner. Interkulturelle Begegnung und psycho-soziale Praxis auf fünf Kontinenten* (pp. 30-49). Klagenfurt: Drava.

Ramphele, M. (1997). Political widowhood in South Africa: The embodiment of ambiguity. In A. Kleinman, V. Das & M. Lock (Eds), *Social suffering* (pp. 99-118). Berkely: University of California Press.

Rando, T. A. (1992-1993). The increasing prevalence of complicated mourning: The onslaught is just beginning. *Omega*, 26(1), 43-59.

———. (1993). *Treatment of complicated mourning.* Ottawa: Research Press.

Rando, T. (2003). Public tragedy and complicated mourning. In M. Lattanzi-Licht & K. J. Doka (Eds), *Coping with public tragedy. Living with grief* (pp. 263-274). New York: Brunner-Routledge.

Reddemann, L. (2004). *Eine Reise von 1.000 Meilen beginnt mit dem ersten Schritt.* Freiburg i.Br.: Herder.

———. (2011). *Psychodynamisch Imaginative Traumatherapie PITT—Das Manual. Vollständig überarbeitete Neuauflage.* Stuttgart, Klett-Cotta.

Rehberger, R. (2004). *Angst zu Trauern. Trauerabwehr in Bindungstheorie und psychotherapeutischer Praxis.* Stuttgart: Pfeiffer bei Klett-Cotta.

Remmers, S. (2009). Wie der Verlust des Ehepartners bewältigt wird: Eine Längsschnittstudie zur Erfassung des Trauerverlaufs innerhalb des ersten Jahres nach demTodesereignis. Dissertation an der Universität Koblenz-Landau. Göttingen: Cuvillier Verlag.

Reynolds, M. (2000, September 17). War has no rules for Russian forces fighting in Chechnya. *The Los Angeles Times*. Retrieved from http://articles.latimes.com/2000/sep/17/news/mn-22524 (accessed on 19 January 2015).

Ritterman, M. K. (1991). *Under siege. Terror and family support in Chile*. New Jersey: Norwood.

Riquelme, H. (2001). *Die Belagerung des Gedächtnisses. Leben und Arbeit von Psychologen unter den Militärdiktaturen Südamerikas*. Bonn: Deutscher Psychologen Verlag.

Robins, S. (2012, April 1). Constructing meaning from disappearance: Local memorialisation of the missing in Nepal. Paper submitted to ISA San Diego. Panel: In Search for Truth and Reconsiliation.

Rogers, J., Spencer J., & Uyangoda, J. (1998, July). Sri Lanka. Political violence and ethnic conflict. *American Psychologist*, 53(7), 771–777.

Roginsky, A. (2009). The embrace of Stalinism. *Orthodoxy Today.org*. Available at http://www.orthodoxytoday.org/articles-2009/Roginsky-The-Embrace-Of-Stalinism.php (accessed on 18 October 2012).

Roth, J. (2010). *Job*. Dexter: Archipelago.

Rothschild. B. (2006). *Help for the helper. Self-care strategies for managing burnout and stress*. New York: Norton.

Rousseau, C., Said, T., Gagne M., & Bilbea, G. (1998). Resilience in unaccompanied minors from the north of Somalia. *Psychoanalytic Review*, 85(4), 615–637.

Rütsche, B. (2003). Die Stimme der Verschwundenen lassen wir nicht zum Schweigen bringen! *Kolumbien-Monatsbericht*, 9, 1–6.

Sabin, M., Lopes, Cardozo B., Nackerud, L., Kaiser R., & Varese, L. (2003). Factors associated with poor mental health among Guatemalan refugees living in Mexico 20 years after civil conflict. *Journal of the American Medical Association*, 290(5), 635–642.

Salahu-Din, Sakinah N. (1996). A comparison of coping strategies of African American and Caucasian widows. *Omega*, 33(2), 103–120.

Saldinger, A., Cain, A., Kalter, N., & Lohnes, K. (1999). Anticipating parental death in families with young children. *American Journal of Orthopsychiatry*, 69(1), 39–48.

Sangster, K. (1999). Truth commissions: The usefulness of truth-telling. *Australian Journal of Human Rights*, 136–158.

Schaffer, H. R., & Emerson, P. (1964). The development of social attachments in infancy. Child Development Publications of the Society for Research in Child Development, 29 no. 3, Serial no. 94.

Scheffer, D. J. (2002, December 21). Justice for Cambodia. *New York Times*, p. 3.

Scherbakova, I. (2002, January). 'Memorial' und 'Opfer zweier Diktaturen.' *OST-WEST. Europäische Perspektiven (OWEP)*, pp. 12–19.

Schindler, R. (1996). Mourning and bereavement among Jewish religious families: Atime for reflection and recovery. *Omega*, 33(2), 121–129.

Schmidt-Häuer, C. (2002). Eva in der Mördergrube. Eine Anthropologin aus Island gibt den namenlosen Opfern in den Massengräbern des Bosnienkriegs ihre Identität zurück. *Die Zeit*, 52. Retrieved from http://www.zeit.de/2002/52/N-Totengr_8aberin (accessed 10 February 2015).

Schreier, H., & Heyl, M. (Eds). (1994). *Die Gegenwart der Schoah. Zur Aktualität des Mordes an den europäischen Juden*. Hamburg: Krämer.

Schrepfer-Proskurjakov, A. (2004). Russlands Krieg in Tschetschenien. *asyl aktuell*, 3, 2–7.

Seven Sisters Post. (2012, August 20). *Mizo villagers bid adieu to 'missing' teenage couple,* p. S. 4.
Shapiro, E. R. (1994). *Grief as a family process. A developmental approach to clinical practice.* New York: The Guilford Press.
Sharma, P. C. (2007). Report of the NHRC Committee on Missing Children. Retrieved from http://www.childlineindia.org.in/CP-CRDownloads/Missing%20Child%20report%NHRC.pdf (last accessed on 10 February 2015).
Simpson, J., & Bennett, J. (1985). *The disappeared and the mothers of the Plaza. The story of the 11 000 Argentino who vanished.* New York: St. Martin's Press.
Sluzki, C. (1990). Disappeared: Semantic and somatic effects of political repression in a family seeking therapy. *Family Process, 29,* 131–144.
———. (1994). Reclaiming words, reclaiming worlds. *Journal of Reviews and Commentary in Mental Health, 9*(2), 4–7.
Smith, A. L. (1992). *Die 'vermißte' Million. Zum Schicksal deutscher Kriegsgefangener nach dem Zweiten Weltkrieg. Schriftreihe der Vierteljahresreihe für Zeitgeschichte.* München: Oldenbourg.
Smith, D. N. (1998). The psychocultural roots of genocide. Legitimacy and crisis in Rwanda. *American Psychologist, 53*(7), 743–753.
Society for Threatened Peoples [Gesellschaft für Bedrohte Völker]. (2004). Auch Jugendliche 'verschwinden'. Retrieved from www.gfbv.de/voelker/asien/lttememo.html
Solzhenitsyn, Aleksandr I. (2002). *The Gulag Archipelago 1918–1956.* New York: Perennial.
Somasundaram, D., & Jamunanantha, C. S. (2002). Psychosocial consequences of war. Northern Sri Lankan experience. In J. de Jong (Ed.), *Trauma, war, and violence. public mental health in socio-cultural context.* New York: Kluwer Academic/Plenum Publishers.
Spitz, R. (1967). *Vom Säugling zum Kleinkind.* Stuttgart: Klett Cotta.
Spolyar, L. (1975). Die grieving process in MIA wives. In I. Mccubbin Hamilton et al. (Eds), *Family separation and reunion. families of prisoners of war and servicemen missing in action* (pp. 77–84). Washington, D.C.: US Government Printing Office.
Staub, E. (1998). Breaking the cycle of genocidal violence: Healing and reconciliation. In J. H. Harvey (Ed.), *Perspectives on loss. A sourcebook.* Philadelphia, PA: Brunner/Mazel.
———. (2000). Genocide and mass killing: Origins, prevention, healing and reconciliation. *Political Psychology, 21,* 367–382.
Staub, E., &. Pearlman, L. A. (2006). Advancing healing and reconciliation. In L. Barbanel & R. J. Sternberg (Eds), *Psychological interventions in times of crisis* (213–244). New York: Springer.
Stroebe, M., & Schut, H. (1999). The dual process model of coping with bereavement: Rationale and description. *Death Studies, 23,* 197–224.
———. (2010). The dual process model of coping with beraeavement: A decade on. *Omega, 61*(4), 273–289.
Stroebe, M., Schut, H., & Stroebe, W. (1998). Trauma and grief: A comparative analysis. In J. H. Harvey (Ed.), *Perspectives on loss. A sourcebook* (pp. 115–132). Philadelphia, PA: Brunner/Mazel.
Stroebe, M., Gergen, M.M., Gergen, K.J., & Stroebe, W. (1992). Broken hearts or broken bonds: Love and death in historical perspective. *American Psychologist, 47,* 1203–1212.
Summerfield, D. (1998). The social experience of war and some issues for the humanitarian field. In J. Bracken & C. Perry (Eds), *Rethinking the trauma of war* (pp. 9–37). London/ New York: Free Association Books.
Talbot, K. (1997–1998). Mothers now childless: Structures of the life-world. *Omega, 36*(1), 45–62.
Tamil Times. (1996, December 15). HRTF Probes 'Missing Persons'. *Tamil Times,* No. 12, 5.
Tauber, Y., & Van der Hal, E. (1998). Countertransference and life-and-death issues in group psychotherapy with child Holocaust survivors. *American Journal of Psychotherapy, 52*(3), 301–313.

Taylor, D. (1997). *Disappearing acts.* Durham/London: Duke University Press.
Thangavelu, V. (2001). *The rape and murder of teen aged Krishanti Kumaraswamy by Sinhalese soldiers.* Retrieved from http://www.sangam.org/JANAKA/Thanga6_21_01.htm (last accessed on 10 February 2015).
Thiruchandran, S. (1999). *The other victims of war. Emergence of female headed households in eastern Sri Lanka.* Colombo: Vikas Publishing House.
Thornton, S. W. (2000). Grief transformed: the mothers of the Plaza de Mayo. *Omega, 41*(4), S. 279–289.
Towell, L. (1994). *House on Ninth Street.* Dunvengan/Ontario: Cormorant Books.
Tschetschenien-Komitee. (2004). *Tschetschenien. Die Hintergründe des blutigen Konflikts.* Kreuzlingen/München: Heinrich Hugendubel Verlag.
Ullmann, K., & Donat, U. (2004). *Justiz in Ruanda 2004.* Retrieved from www.rav.de/infobrief93/ullmann.htm (accessed on 19 January 2015).
Ung, Loung. (2000). *First they killed my father.* New York: HarperCollins.
United Nations Human Rights. (n.d.). *International convention for the protection of all persons from enforced disappearance.* Retrieved from http://www.ohchr.org/EN/HRBodies/CED/Pages/ConventionCED.aspx (accessed on 12 July 2013).
United Nations Treaty Collection. (2006). Chapter IV. Human Rights. 16. International Convention for the Protection of all Persons from Enforced Disappearance. Retrieved from http://treaties.un.org/Pages/ViewDetails.aspx?src=TREATY&mtdsg_no=IV-16&chapter=4&lang=en (accessed on 19 January 2015).
Valent, P. (1998). Resilience in child survivors of the Holocaust: Toward the concept of resilience. *Psychoanalytic Review, 85*(4), 517–535.
Van der Kolk, B. A. (1985). Adolescent vulnerability to post traumatic stress disorder. *Psychiatry, 48,* 365–370.
———. (1987). *Psychological trauma.* Washington, D.C.: American Psychiatric Press.
Van der Veer, G. (1992). *Counselling and therapy with refugees. Psychological problems of victims of war, torture and repression.* West Sussex: John Wiley & Sons.
Van Dexter, J. (1986). Anticipatory grief: Strategies for the classroom. In T. A. Rando (Ed.), *Loss and anticipatory grief* (pp. 155–173). Massachusetts: Lexington Books.
Varier, T. V. E. (2004). *Memories of a father.* Hong Kong: Asian Human Rights Commission.
Varvin, S. (1998). Psychoanalytic psychotherapy with traumatized refugees: Integration, symbolization, and mourning. *American Journal of Psychotherapy, 52,* 64–71.
Veith, C. (2008). *Die Bindungstheorie. Überblick und neuere Forschungsansätze.* Innsbruck: SPI-Schriften.
Vesti, P., Somnier, F.E., & Kastrup, M. (1992). *Psychotherapy with torture survivors.* Copenhagen: RCT/IRCT.
Volkan, V. D. (1981). *Linking objects and linking phenomena.* New York: International Universities Press, Inc.
Volkan, V., & Zintl, E. (2000). *Wege der Trauer. Leben mit Tod und Verlust [Life After Loss. The Lessons of Grief].* Gießen: Psychosozial Verlag [New York: Charles Scribner's Sons].
Weisaeth, L., & Eitinger, L. (1991). Research on PTSD and other posttraumatic reactions: European literature. *PTSD Research Quarterly,* Spring, *2*(2), 1–2.
Welt, S. R., & Herron, W. G. (1990). *Narcissim and the psychotherapist.* New York: Guilford Press.
Welzer, H. (1997). *Verweilen beim Grauen. Essays zum wissenschaftlichen Umgang mit dem Holocaust.* Tübingen: Edition Diskord.
Winnicott, D. W. (1951). 'Transitional Objects and Transitional Phenomena', in Winnicott, D.W. 1975. *Through Paediatrics to Psycho-Analysis.* London: Hogarth, 229–242.

Winnicott, D. W. (1953). Transitional Objects and Transitional Phenomena. *International Journal of Psycho-Analysis, 34*, 89–97.
———. (1956). Primary maternal preoccupation. *Collected papers: Through paediatrics to psycho-analysis* London: Tavistock (pp. 300–305).
———. (1965). *The maturational processes and the faciliatory environment: Studies in the theory of emotional development.* New York: International Universities Press.
———. (1971). *Playing and reality.* London: Tavistock Publications.
Wistrich, Robert S. (2002). *Who's who in Nazi Germany.* Oxon: Routledge.
Zalaquett, J. (1992). Balancing ethical imperatives and political constraints: The dilemma of new democracies confronting past human rights violations. *Hastings Law Journal, 43*(6), 1425–1438.
Zelman, L. (1998). *After survival: One man's mission in the cause of memory.* New York: Holmes & Meier.
Zepf, S. (2001). Trauma, Reizschutz und traumatische Neurose. Versuch einer Klärung der Konzepte Freuds. *Forum der Psychoanalyse, 17*, 332–349.
Zisook, S., & DeVaul, R. (1983). Greif, unresolved grief, and depression. *Psychosomatics 24*(3), 247–256.
Zuckermann, M. (1998). *Zweierlei Holocaust. Der Holocaust in den politischen Kulturen Israels und Deutschland.* Göttingen: Wallstein Verlag.
Zvizdic, S., & Butollo, W. (2000). War-related loss of one's father and persistent depressive reactions in early adolescents. *European Psychologist, 5*(3), 204–214.

# Further Readings

Genfer Rot Kreuz Abkommen [Geneva Conventions of 1945]. Retrieved from http://www.icrc.org/applic/ihl/ihl.nsf/Comment.xsp?viewComments=LookUpCOMART&documentId=16B0826A9E1C3FB0C12563CD0041F8C0&action=openDocument (accessed on 26 February 2015).
Inter Agency Standing Committee: IASC Guidelines on Mental Health and Psychosocial Support in Emergency Settings. Retrieved from http://www.humanitarianinfo.org/iasc/pageloader.aspx?page=content-subsidi-common-default&sb=72 (accessed on 26 February 2015).
International Coalition against Enforced Disappearances. Retrieved from http://www.icaed.org/ (accessed on 26 February 2015).
International Convention for the Protection of All Persons from Enforced Disappearance Volltext (englisch) [full text]. Retrieved from http://www.ohchr.org/EN/HRBodies/CED/Pages/ConventionCED.aspx (accessed on 26 February 2015).
Protocol Additional to the Geneva Conventions of 12 August 1949, and relating to the Protection of Victims of International Armed Conflicts (Protocol I), 8 June 1977. Retrieved from http://www.icrc.org/ihl.nsf/INTRO/470 (accessed on 26 February 2015).
Stand der Ratifizierung [Status of ratification]. Retrieved from http://treaties.un.org/Pages/ViewDetails.aspx?src=TREATY&mtdsg_no=IV-16&chapter=4&lang=en; http://www.ohchr.org/EN/HRBodies/CED/Pages/CEDIndex.aspx (accessed on 26 February 2015).
UN Working Group on Enforced or Involuntary Disappearance. Retrieved from http://www.ohchr.org/EN/Issues/Disappearances/Pages/DisappearancesIndex.aspx (accessed on 26 February 2015).

# Index

absentee as centre of the family, 4
act of saying goodbye, 1–2
　rituals for, 32–33
adolescence/adolescents, 13–14
　autonomy and, 13
　feeling of belonging, 14
　gender differences in behaviour, 14
　peer group influence, 13
　phases of, 13
Asia mourning rites, 36
attachment
　Bowlby's theory, 7–10
　mother–child, 5–7
9/11 attacks and disappearances, 62–66
　psychological counselling and support for relatives of 'missing' people, 64–65
　rituals, 65–66
avoidance of grief, 29

black dress, as a symbol of mourning, 36–37
Bolshevik Revolution in Russia in 1917, 51
Bosnia, disappearances in, 75
Bowlby, John
　attachment theory, 7–10
　factors of mourning, 26–27
　four phases of mourning, 24–27

Cambodia under the Khmer Rouge, enforced disappearances in, 66–69
Chechnya, disappearances in, 76–78
children/childhood
　effects of loss of father, 74–76
　experiences of loss during, 14
　strategies for coping with grief, 15–16
　structural violence and 'disappeared' children, 84–85
　telling children the truth, 21–22

CINTRAS, 178–180
collective forms of coping. *See* coping with grief
FEDEFAM, 97
formation of support groups for relatives of the 'disappeared', 93–95
ICMP, 97
justice, demand for, 111–112
'Mothers of the Plaza de Mayo', 90–93
reconciliation, demand for, 112
sense of coherence and resilience, 112–113
transformation of grief and traumatisation into political action, 95–96
truth commissions, 98–100
commemoration, heteronomous and autonomous forms of, 108–109
community-based interventions, 176–180
　central subject areas, 177–178
　psychoeducation, 176–178
　psychological group therapy in a village in Chile, 178–180
　trauma counselling during and after a catastrophe, 181–185
complicated mourning, 29–30
conjugal bereavement, 37
connectedness, psychosomatics as symbols and forms of, 145–150
　delayed rituals, 148–150
　eating disorders, 146–147
　fear and worry, 147–148
connection/attachment, 5
coping with grief. *See* collective forms of coping; psychological and psychosocial support programmes; self-care during crisis
　acceptance and denial factors, 28
　Antonovsky's SOC, 88–90

with bereavement and dissociation, 27–29
children's strategies for, 15–16
dual process model (DPM), 27
loss of a child, 42–43
loss of one or both parents, 40–41
loss through an 'enforced disappearance', 41–42
mourning 'disappeared' relatives, 31–32
over loss of one's spouse/life partner Shapiro's view, 23
support via social network, 33
violent death of a child, 43–44
countertransference, 122–127, 145, 195–198

death certificates, need for, 100–102
death equivalents, 5
denial or rationalisation of traumatic events, 27–28, 124, 179, 203–204
depression
loss as risk factor for, 37
disorganisation and despair phase, 25
dissapearance/disappeared person, 4.
*See also* enforced disappearances; symbolic and virtual memorial places
Böhme's interpretation, 50–51
categories 'imprisonment' and 'death', 50
children of 'disappeared' soldiers, 74–76
as a consequence of war, 49–51
in course of a natural catastrophe, 85–87
death certificates, need for, 100–102
effective identification of exhumed persons, 102–106
in Greek mythology, 48–49
justice, demand for, 111–112
during Nazi Regime, 50
reconciliation, demand for, 112
of refugees, 83–84
structural violence and 'disappeared' children, 84–85
use of mysticisms and supernatural phenomena to search, 73–74
war memorials listings, 49
dissociation, coping with, 27–29
dual process model (DPM) of coping with bereavement, 27

emotional conditions of bereaved, 23
enforced disappearances. *See* disappearance/disappeared person; family response to 'enforced disappearance'
in Cambodia under the Khmer Rouge, 66–69
in Chechnya, 76–78
of children, 44–45
as a consequence of war and terror, 62–87
as a form of terror against political/ethnic/religious opponents, 2–3
forms of traumatisation, 29
in the history of Russia, 51–52
loss of one or both parents through an, 41–42
by 'Nacht-und-Nebel-Erlass' (Night and Fog Decree), 53
as a part of Holocaust, 53–61
by political arbitrariness, 66–69
rituals for victims of, 33–34
in Sri Lanka, 69–72
as systematic violations of human rights, 78–82
exhumations, 102–106
phases of processes, 103
psychological support of relatives during, 103–105

family response to 'enforced disappearance'. *See* enforced disappearances
aggression towards weaker family members, 158–161
children as carriers of symptoms, 154
children supporting children, 161
desire to protect children, 155–158
psychosocial work with affected families, 163–166
regressive behaviour, 154–155
relationship between spouses or partners, 161–162
taking over roles, 151–154
father–son bond, 22
FEDEFAM, 97
frozen time, 23

grief counselling, 119–120
grief/grieving, 204–205
    age-dependent reactions, 12–13
    age-independent reactions, 18
    aspects of Holocaust survivors, 31
    avoidance of, 29
    children and, 175–176
    definition of, 30
    expression of, 32–36
    of loss through an 'enforced
        disappearance', 41–42
    over loss through act of political
        repression, 41
    of parents mourning a child, 42–43
    pathological grief reactions, 42
    process, 22–24
    process of facilitating, 12–13
    PTSD and, 30–31
    Rando's six 'R' process, 24
    regressive behaviour, 15–16
    Rehberger's views, 23–24
    social context, 36
    spontaneous expressions of, 33
    violent death of a child, 43–44

hidden mourning, 186–188
Historical Clarification Commission, 104
Holocaust, enforced disappearances a part
        of, 53–61
    attempts to avoid further losses, 60–61
    life in the ghetto, 56
    searching for surviving relatives after
        the War, 58–59
    separation in the concentration camp,
        57–58
    statistics, 55
    therapeutic sessions for coping, 61
    ways of remembering lost relatives,
        59–60
    *Wiedergutmachung*, 61

ICMP, 97
individual reactions to enforced
    disappearances, 128–130
    aggression and anger, expressions of,
        137–141

aggressive behaviour towards children
    or other weaker members, 139–141
attempted suicides and auto-aggressive
    behaviour, 138–139
avoiding the topic, 134–136
difficulty of entering into new
    relationships, 141–143
experiences in psychotherapeutic settings
    after traumatic situations, 140
helplessness, 143–145
longing for a reunion with the
    'disappeared' person, 132–134
post-traumatic factors, 205
pre-traumatic factors, 205
traumatic factors, 205
ways of searching for 'disappeared'
    relatives, 130–131
Inter-Agency Standing Committee (IASC),
        176
interventions for communities after
        'disappearances'
    psychological support, 167–176

Jewish mourning rites, 36–37
justice, demand for, 111–112

Klüger, Ruth, 61
Krystal, Henry, 31

loss
    of a child, 42–43
    experiences during childhood, 14–22
    of one or both parents, form of
        mourning in children, 40–41
    of one or both parents through an
        'enforced disappearance', 41–42
    of one's spouse/life partner, coping
        strategies for, 37–38
    primary reaction to, 36
    siblings of children that have died or
        have 'disappeared', 45–46
    social roles, changes connected to,
        36–46
    through acts of political repression, 41
loss-oriented pole, 27

Index   225

Memoria Abierta organisation, 110
missing/'missing in action (MIA)', 39–40
missing-person-flyers, 65–66
mother–child attachment, 5–7
'The Mothers of the Plaza del Mayo', 39
'Mothers of the Plaza de Mayo', 90–93
mourning
    age and sex of the person bereaved, role in, 26
    age-dependent reactions, 12–13
    black dress, as a symbol of, 36–37
    Bowlby's four phases of, 24–27
    causes and circumstances of loss and, 26
    complicated, 29–30
    definition of, 31
    for 'disappeared' relatives, 31–32
    healthy, 40
    hidden, 186–188
    loss of one or both parents, in children, 40–41
    perceived as a betrayal of 'disappeared', 3
    psychological circumstances affecting, 26
    relationship with the lost person and, 26
    rituals, 3, 33
    second phase of, 36
    social and psychological circumstances affecting, 26
    social context, 36–37
    stable relationships, effect on, 27
    symbolic rituals, 35–36
    third phase of, 37
    of violent death of a child, 43–44
    of widows and widowers, 38–39
    by wives of 'missing in action (MIAs)', 39

Nacht-und-Nebel-Erlass, 53
National League of Families, 39
Noor, Queen, 48
numbing phase, 25

organised mental hygiene, forms of, 200–202
    positive working climate, 201–202
    psychological first-aid interventions, 200–201
    supervision sessions, 201

parental home, 13–14
peer group, 13–14
post-traumatic stress disorder (PTSD), 26, 30–31, 76, 124
pre-conflict phase, 18
primary reaction to a loss, 36
progressive attrition, 17
psychological and psychosocial support programmes. *See* coping with grief
    9/11 attacks and disappearances, 64–65
    cooperation between medicine and psychotherapeutic support, 116–117
    direct support of children in times of crisis, 170–176
    forms of self-expression, 173–175
    with Holocaust survivors, 126
    long-term communal programmes, 176–180
    psychological first-aid interventions, 200–201
    safe counselling relationship, 115–116
    supporting children by supporting their adult caregivers, 168–170
    at time of exhumations, 103–105
    transference and countertransference, 122–127
    trauma-related psychotherapy, 114–115
    2004 tsunami, 86–87
    work together with interpreters, 117–118
psychological circumstances affecting mourning, 26
psychosocial work with affected families, 163–166
    helping single parents, 165–166
    sharing of opinions and beliefs with each other, 163–164
    supporting families find their own rituals, 166
    supporting families in (re)building family structure, 164–165
psychotherapeutic process
    aim of psychotherapy, 118–119
    concluding, 121
    dealing with traumatisation through violations of human rights, 120–121
    grief counselling, 119–120
    psychotherapeutic sessions, 119

'Rajan Memorial' ward, 109–110
Rando, T. A.
  risk of complicated mourning, 29
  six 'R' process, 24
reappearance of 'disappeared' person,
    coping with
  counselling and psychotherapy, role in
    reuniting, 193–194
  relationships lost and ended, 189–191
  renewal of injury, 188–189
  willing to accept the time apart, 192–193
reconciliation, demand for, 112
recovering and identifying bodies, process
    of, 104
reorganisation phase, 25
rituals, 173
  for act of saying goodbye, 32–33
  in community settings, 32–33
  in context of the therapy, 149
  cultures and mourning, 36–37
  delayed, 148–150
  in intercultural, interreligious setting, 150
  mourning, 3, 33
  of posting and visiting the missing-
    person-flyers, 65–66
  symbolic mourning, 35–36
  transition, 37
  urbanisation and changing mode of, 33
  for victims of enforced disappearances,
    33–34
Roginsky, Arseny, 52


safe islands, 172–173
Salud Mental, 105
Saravanumuttu, Manorani, 111–112
self-care during crisis
  after a traumatic event, 198
  in the long-term process, 199–200
'Sense of Coherence' (SOC)
  comprehensibility, 88
  manageability, 88
  meaningfulness, 89
separation, 3, 5
sequential traumatisation in children, 16–20
  beginning of the persecution, 19
  different age groups, 18
  direct persecution, acute terror and
    relative calm chronification, 19

  following uprisings of the Arab Spring
    Movement, 19
  Keilson's study, 18
  phase of transition, 19
  post-conflict situation, 19
  post-traumatic sequence, 17
  pre-conflict phase, 18
  pre-traumatic sequence, 17
  psychological experiences of a 'general
    atmosphere of menace', 17
  story of Esther, 20
  traumatic sequence, 17
silent camps, 51
social circumstances affecting mourning, 26
social projects in the name of the
    'disappeared', 109–110
social roles, changes connected to loss,
    36–46
  loss of one or both parents, 40–41
  parents of children that have
    'disappeared', 44–45
  siblings of children that have died or
    have 'disappeared', 45–46
  spousal bereavement, 37–38
  spouses of missing/'missing in action
    (MIA)', 39–40
  violent death of a child, 43–44
  widows and widowers, 38–39
Solzhenitsyn, Aleksandr, 52
spousal bereavement, coping strategies
    for, 37–38
Sri Lanka, enforced disappearances in,
    69–72
stable relationships, effect on mourning, 27
structural violence and 'disappeared'
    children, 84–85
symbolic and virtual memorial places
  embroidered names of the
    'disappeared', 107–108
  heteronomous and autonomous forms
    of commemoration, 108–109
  memorial parks and memorial
    museums, 110
  pictures of the 'disappeared', 106–107
  social projects in the name of the
    'disappeared', 109–110
  virtual cemetery online, 110
symbolic funeral, 34
symbolic mourning rituals, 35–36

transference, 122–127
transitional objects, 10–13, 173
transitional phenomena, 10–13
trauma counselling during and after a catastrophe, 181–185
    guidelines for psychological counsellors, 182–185
trauma healing, 87
trauma-related psychotherapy, 114–115
Treaty of Brest-Litovsk, 51
truth commissions, 98–100

Varier, E., 109
violent aggression, 21

violent death of a child, grieving process of, 43–44
    fate of Bessie K., 43–44

war and terror, disappearances as a consequence of, 49–51, 62–87
    9/11 attacks, 62–66
    in Bosnia, 75
    in Chechnya, 76–78

yearning and searching phase, 25

Zelman, Leon, 57–58
Zvizdic, Sibela, 74

# About the Author and Translator

**Barbara Preitler** works as trauma therapist and is a supervisor for psychotherapists and social workers. She is a Lecturer at University of Klagenfurt, Austria. Her main areas of research are psychotraumatology, trauma and grief and psychological aspects of international development cooperation. Dr Preitler has published numerous articles and has also developed diploma courses on trauma counselling in Austria and Sri Lanka.

## About the Translator

**Julia Skala** is currently a Lecturer and Research Assistant in the field of theoretical linguistics at the department of English and American studies, University of Vienna. She has also studied English and Mandarin at the University of Vienna.

**Zukunftsfonds Österreich** is the agency that sponsored the English translation of the revised German edition of *Ohne jede Spur... Psychotherapeutische Arbeit mit Angehörigen "verschwundener" Personen.*